# Ontario BICYCLE *Touring Atlas*

**Bike ON Tours**

## Get out your bicycle and enjoy touring in Ontario!

These routes were developed over more than fifteen years of selecting quiet scenic roads for enjoyable cycling and from responding to requests for routes through various areas. This publication puts all of these routes together. You will find useful information on towns, attractions, bicycle repair shops, libraries for internet access while you are travelling and a selection of the most convenient and best restaurants, bed and breakfasts, inns, motels and camping. Also included is information on wineries, theatre festivals, beaches, natural areas, historic sites, Mennonite and Native Canadian communities. There are long distance linear routes across the province and loop routes, suitable for day trips.

To facilitate navigation, GPS geocoding is included for all of the places in the Community Guide Index and Accommodation Partners. New for 2012, quiet paved road routes have been added, particularly in Chatham Kent and in the Peterborough area. New trails that are good for cycling are included from Brantford south to Waterford and from Peterborough to Lindsay and Durham Region. More information about listed services and events is easily accessible on the internet with the urls included.

## CONTENTS

PHOTOS COURTESY OF
HOWARD PULVER ©2009

**Credits:**
Maps ©2012 **mapmobility** corp.
Bicycle routes & touring information compiled and written by Howard Pulver, ©2012 Bike On Tours

Fifth Edition
ISBN 978-1894955218

For more detailed information and customized trip planning, contact:

Bike On Tours
75 Thornton Avenue
London, ON N5Y 2Y4
E-Mail info@bikeontours.on.ca
www.bikeontours.on.ca

Designed & Published By:
**mapmobility** corp.

50 Ronson Dr., Suite 150
Toronto, ON M9W 1B3
Tel: 416-244-7881
Fax: 416-244-5422
E-Mail: info@mapmobility.com
www.mapmobility.com

# Touring Areas by Howard Pulver

## THAMES - AVON

### STRATFORD - LONDON - ST. MARYS

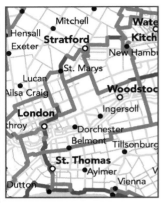

**Features:** London Bike Paths, historic, river valley, Theatre [Shakespeare Festival] - moderate, flat to rolling.

Go for the Theatre at the Stratford Festival and stay to bicycle. Every year from May to early November Stratford attracts visitors from Canada, the United States and around the world to the Stratford Festival for Theatre on four stages. The gardens, lakeside parks, restaurants and downtown shopping area make this an attractive place to stay a while and enjoy bicycling on tree lined country roads through scenic farmland.

Bicycle 25 kilometres from Stratford to visit St. Marys with a wonderful main street of Victorian stone buildings, Canada's largest outdoor swimming pool in an old quarry, the Canadian Baseball Hall of Fame and Museum and a scenic riverside promenade.

There are a number of bicycling options in this area including a 60 kilometre ride, which takes you to London and Fanshawe Park Conservation Area where you can camp, swim and visit the pioneer village. Continue into London and enjoy the outdoor festivals in the downtown area amid the Thames River parks and tree-lined streets.

Theatre lovers might also wish to try a bike route with a special appeal! Take a tour between the Shaw Festival in Niagara-on-the-Lake and the Shakespearian Festival in Stratford. A package route guide is available for a 5-day "Theatre to Theatre Ride" with 110 kilometre average distance per day. The package includes turn-by-turn directions, accommodation suggestions and attractions. Start at Niagara-on-the-Lake or Stratford. You bike through Six Nations First Nation, along the Grand River through Brantford, then northwest to Stratford. From Stratford you ride to Lake Erie to Port Dover along the Niagara Parkway past Niagara Falls.

For Information see: www.bikeontours.on.ca/custom.htm

## ST. LAWRENCE - RIDEAU

### GANANOQUE - KINGSTON - OTTAWA - BROCKVILLE PRESCOTT - MERRICKVILLE

**Features:** Waterfront Trail, Ottawa Bike Paths, Rideau

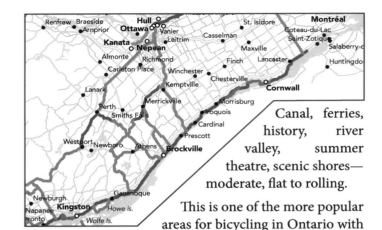

Canal, ferries, history, river valley, summer theatre, scenic shores— moderate, flat to rolling.

This is one of the more popular areas for bicycling in Ontario with scenic quiet roads and charming towns. Kingston is a popular historic waterfront city with a ferry to Wolfe Island and New York State. Bike 30 kilometres east on the Waterfront Trail to Gananoque, the gateway to the Thousand Islands. Along the way you can take a short ferry ride to Howe Island. Gananoque has a lively waterfront featuring the riverfront Heritage Centre, island boat cruises, theatre at the Thousand Islands Playhouse and the Festival of The Islands in August.

Enjoy the 70 kilometre scenic Thousand Islands Parkway bikeway and Waterfront Trail between Gananoque to Brockville. Brockville's Riverfest offers many days of concerts and entertainment starting the last week of June but there are also lots of regular attractions at this historic city on the St Lawrence River including the farmers market, historic railway tunnel, Theatre Brockville, the Brockville Museum and Fulford House 1900's Edwardian mansion.

From Brockville you continue on the Waterfront Trail 50 kilometres to Prescott with historic Fort Wellington, on the St. Lawrence River.

Follow quiet historic routes north to Kemptville leading to the wonderful old stone buildings and Blockhouse Museum in the historic Rideau Canal town of Merrickville. Continue along the Rideau Canal from Kemptville to Parliament Hill in Ottawa. The nation's capital has a great system of bike paths and an unequalled array of attractions, museums, restaurants and accommodation. It is 40 kilometres from Brockville to Kemptville and an additional 30 kilometres to Ottawa.

A package route guide is available for a 5 day "St. Lawrence and Rideau Canal Ride" with 58 kilometre average distance per day including turn-by-turn direction, accommodations suggestions and attractions. Starting at Gananoque, you bike east along the Thousand Island Parkway and then north to Rideau Canal visiting several canal lock towns. Luggage transfer and accommodation reservations are available. For information see: www.bikeontours.on.ca/custom.htm

## PORTS OF LAKE ERIE

PORT DOVER - PORT ROWAN - PORT BURWELL
PORT STANLEY

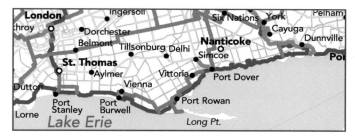

**Features:** Beaches, bird watching, historic, summer Theatre, waterfront - moderate, flat with a few short hills.

This is one of the best areas for bicycle touring in Ontario. It is a place that time forgot; a gem of historic lakefront ports and an easy ride on traffic free paved roads making it truly a cyclists' paradise.

Bike close to the Lake Erie shore with many newly added options for shorter distances and loops. It is about the same distance - 40 kilometres - between Port Dover, Port Rowan and Port Stanley.

The settlements, which date from the early 1800's include the early regional capital at Vittoria, Port Burwell with an 1840 lighthouse and the picturesque hamlets of Normandale and Port Ryerse. You can rest on the Lake Erie beaches and camp at the Provincial Parks at Long Point, Turkey Point or Port Burwell. Long Point is also a UN designated natural area. The Backus Conservation area near Port Rowan has a heritage village with an original operating 1798 water powered mill and camping facilities.

Both Port Stanley and Port Dover have summer Theatre. Port Dover is a tourist centre with restaurants featuring fresh Lake Erie perch and pickerel. Should you happen to visit there on any Friday the thirteenth you will find yourself a part of as unique celebration with hundreds of recreational motorcyclists from near and far.

PORT ROWAN

PORT BURWELL

GLENORA FERRY, PICTON

## PRINCE EDWARD COUNTY

PICTON - BELLEVILLE - DESERONTO - NAPANEE

**Features:** Waterfront Trail, beaches, bird watching, cheese factories, ferry, historic, First Nations, waterfront, wineries - moderate, flat to rolling.

This is one of the most popular areas for bicycling in Ontario, centered on the peninsula of Prince Edward County. Enjoy scenic rolling countryside, waterfront views, sand beaches, camping and great restaurants. Sample the wines and cider near Wellington, Waupoos and Milford. Bike on quiet country roads, explore historic villages and visit cheese factories. Stop at Lake on the Mountain to enjoy the panoramic view of the Glenora Ferry.

Take the bridge across the Bay of Quinte to visit the native craft shops of the Tyendinaga First Nation near Deseronto, to see Belleville's revitalized waterfront and the Glanmore Victorian mansion National Historic Site. The Glenora Ferry takes you across the bay to continue east to Napanee or historic Kingston.

Picton is a great starting point for multiday bike ride loops going west or east on the Waterfront Trail and then north to Rice Lake, Campbellford and Tweed. A package route guide is available for a 5 day "Lake Ontario and Trent Canal Ride" with a 60 or 100 kilometre average distance per day including turn-by-turn directions, accommodation suggestions and attractions. Starting at Picton, you bike through Cobourg or Port Hope north to Rice Lake and the Trent Canal. The 60 kilometre per day ride crosses the Bay of Quinte at Belleville. The 100 kilometre per day ride includes Kingston and the Glenora Ferry. Luggage transfer and accommodation reservations are available.

For information see: www.bikeontours.on.ca/custom.htm

WELLAND CANAL

## NIAGARA

NIAGARA FALLS - NIAGARA ON THE LAKE - FORT ERIE
PORT COLBORNE - DUNNVILLE - GRIMSBY

**Features:** Niagara Parkway, Friendship Trail and Welland Canal Trails, beaches, historic, ships on Welland Canal, Theatre [Shaw Festival], waterfalls, lakeshore, wineries—moderate, mostly flat except escarpment hills.

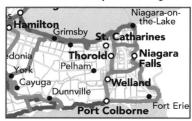

The Niagara Falls region is one of the best areas for bicycling anywhere in North America as a result of the unrivalled scenery of Niagara Falls, the Niagara Parkway and many bike paths. Niagara is also Ontario's oldest wine producing area with a growing number of wineries welcoming visitors. The terrain is quite flat except for where you climb and descend the Niagara Escarpment. Starting on the shore of Lake Ontario in the charming and historic town of Niagara-on-the-Lake, you can bike 60 kilometres through the manicured parkland of the Niagara Parkway. The Niagara-on-the-Lake to Niagara Falls section is best enjoyed if you can avoid the busy holidays and summer weekends. The parkway is a limited speed roadway, with a bike path beside it, following the Niagara River through Niagara Falls all the way to Fort Erie, on Lake Erie, across from Buffalo, New York.

From there the Friendship Trail takes you 25 kilometres to Port Colborne where you can join the Welland Canals Parkway. You will see ocean going ships travel through the locks and you can ride across the canal on the pedestrian ferry at Port Robinson. Follow the bike paths along the canal for 40 kilometres to return to Lake Ontario. For a longer ride, bicycle west to Dunnville and take the scenic River Road along the edge of the Grand River to York, then cross the Niagara Peninsula to Lake Ontario at Grimsby.

You might wish to try out the bike route with a special appeal for Theatre lovers, between the Shaw Festival in Niagara on the Lake and the Shakespearian Festival in Stratford. A package route guide is available for a 5 day "Theatre to Theatre Ride" with 110 kilometre average distance per day including turn-by-turn directions, accommodation suggestions and attractions is available. Starting at Niagara on the lake you bike through Six Nations First Nation, along the Grand River through Brantford and Paris north and west to Stratford. You return along Lake Erie and the Niagara Parkway through Port Dover, Fort Erie and Niagara Falls with stops in Ohsweken, Stratford, Port Dover and Port Colbourne.

A package route guide is available for a 4 day "Grand Niagara Ride" with 65 kilometre average distance per day including turn-by-turn directions, accommodation suggestions and attractions.
For information see: www.bikeontours.on.ca/custom.htm

## HURON SHORE

GODERICH - BAYFIELD - IPPERWASH BEACH -
GRAND BEND - SARNIA

**Features:** St. Clair Parkway and Sarnia Lakeshore Trails, beaches, ferries, history, First Nations, ships on St. Clair

BLUE WATER BRIDGE, SARNIA

River, waterfront – moderate, rolling to flat.

Historic Bayfield Village, although a lively port for small boats, looks pretty much as it did in the 1840's with its quaint main street including two historic hotels. You can check out the nearby Folmar Windmill, flea markets or shop for fresh and smoked fish. A back road route takes you 20 kilometres to Goderich, with its unique octagonal town square, lighthouse and beaches on Lake Huron. The town square is the location of the Saturday Farmers Market. The restored mills of Benmiller provide a scenic and peaceful luxury resort. There are a number of loop routes in this area.

Enjoy peaceful roads with cottages along Lake Huron, a back road connection to Pinery Provincial Park and the Rotary Trail (adjacent to Highway 21) to Grand Bend, the Kettle Point First Nation community and fruit growing areas; away from heavy motor vehicle traffic on Highway 21.

Ipperwash Beach is a broad sand beach with a shallow shoreline and spectacular sunsets. Best of all, you can enjoy it all day and park your motor vehicle at no charge. Take the 80 kilometre loop route to Arkona and the adjacent Rock Glen Conservation Area, the scenic centre of a tender fruit growing area, with cherries, peaches and apples.

The Sarnia area has bike paths from Errol on Lake Huron continuing 20 kilometres under the Blue Water Bridge. Heading south, the St. Clair Parkway is a 40 kilometre route all the way to Wallaceburg. Small ferries connect to the Bridge to Bay Trail in Michigan at Sombra [Marine City] and Walpole Island [Algonac].

CHANTRY ISLAND, SOUTHAMPTON

**Features:** Bike paths, beaches, historic, theatre, ferry, waterfront along Lake Ontario and St. Lawrence River, moderate—flat to rolling Area Map

This wonderful greenway traverses the largest urban areas in Ontario, yet is still very scenic and follows the shore of Lake Ontario and the St. Lawrence River. You can bicycle all the way from Niagara to the border of the Province of Quebec, east of Cornwall.

Starting from picturesque and historic Niagara-on-the-Lake, you'll pass through Toronto's Harbourfront, attractive beachfronts, and residential neighbourhoods, to quiet lakefront roads, farmland and small historic towns including charming Port Hope & Cobourg, Bloomfield, Picton, and on to the Glenora Ferry. Enjoy the bike paths of the Loyalist Parkway and Thousand Islands Parkway, Kingston, "the Limestone City", Fort Henry and historic Brockville and Prescott. This is wonderful ride with all of the tourist services that you could desire. Easy, flat to slightly rolling.

The Waterfront Trail is also a great starting point for multiday bike ride loops going west or east on the Waterfront Trail and then north to Rice Lake, Campbellford, Perth and all the way to Ottawa. Route information packages with turn-by-turn route guides are available at www.bikeontours.on.ca/custom.htm.

One of the package route guides available is a 5 day "Lake Ontario and Trent Canal Ride" with either 60 or 100 kilometre average distances per day, accommodation suggestions and attraction details. Starting at Picton, you bike through Cobourg or Port Hope north to Rice Lake and the Trent Canal.

From there, the 60 kilometre per day ride crosses the Bay of Quinte at Belleville. The 100 kilometre per day ride includes Kingston and the Glenora Ferry. Luggage transfer and accommodation reservations are available. For information see: www.bikeontours.on.ca/custom.htm

## WATERFRONT TRAIL

NIAGARA-ON-THE-LAKE - HAMILTON
TORONTO - COBOURG - KINGSTON
BROCKVILLE - CORNWALL

## BRUCE PENINSULA

OWEN SOUND - COLLINGWOOD
PORT ELGIN - KINCARDINE - PAISLEY - MARKDALE

**Features:** Georgian Trail, Saugeen Trail, beaches, breweries, First Nations, Mennonite, waterfalls, waterfront — easy to difficult, flat to rolling hills..

A quiet and scenic area which goes from the port of Owen Sound, past the rugged rocky shores and clear water of Georgian Bay and Colpoys Bay, to miles of quiet sand beaches on Lake Huron, and through peaceful farming areas. See the cascading eighty foot high waterfall at Inglis Falls near Owen Sound and visit the home of Wiarton Willie, the world famous groundhog weather forecaster who makes his prediction each February. It is a pleasant 80 kilometre ride from Owen Sound to Southampton and Port Elgin on Lake Huron.

Enjoy the popular Summerfolk Music and Craft Festival, late August in Owen Sound and check for local special events happening most summer weekends in the resort towns of Port Elgin and Southampton.

The Beaver Valley is unique and scenic with steep hills on each side, which meet at Kimberley. This is a beautiful area which suits cyclists at all levels–an easy ride on the hard packed gravel Georgian Trail with an access to beaches on Georgian Bay between Meaford and Collingwood, a moderate 20 kilometre ride up the scenic valley to Kimberley or a challenging 40 kilometre ride on to Flesherton and Markdale.

The Saugeen River valley is a rural countryside experience with small towns, quiet roads and an Amish Mennonite farming area. Bicycling between Paisley, Chesley, Hanover, Mildmay and Formosa makes a pleasant 100 kilometre ride. The reminders of the past are everywhere with rushing water past mills and mill ruins. Visit and sample the brew from two historic breweries still in operation on the route, the 1859 Neustadt Springs Brewery and the 1870 Formosa Springs Brewery. The area is also well known as a great place for canoeing and kayaking.

A package route guide is available for a 4 or 6 day "Bruce Peninsula Ride" with a 57 or 85 kilometre average distance per day including turn by turn directions, accommodation suggestions and attractions. Starting from Owen Sound, you bike close to the shore of Georgian Bay and Colpoys Bay through Wiarton to the shore of Lake Huron traveling south to Kincardine and Point Clark. Return through Mennonite farming countryside and historic mill towns on the Saugeen River. For information see: www.bikeontours.on.ca/custom.htm

## NORTHUMBERLAND

COBOURG - PORT HOPE - RICE LAKE - COLBORNE
BRIGHTON

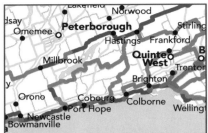

**Features:** Waterfront Trail, Trent Canal, apple orchards, beaches, historic, First Nations, waterfront - moderate to difficult, hilly north of Lake Ontario.

You can enjoy an easy ride along Lake Ontario through the old fashioned main streets of delightful heritage towns. In Port Hope enjoy Theatre and music at the atmospheric Capitol Theatre; visit the Canadian Firefighters Museum or shop for antiques and collectibles on the unique mid-19th century main street. Cobourg, with its beach and boardwalk on Lake Ontario, offers Theatre at the 1860 Victoria Hall. Continue on the Waterfront Trail to visit the landmark "Big Apple" in Colborne, with a charming town square. Near Brighton, Presqu'ile Provincial Park offers beaches and natural areas to explore. It is 14 kilometres from Port Hope to Cobourg, a further 25 to Colborne and an additional 15 to Brighton.

You'll encounter picture perfect rolling farmland with wooded hills on your way to naturally beautiful Rice Lake and the Alderville First Nation community. Try the 150 kilometre challenging loop route from Cobourg through Port Hope to Rice Lake and Warkworth, returning under Highway 401 along scenic Shelter Valley Road.

The lakeshore towns of Northumberland are great starting points for multiday bike ride loops. A package route guide is available for a 5 day "Lake Ontario and Trent Canal Ride" with a 60 or 100 kilometre average distance per day including turn by turn directions, accommodation suggestions and attractions. Starting at Picton, you bike through Cobourg or Port Hope north to Rice Lake and the Trent Canal. The 60 kilometre per day ride crosses the Bay of Quinte at Belleville. The 100 kilometre per day ride includes Kingston and the Glenora Ferry. Luggage transfer and accommodation reservations are available.

POINT PELEE BOARDWALK

## ERIE SHORES

### WINDSOR - LEAMINGTON - KINGSVILLE - CHATHAM PELEE ISLAND

**Features:** Chrysler Greenway Trail, beaches, bird watching, ferry, French Canadian, historic, waterfront, wineries–easy, flat.

You can bike through the most southerly part of Canada, close to the shore of the Detroit River, Lake St. Clair, the Thames River and Lake Erie. This area is very flat, making it perfect for an easy early or late season rides since it is frost free a month longer than the rest of Ontario.

The Chrysler Canada Greenway Trail follows an abandoned rail line from the paradise of Colisanti's Tropical Gardens to the Colio Winery in Harrow and the south side of Windsor.

Leamington makes a great centre for exploring this area and a number of loop routes are available. From there you can bicycle 15 kilometres to Point Pelee, 50 kilometres to Amherstburg, 70 kilometres to Windsor or 80 kilometres to Chatham.

Enjoy scenic countryside including the French Canadian community of Pain Court as well as the settlements of black slaves who escaped from the United States at North Buxton. Learn about the history of this area by visiting the restored Buxton National Historic Site and Museum, 1850 John Park homestead on the lake at Colchester, and Fort Malden on the river in historic Amherstburg.

This area is home to one of Ontario's oldest wineries, the Pelee Island Winery in Kingsville, as well as a growing number of new ones close to Lake Erie. This unique natural area produces an abundance of fresh fruit and vegetables from the fields and acres of greenhouses.

Explore the boardwalk, nature trails and beaches of Point Pelee National Park, featuring a tree canopied paved road down to the tip. Pelee Island makes an interesting day trip from Leamington or Kingsville harbour along quiet lakefront roads.

A package route guide is available for a 4 or 5 day "Erie Shores and Pelee Ride" with a 63 kilometre average distance per day including turn by turn directions, accommodation suggestions and attractions. Starting from Windsor or Amherstburg, you bike close to the shore of Lake Erie, the Thames River and Lake St. Clair including Point Pelee National Park. The 5th day is an optional day trip travelling by ferry to bicycle Pelee Island. Luggage transfer and accommodation reservations are available. For information see: www.bikeontours.on.ca/custom.htm

## GRAND RIVER

### BRANTFORD - PARIS - SIX NATIONS TERRITORY ST. JACOBS - ELORA

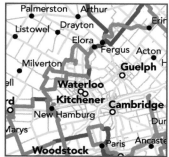

**Features:** Grand River Trails, Hamilton - Brantford Rail Trail, covered bridge, historic, First Nations, Mennonite, river valley– moderate, rolling.

Encounter horses and buggies and cross Ontario's last remaining covered bridge at West Montrose. You are certain to see Mennonites at work in the fields, travelling to town or to the meetinghouses on Sunday in Elmira, near Floradale and near Linwood. This is one of the few areas in Ontario where the Amish and old order Mennonites are living much as they did when they first settled in the early 1800's.

A 130 kilometre loop route takes you from St. Jacobs across the covered bridge to Fergus, returning through Elmira and Wellesley. Follow the Grand River and see the scenic Elora Gorge from the 1870 Elora Mill – now an inn and restaurant – or explore the gorge by taking a short walk from town.

There is a 160 kilometre loop route centred the Grand River towns around Brantford including Paris, Ancaster and the Six Nations Territory.

The Grand River is a designated Canadian Heritage River and it's a wonderful natural resource for hiking, canoeing, bird watching, fishing and camping as well as bicycling. Enjoy the scenic valley towns, lush rolling countryside and the large Six Nations native settlement of loyalist natives who relocated from the Mohawk valley of New York State in 1784.

The family home of Alexander Graham Bell overlooks the Grand River, where he developed the principle of the telephone in 1874. From here, the first long distance telephone call was made, to Paris, ON. Other attractions in Brantford include a native cultural centre, replica 17th century Iroquoian village, a restored 1919 performing arts centre, military heritage and motorcycle museums.

MENNONITE TRANSPORT

## Ten Tips For Enjoyable Bicycle Touring

1. Wear A Helmet - Helmets save lives and prevent serious injuries. While other injuries can heal, a head injury can lead to disability or death.

2. Check Your Bike - Use a bike with a lightweight alloy frame and have it checked out by a trained bicycle mechanic if you are not certain that it is in good condition. Carry an inner tube to fit your tires, a tire pump and tools to change a flat.

3. Train To Enjoy The Ride - Ride 30 kilometers (20 miles) or more several times each week. Ride the distance that you plan to ride in a day at least once prior to the trip

4. Ride Safely And Be Visible - Always follow the rules of the road. Wear bright colours to increase your visibility. Use a headlight and rear light at night.

5. Be Alert - Look ahead constantly for hazards including turning vehicles, rail tracks, sewer grates, road debris and broken pavement.

6. Drink Water - Take a large water bottle and drink before you are thirsty to avoid dehydration.

7. Pack A Snack - Carry your favourite snack such as fruit, fruit juice and granola bars to eat on the road. Eating dairy products (other than yogurt) and large meals on a strenuous ride may cause indigestion.

8. Dress For Comfort - Wear purpose designed bike shorts to protect the bike seat contact area (available in styles that look like walking shorts or form fitting lycra shorts). Dress in layers on cool days so that you can adjust your clothing to stay comfortable.

9. Lock Your Bike - When your bike is out of sight lock the rear wheel, frame (and front wheel if possible) to a secure object. A "U" shaped security lock is best.

10. Reserve Ahead - Always reserve needed overnight accommodation in advance. Be certain that you will have a comfortable place to rest and a secure place for your bicycle at the end of the ride.

> For a complete marked Route Map and turn by turn Route Description with Attractions, Accommodation, Restaurant and Bike Repair Shop List; customized to meet your specific needs and the locations that you want to travel, contact Bike On Tours.
> E-mail to info@bikeontours.on.ca

WELLAND CANAL

## Touring Resources

You may also find the following list of resources useful when planning a bike trip in Ontario:

**Ontario Travel Information**
www.ontariotravel.net
www.ontariooutdoor.com
Tel: (800) 668 2746

**Bicycle Ontario**
www.bicycleontario.ca

**Via Rail**
Trains with bike racks in Ontario and Quebec between Windsor, London, Toronto, Ottawa, Montreal, Quebec City, Senneterre, Jonquiere
www.viarail.ca/en/bike

**Waterfront Trail**
Niagara on the Lake – Toronto – Cornwall – Quebec Border
www.waterfronttrail.org

**Share The Road Cycling Coalition – Ontario Cycling Advocacy**
www.sharetheroad.ca

**Quebec's Route Verte**
**Bicycle Routes in Quebec**
www.routeverte.com/rv/index2010_e.php

**Quebec Tourism**
www.bonjourquebec.com/ca-en/accueil0.html

**Manitoba Tourism**
www.travelmanitoba.com

**Adventure Cycling Association**
**United States Bicycle Routes And Touring Information**
www.adventurecycling.org/cyp/index.cfm

**Total Bike - Bicycle Repair Guide**
www.totalbike.com/repair/

**Cycling Performance Tips - Training and diet advice**
www.cptips.com

### Share Your KNOWLEDGE
With your feedback, we can make this atlas even better!
E-mail your comments to info@mapmobility.com

# Map Section Contents

# Ontario BICYCLE *Touring Atlas*

## Legend

Bike On Tours route - paved

Bike On Tours route - unpaved

Other bike route - paved

Other bike route - unpaved

⚠ Caution - hazard for cyclists
*(Note: These aren't the only hazards you could encounter!)*

Steep Incline (showing direction of slope)

· · · · Hiking Trail

· · · · Bicycle / Hiking Trail
*(Surface type and conditions unverified; inquire locally)*

Primary Highway

Secondary Highway

County / Regional Road

Other Road

Scenic Parkway

Expressway

Toll Expressway

Undivided expressway

Interchange / Partial interchange

**661** Interchange Exit Number

**400** Ontario King's Highway

**71** County / Regional Highway

**600** Secondary Highway

**17** Trans-Canada Highway

Ferry (automobile)

Ferry (passenger)

Parks Canada Waterway

Lake

Stream / River

Public Forest

Park

T Wildlife Reserve

General Built-Up Area

● Point of Interest

✈ Major Airport

✦ Minor Airport

❂ Ontario Provincial Police

▲ Service Centre

⛱ Picnic Area

▼ 19 ▼ Distance in Kilometres

▼ 78 ▼ Cumulative Distance (kms)

🅿? Tourist Information-Provincial / Regional

Railway

⚒ Ontario Northland Station

🚆 Commuter Train Station

VIA VIA Train Station

⚑⚑ Border Crossing

National Park / Historic Site

Ontario Provincial Park

▲ Camping (Organized Park)

▲ No Camping (Organized Park)

△ Camping (Unorganized Park)

△ No Camping (Unorganized Park)

Ski Area

International Boundary

Provincial Boundary

County / Regional Boundary

Township / Municipal Boundary

**SIMCOE** Incorporated Municipality

**Dunlop** Unincorporated Municipality

■ **LONDON**
■ **SUDBURY**   Type size and dot
■ **Tillsonburg**   indicative of
■ **Lakefield**   population size
● **Arklan**

■ **LONDON**   Highlight indicates
■ **SUDBURY**   that the community has an entry in the
■ **Tillsonburg**   Community Guide index at the end of
■ **Lakefield**   this book
● **Arklan**

## WARNING AND DISCLAIMER:

⚠ Cyclists are solely responsible for risks encountered and for their own safety. The following are potential safety hazards: weather, poor road surface, heavy traffic, reduced visibility, physical or mental well-being, damaged equipment, speed, knowledge or technique, food or drink, road position, improper procedure, protection, scheduling, new or unexpected situation, fatigue, distraction, peer pressure. Neither Bike On Tours, nor the authors and publishers assume any responsibility for the accuracy of this guide and associated maps, the safety or fitness of the suggested routes or any damages and/or claims whatsoever associated with use.

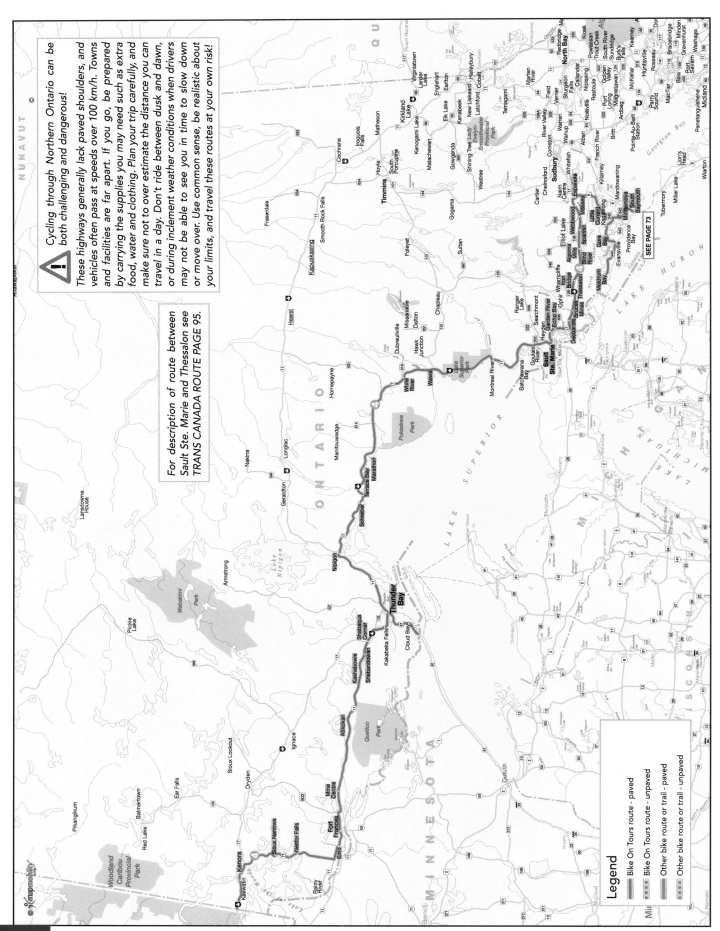

Cycling through Northern Ontario can be both challenging and dangerous!

These highways generally lack paved shoulders, and vehicles often pass at speeds over 100 km/h. Towns and facilities are far apart. If you go, be prepared by carrying the supplies you may need such as extra food, water and clothing. Plan your trip carefully, and make sure not to over estimate the distance you can travel in a day. Don't ride between dusk and dawn, or during inclement weather conditions when drivers may not be able to see you in time to slow down or move over. Use common sense, be realistic about your limits, and travel these routes at your own risk!

For description of route between Sault Ste. Marie and Thessalon see TRANS CANADA ROUTE PAGE 95.

SEE PAGE 73

### Legend

- Bike On Tours route - paved
- Bike On Tours route - unpaved
- Other bike route or trail - paved
- Other bike route or trail - unpaved

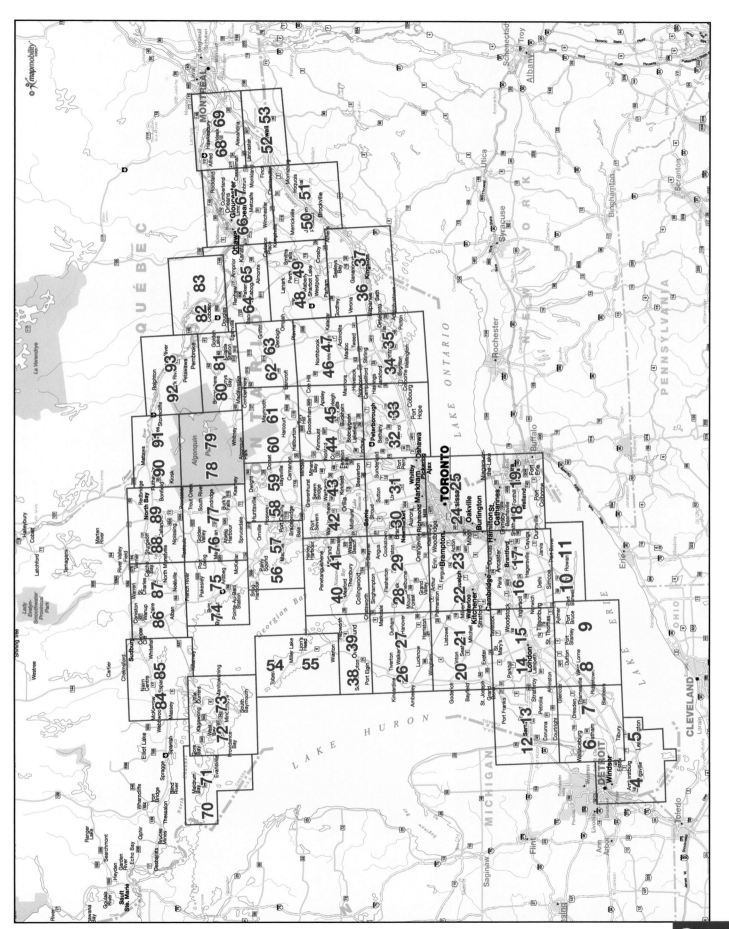

**Southern Ontario Key Map** 3

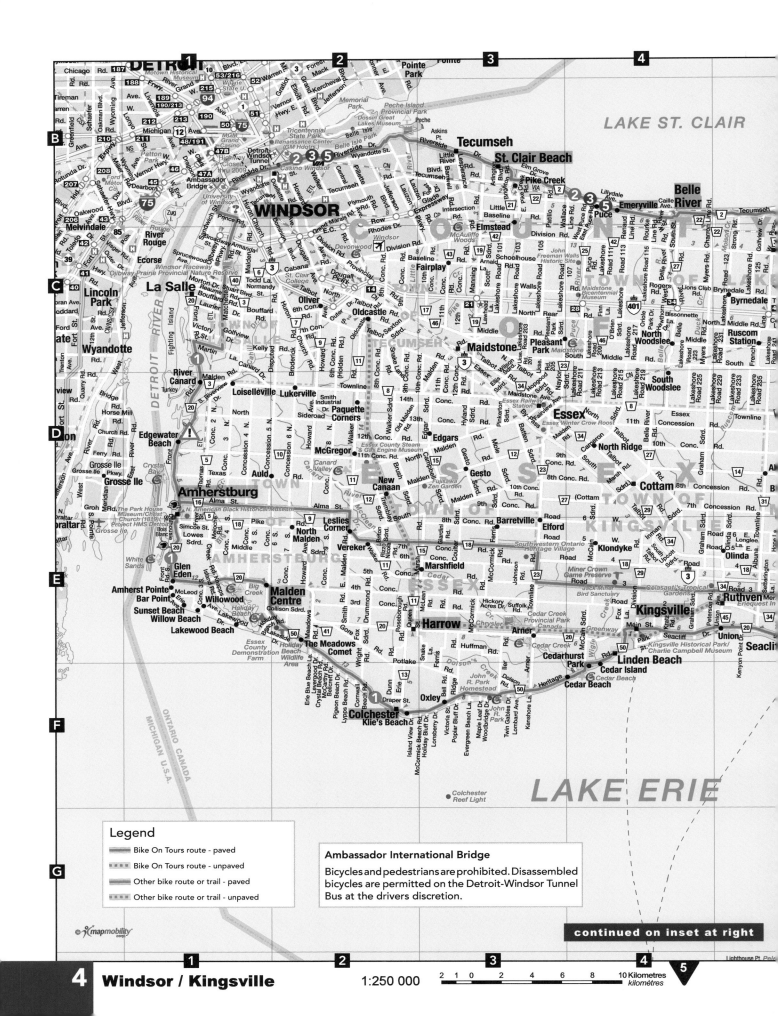

## Legend

- Bike On Tours route - paved
- Bike On Tours route - unpaved
- Other bike route or trail - paved
- Other bike route or trail - unpaved

**Ambassador International Bridge**

Bicycles and pedestrians are prohibited. Disassembled bicycles are permitted on the Detroit-Windsor Tunnel Bus at the drivers discretion.

© mapmobility corp.

**continued on inset at right**

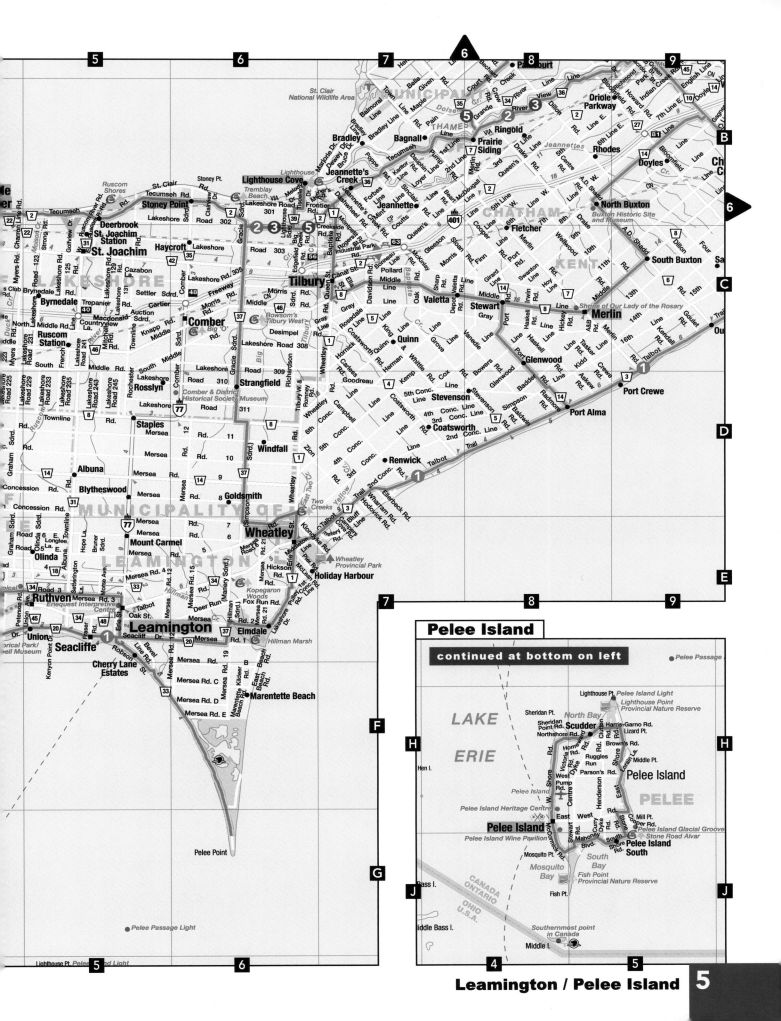

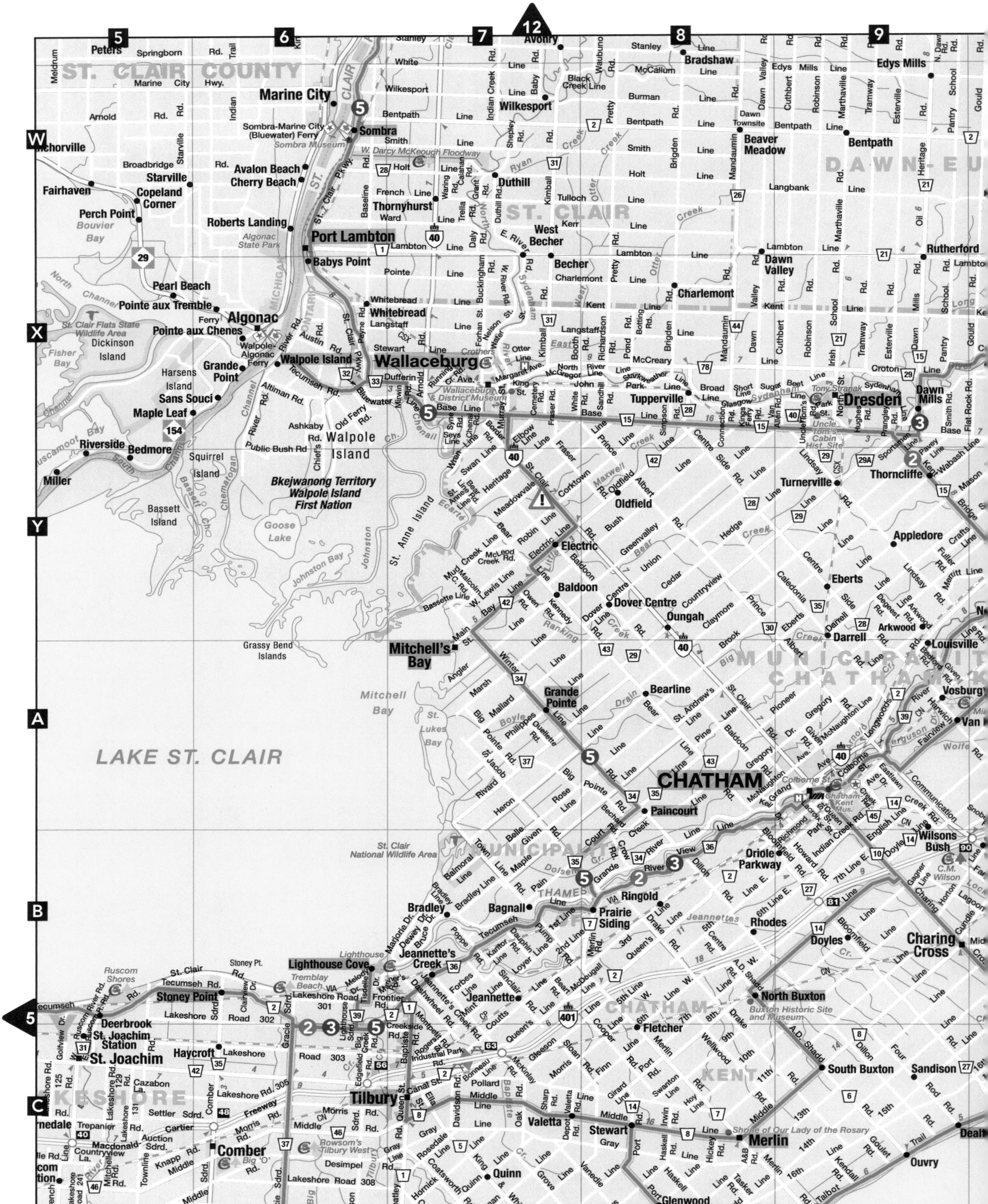
LAKE ST. CLAIR
ST. CLAIR COUNTY
ST. CLAIR
DAWN-EU
MUNICIPALITY CHATHAM-KENT
MUNICIPALITY CHATHAM-KENT
CHATHAM
Marine City
Sombra
Sombra-Marine City (Bluewater) Ferry
Sombra Museum
W. Darcy McKeough Floodway
Avalon Beach
Cherry Beach
Roberts Landing
Algonac State Park
Port Lambton
Babys Point
Starville
Copeland Corner
Fairhaven
Perch Point
Bouvier Bay
Pearl Beach
Pointe aux Tremble
Algonac
Pointe aux Chenes
Walpole-Algonac Ferry
St. Clair Flats State Wildlife Area
Dickinson Island
Fisher Bay
Harsens Island
Grande Point
Walpole Island
Sans Souci
Maple Leaf
Riverside
Bedmore
Miller
Squirrel Island
Bassett Island
Bkejwanong Territory
Walpole Island First Nation
Goose Lake
Johnston Bay
St. Anne Island
Grassy Bend Islands
Mitchell's Bay
Mitchell Bay
St. Lukes Bay
Wallaceburg
Wallaceburg & District Museum
Thornyhurst
Duthill
West Becher
Becher
Whitebread
Wilkesport
Avonry
Bradshaw
Edys Mills
Beaver Meadow
Bentpath
Dawn Valley
Rutherford
Charlemont
Tupperville
Dresden
Uncle Tom's Cabin Hist. Site
Dawn Mills
Thorncliffe
Turnerville
Oldfield
Electric
Baldoon
Dover Centre
Oungah
Appledore
Eberts
Darrell
Arkwood
Louisville
Bearline
Grande Pointe
Vosburg
Paincourt
Chatham-Kent Mus.
Wilsons Bush
C.M. Wilson
Oriole Parkway
St. Clair National Wildlife Area
Bradley
Bagnall
Ringold
Prairie Siding
Rhodes
Doyles
Charing Cross
Lighthouse Cove
Jeannette's Creek
Jeannette
North Buxton
Buxton Historic Site and Museum
Fletcher
South Buxton
Sandison
Ruscom Shores
Stoney Point
Tremblay Beach
Deerbrook
St. Joachim Station
St. Joachim
Haycroft
Tilbury
Rowsom's Tilbury West
Comber
Valetta
Stewart
Merlin
Shrine of Our Lady of the Rosary
Quinn
Glenwood
Ouvry
Lakeshore
Kent
Thames
1:250 000
2 1 0 2 4 6 8 10 Kilometres kilomètres

LAKE ERIE

Legend
▬▬▬ Bike On Tours route - paved
▪▪▪ Bike On Tours route - unpaved
▬▬▬ Other bike route or trail - paved
▪▪▪ Other bike route or trail - unpaved

© mapmobility corp.

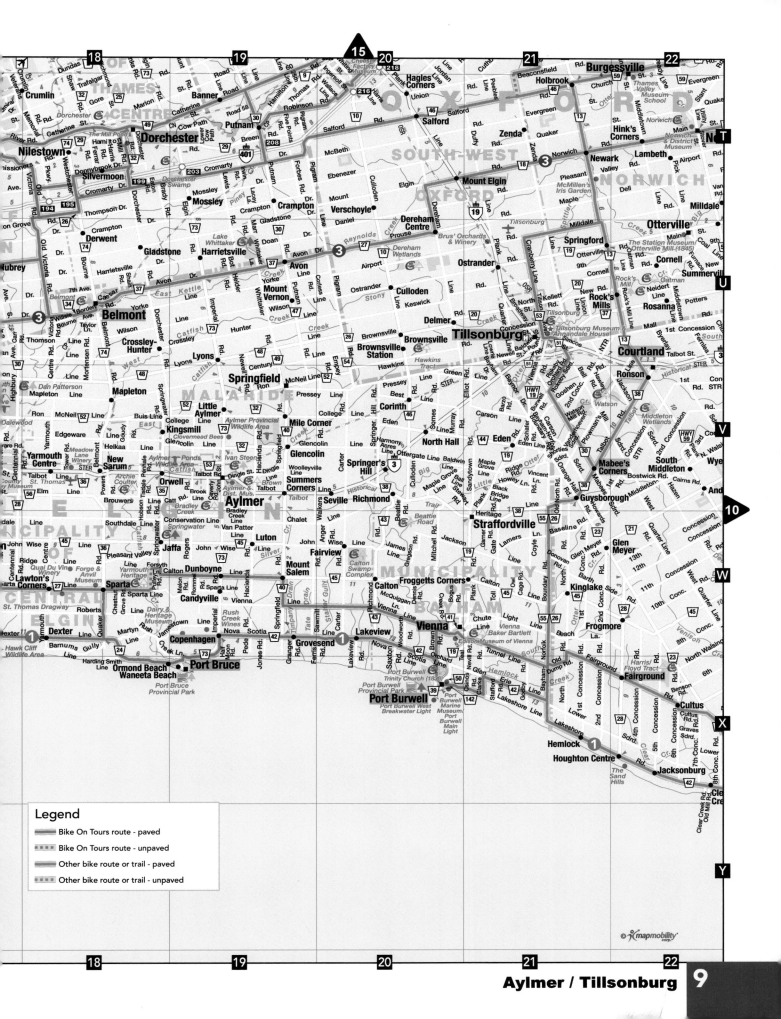

## Legend

Bike On Tours route - paved

Bike On Tours route - unpaved

Other bike route or trail - paved

Other bike route or trail - unpaved

© mapmobility corp.

1:250 000

2 1 0 2 4 6 8 10 Kilometres
kilomètres

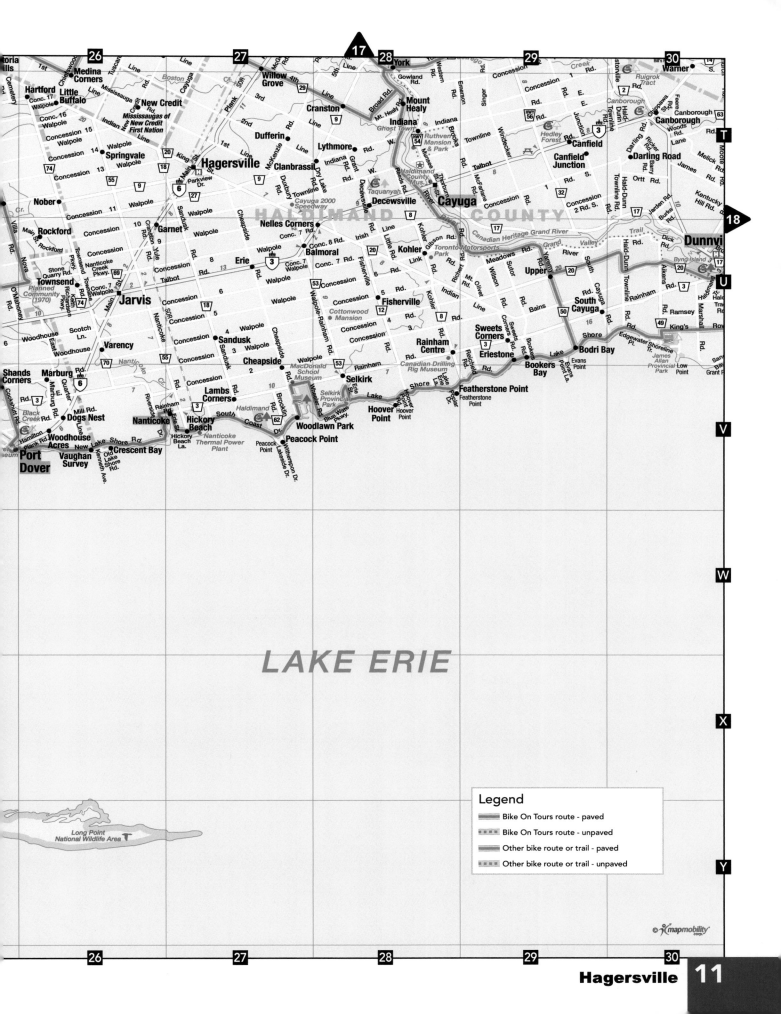

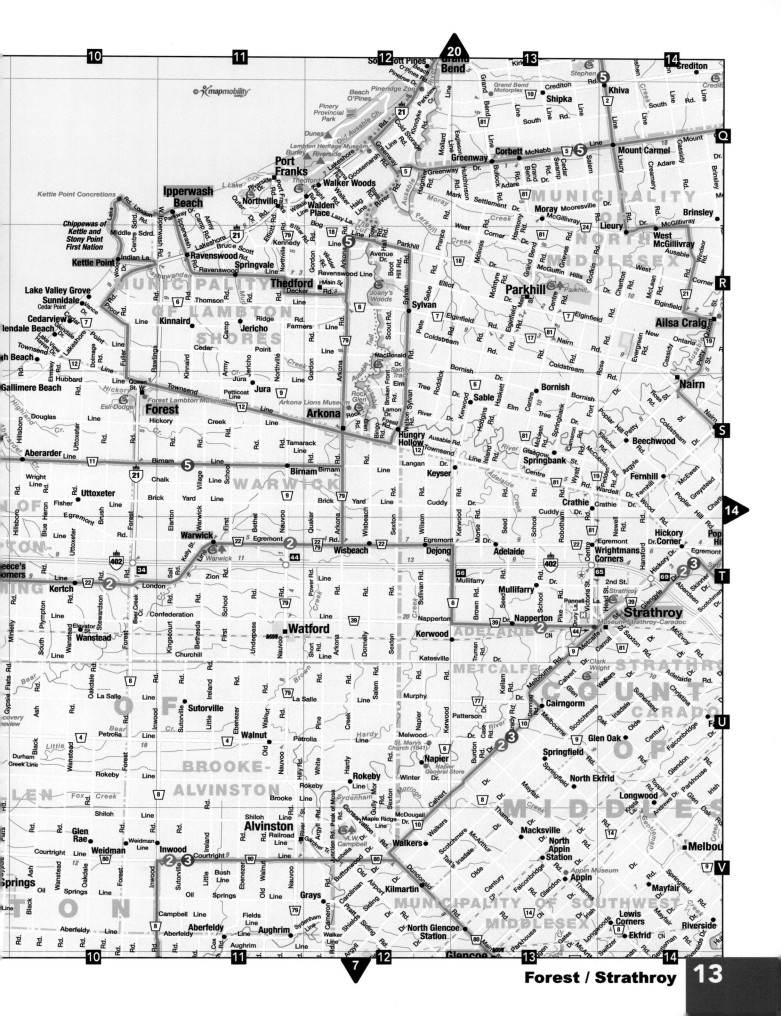

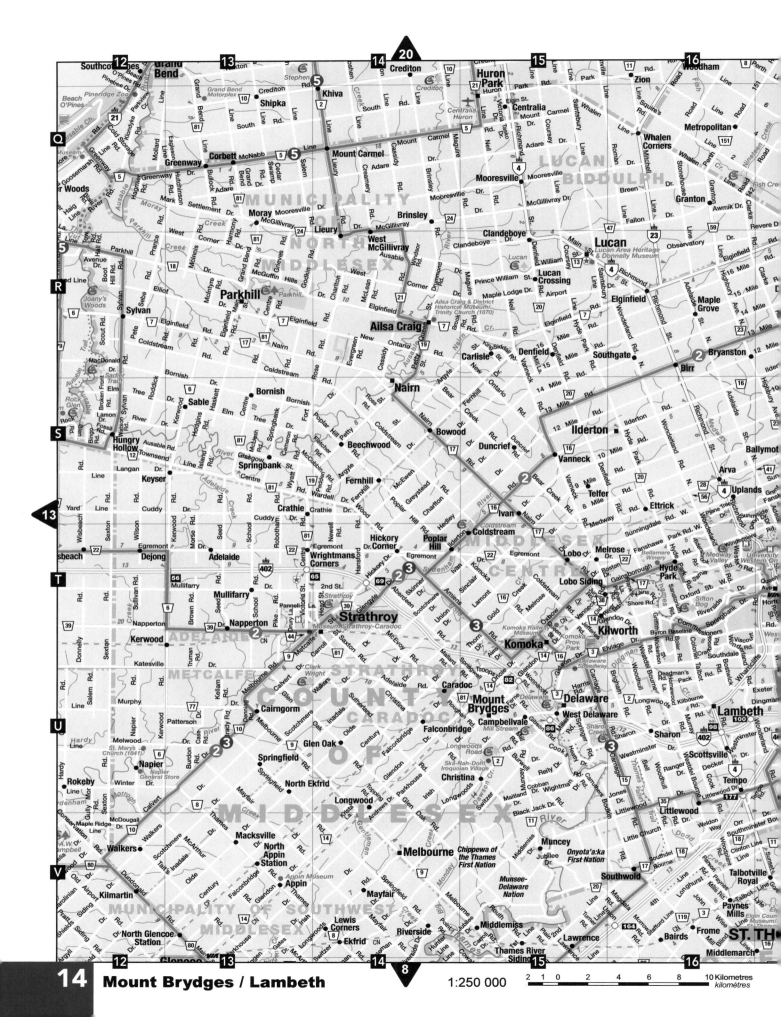

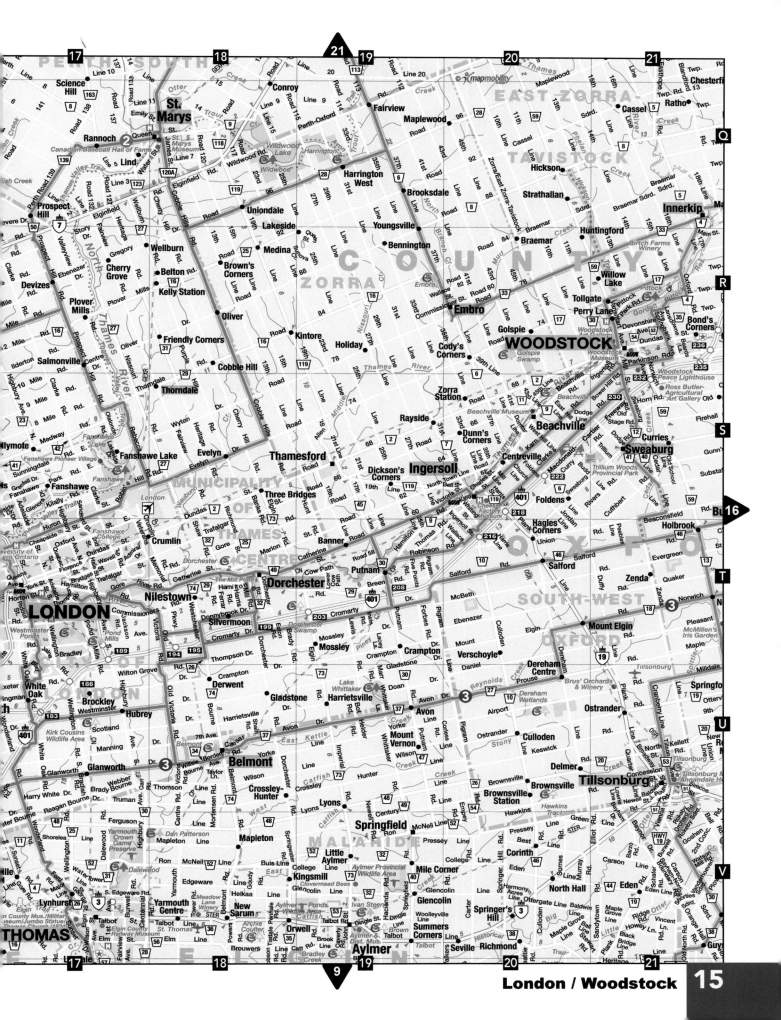

1:250 000

2 1 0 2 4 6 8 10 Kilometres
*kilomètres*

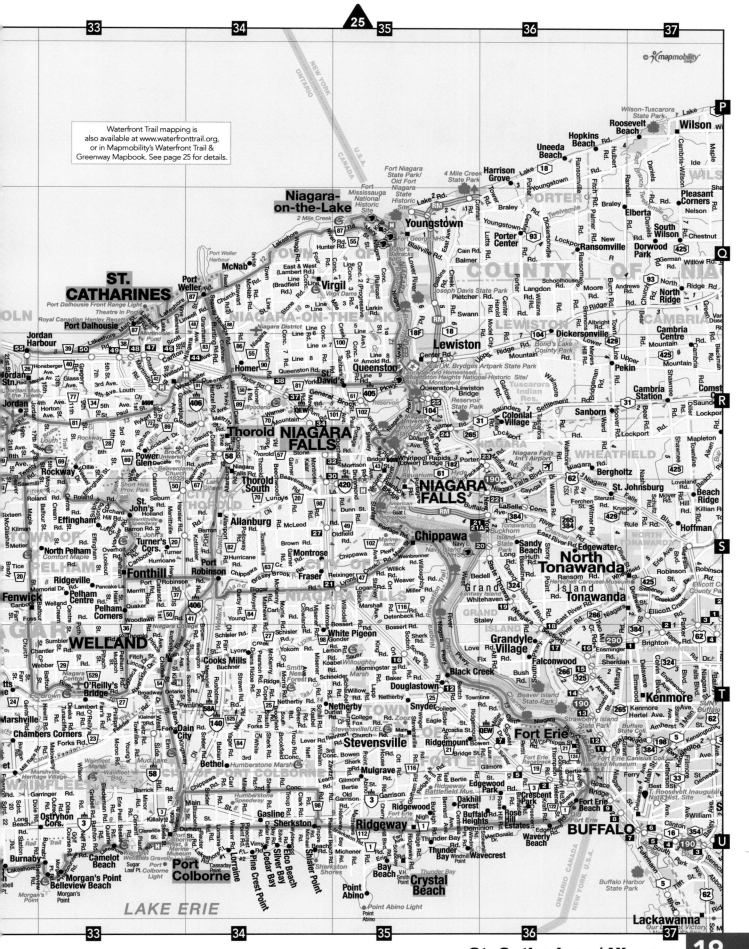

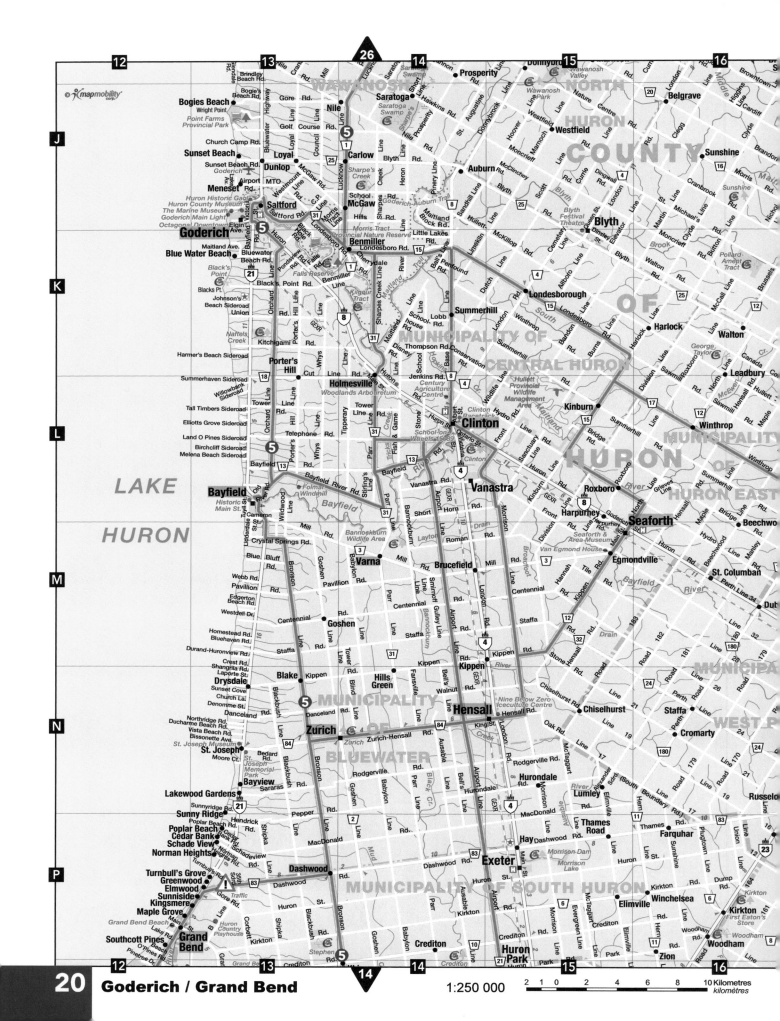

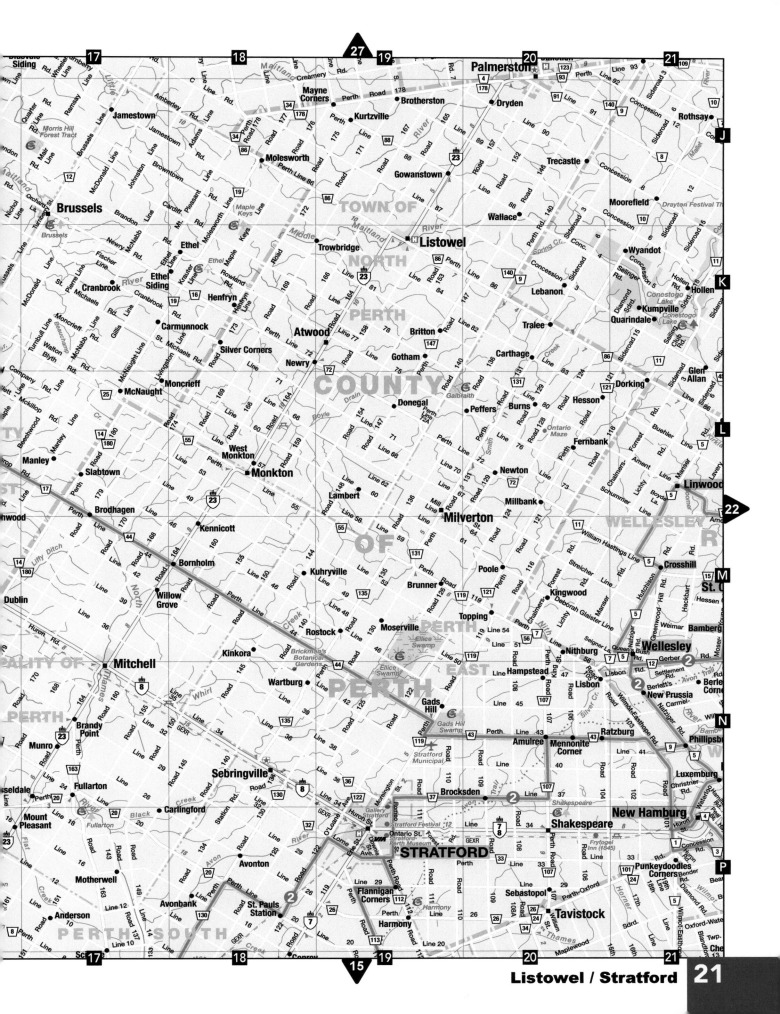

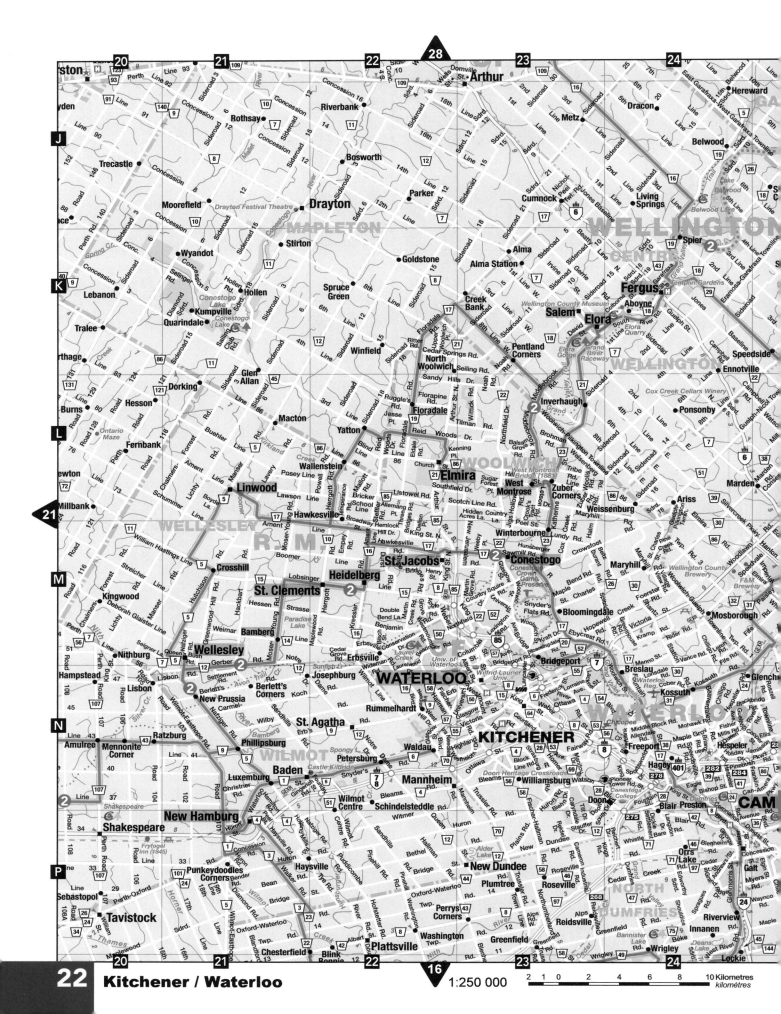

1:250 000

2 1 0 2 4 6 8 10 Kilometres
kilomètres

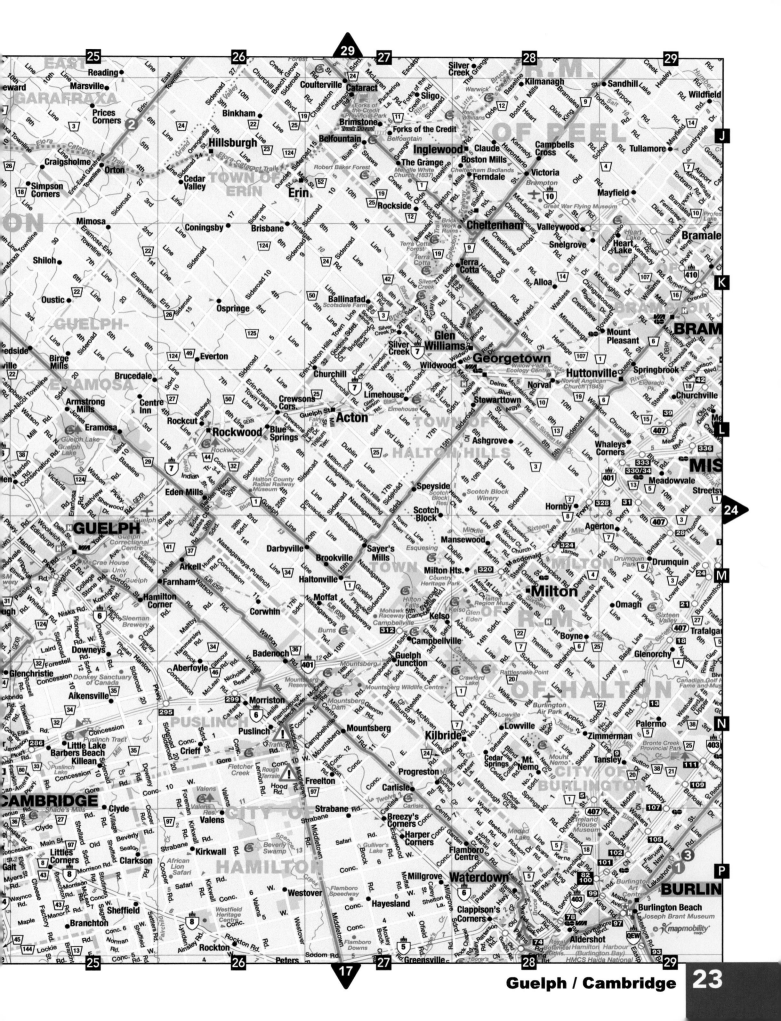

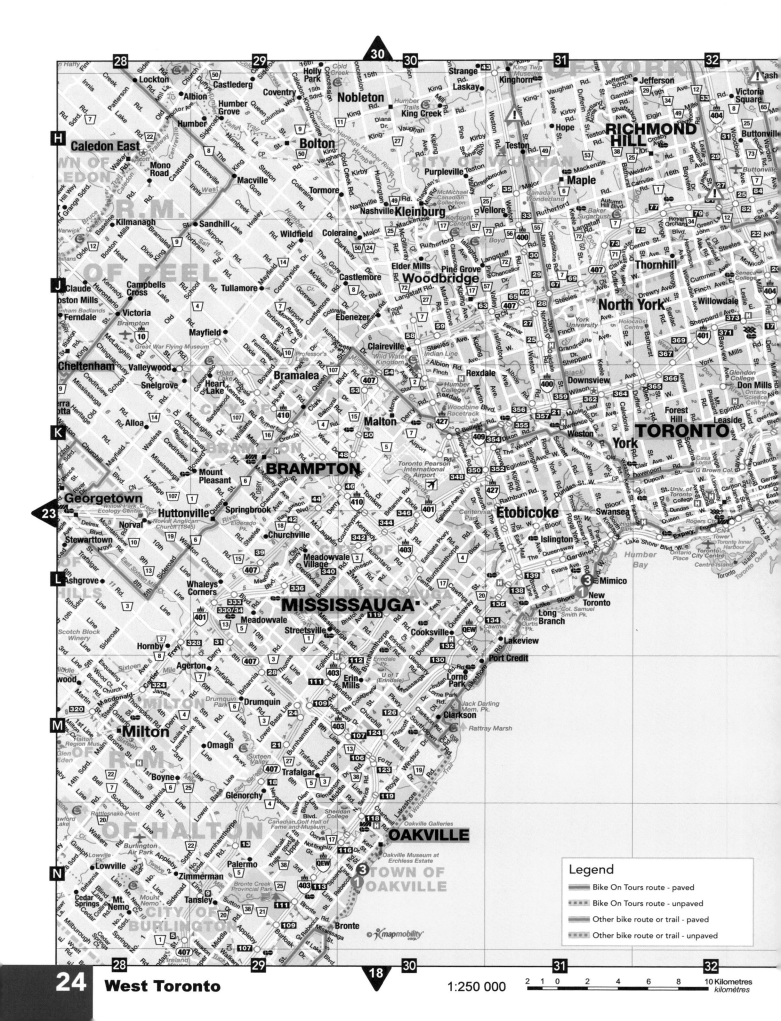

**Legend**

━━━ Bike On Tours route - paved

┅┅┅ Bike On Tours route - unpaved

━━━ Other bike route or trail - paved

┅┅┅ Other bike route or trail - unpaved

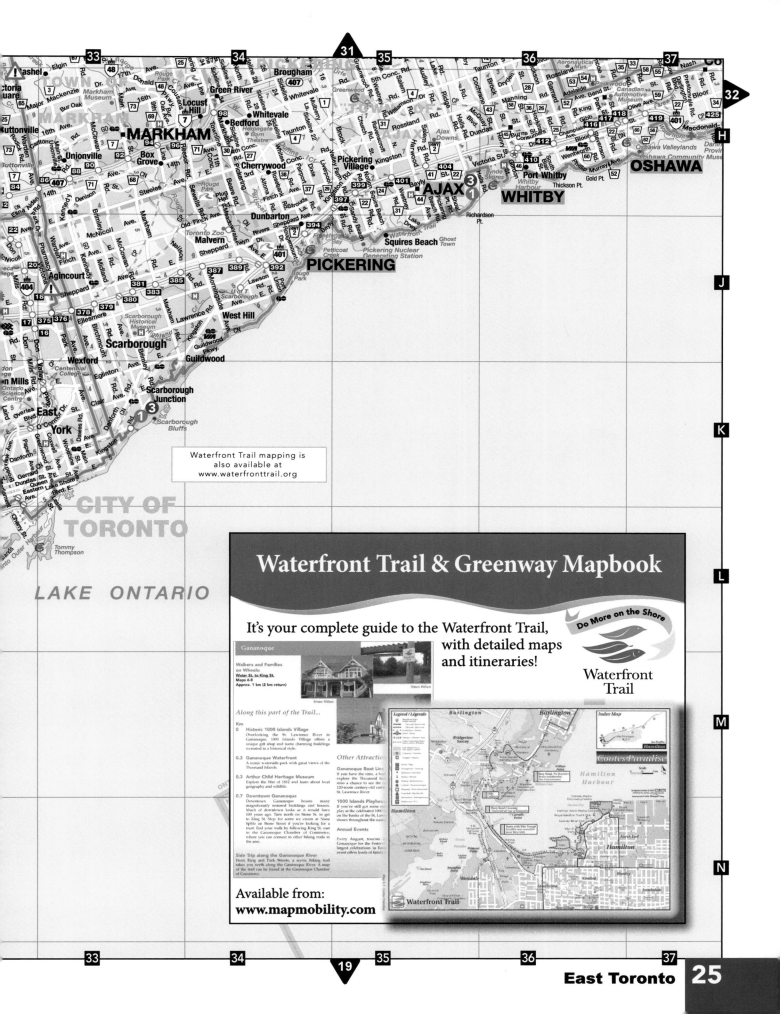

Waterfront Trail mapping is also available at www.waterfronttrail.org

## Waterfront Trail & Greenway Mapbook

It's your complete guide to the Waterfront Trail, with detailed maps and itineraries!

Do More on the Shore

Waterfront Trail

Available from:
**www.mapmobility.com**

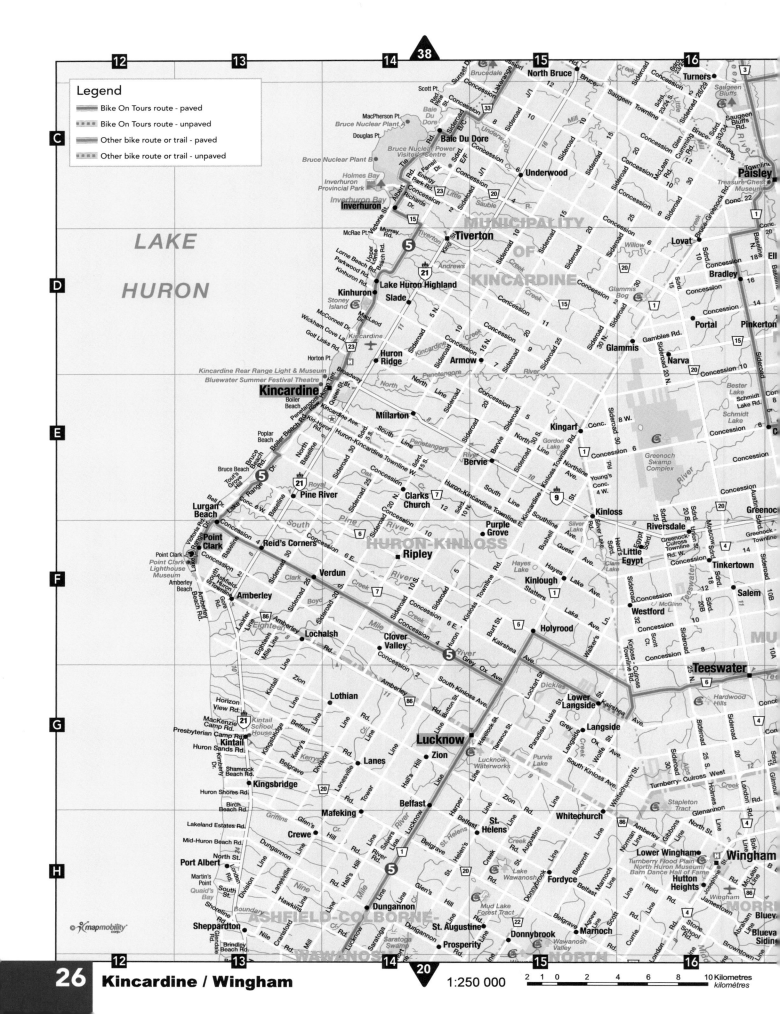

1:250 000

2  1  0    2    4    6    8    10 Kilometres
*kilomètres*

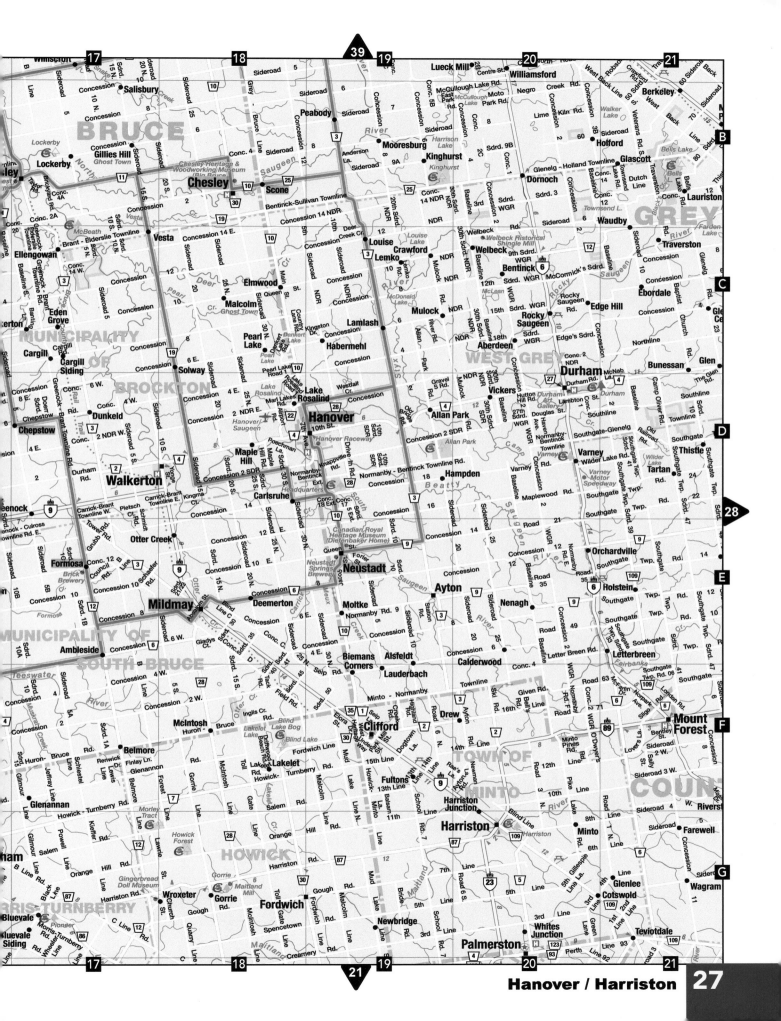

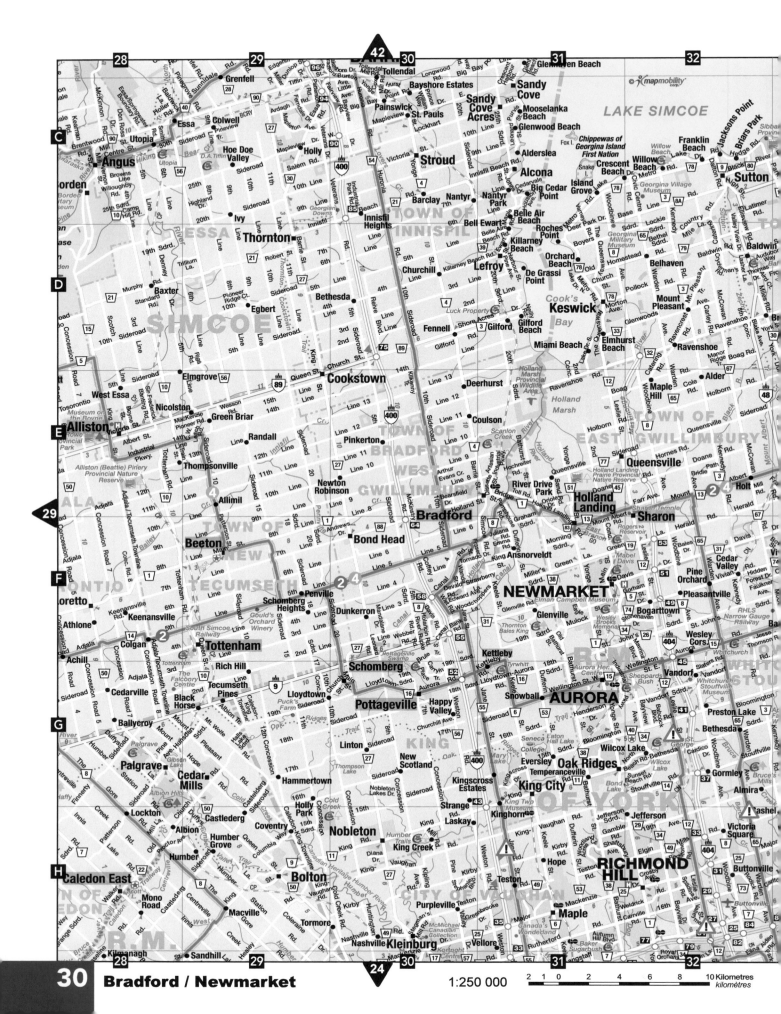

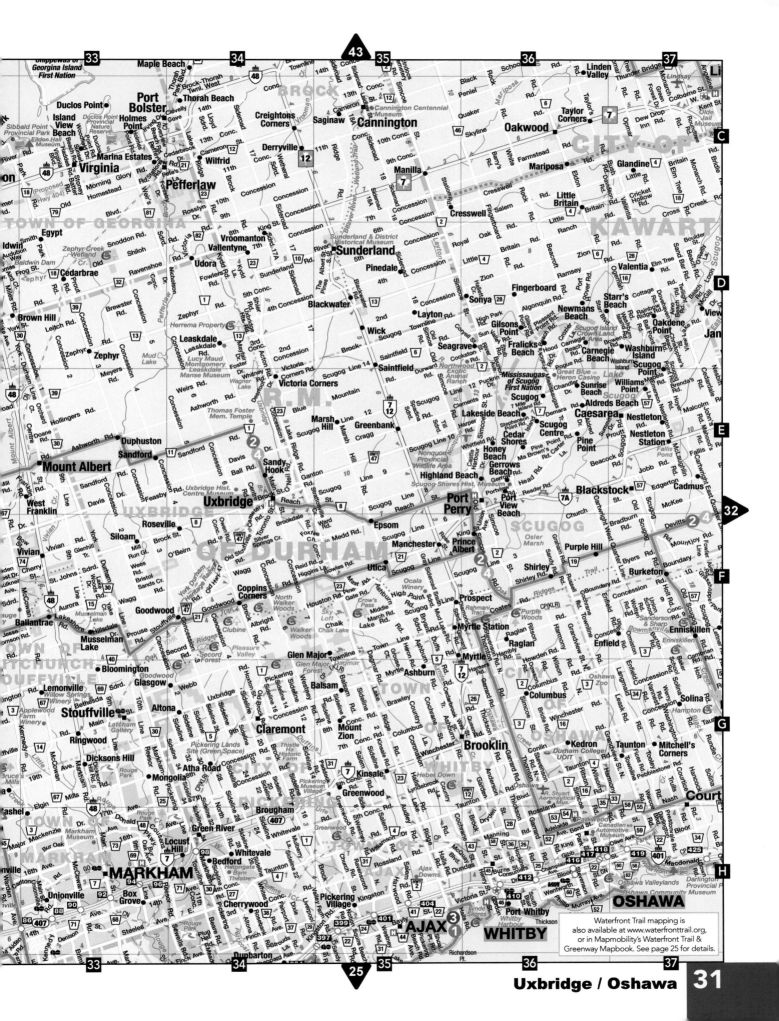

1:250 000

2 1 0   2   4   6   8   10 Kilometres
kilomètres

## Legend

Bike On Tours route - paved

Bike On Tours route - unpaved

Other bike route or trail - paved

Other bike route or trail - unpaved

Waterfront Trail mapping is
also available at www.waterfronttrail.org,
or in Mapmobility's Waterfront Trail &
Greenway Mapbook. See page 25 for details.

**34**   **Trenton / Belleville**      1:250 000    2 1 0   2   4   6   8    10 Kilometres
*kilomètres*

LAKE ONTARIO

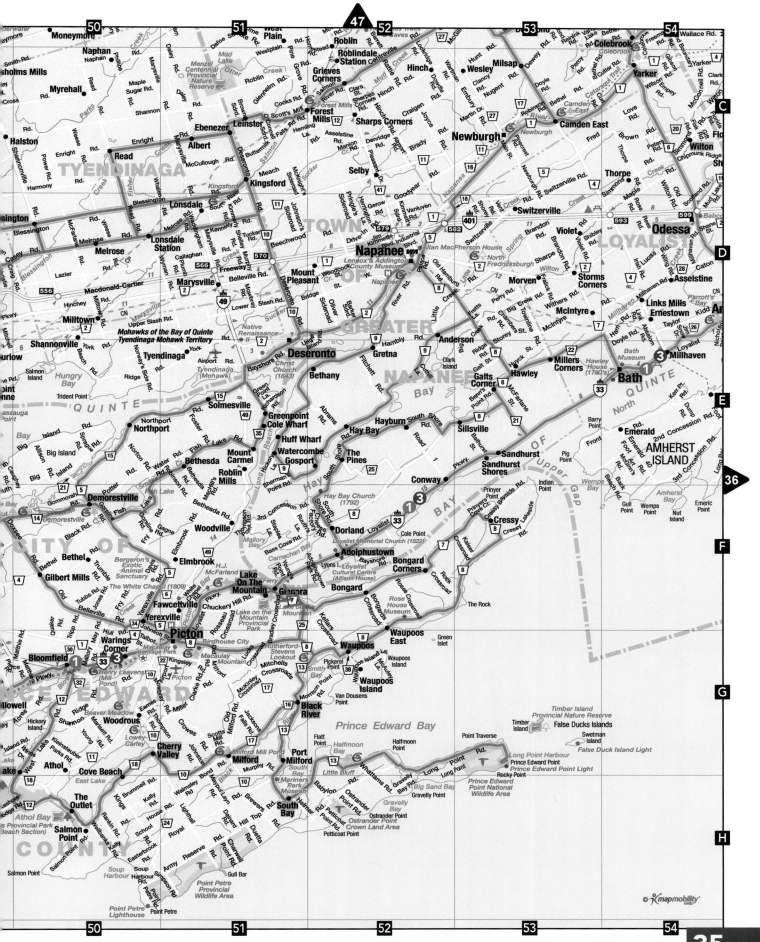

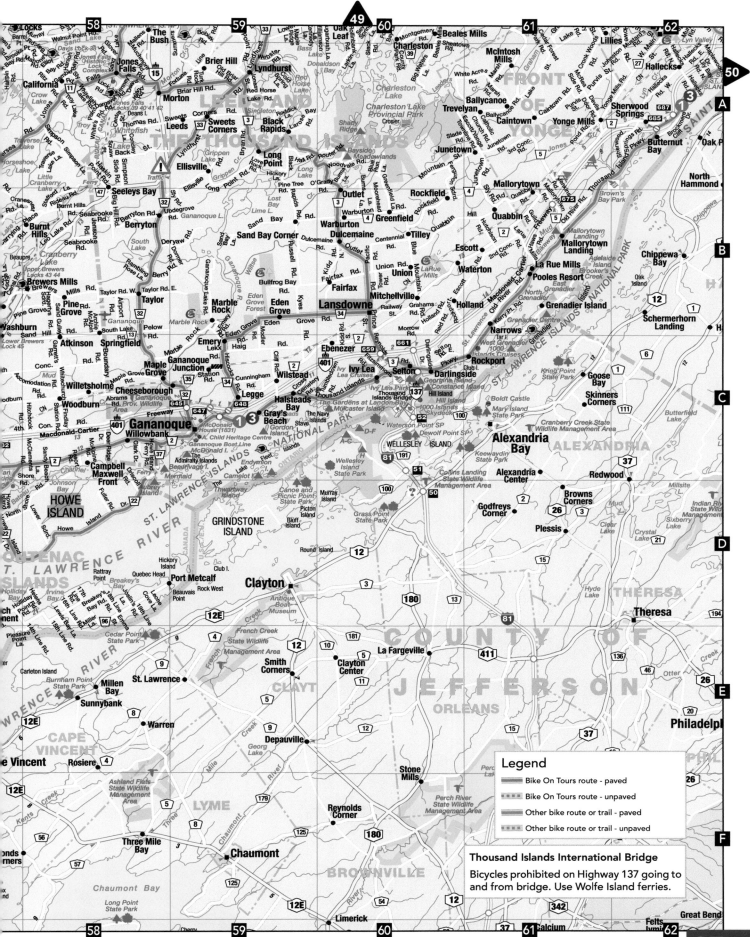

Gananoque **37**

## Legend

- Bike On Tours route - paved
- Bike On Tours route - unpaved
- Other bike route or trail - paved
- Other bike route or trail - unpaved

**LAKE HURON**

**TOWN OF SOUTH BRUCE PENINSULA**

**COUNTY**

**TOWN OF SAUGEEN SHORES**

**MUNICIPALITY OF ARRAN-ELDERSLIE**

Hope Bay
Adamsville
Edenhurst
Little Pike Pt.
Little Pike Bay
Purgatory Cove
Pike Bay
Kolfage Island
Fishing Islands Nature
Howdenvale
St. Jean's Point Nature
Ghegheto Island
Red Bay
Red Bay Nature
Beament Island
Fishing Islands Nature
Evelyn Island
Argyle Island
Burke Island
Main Station Island
Jack Island
Cranberry Island
Smokehouse Island
Vimy Island
Whitefish Island
Mar
Wiarton
Hodgins Lake
Isaac Lake
Boat Lake
Oliphant
Chiefs Pt.
Chiefs Point Bay
Clavering
Sauble Falls
Sauble Falls Provincial Park
Chief's Point Indian Reserve 28
Sauble Beach North
Walker Woods Nature
Tolmie
Sauble Beach
Sauble Beach Amusements
Sauble Beach South
Sauble Speedway
Park Head
Skipness
Maryville Lake Rd.
Frenchman Pt.
Frenchman Bay
Chippewas of Saugeen First Nation
Scotch Settlement
Chippawa Hill
Keewaydin Rd.
Kelly's Corners
Elsinore
Allenford
Southampton
Saugeen Amphitheatre Gardens
Saugeen River Front Range Light
Bruce County Museum
Chantry Island National Migratory Bird Sanctuary
Chantry Island Lighthouse
McNab Pt.
Miramichi Bay
Denny's Dam
Tara
Invermay
Arkwright
Arranvale
Port Elgin
Port Elgin & North Shore "Miniature" Railroad
Burgoyne
Mount Hope
MacGregor Point Provincial Park
MacGregor Pt.
Nipissing
Huron
Algonquin
Brucedale
North Bruce
Dunblane
Williscroft
Turners
Salisbury

© mapmobility corp.

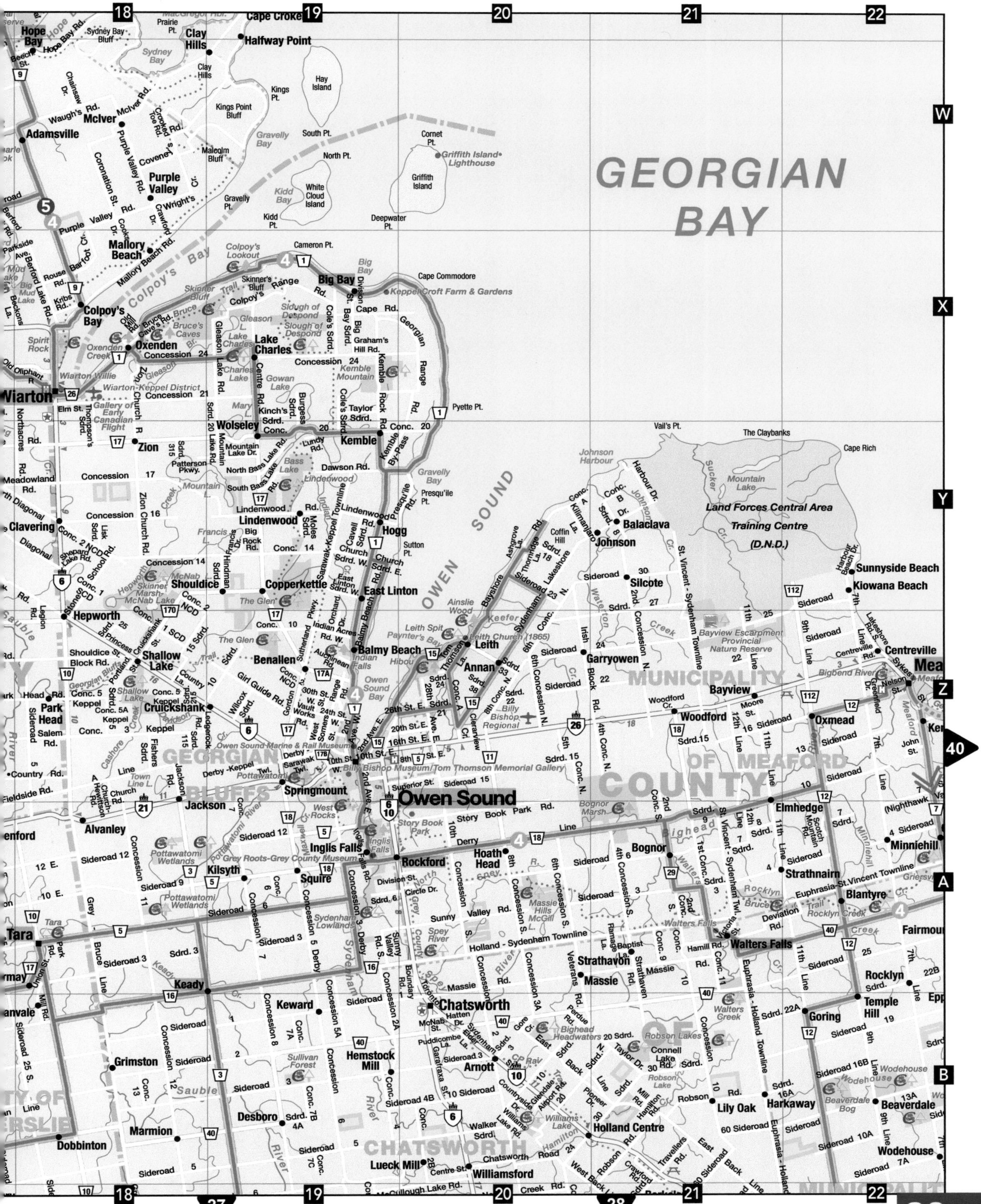

18
19
20
21
22
W
X
Y
Z
A
B
40
27
28
GEORGIAN BAY
OWEN SOUND
Hope Bay
Clay Hills
Halfway Point
Cape Croker
Hay Island
Kings Pt.
Kings Point Bluff
Adamsville
McIver
Purple Valley
Gravelly Bay
South Pt.
North Pt.
Cornet Pt.
Griffith Island Lighthouse
Griffith Island
Malcolm Bluff
Kidd Bay
White Cloud Island
Deepwater Pt.
Mallory Beach
Colpoy's Bay
Colpoy's Lookout
Cameron Pt.
Big Bay
Cape Commodore
Keppel Croft Farm & Gardens
Skinner's Bluff
Slough of Despond
Oxenden
Lake Charles
Kemble Mountain
Wiarton
Wiarton Willie
Wiarton-Keppel District
Gallery of Early Canadian Flight
Pyette Pt.
Wolseley
Kemble
Zion
Vail's Pt.
The Claybanks
Cape Rich
Johnson Harbour
Mountain Lake
Land Forces Central Area Training Centre (D.N.D.)
Gravelly Bay
Presqu'ile Pt.
Lindenwood
Hogg
Balaclava
Johnson
Clavering
Sutton Pt.
Coffin Hill
Sunnyside Beach
Kiowana Beach
Shouldice
Copperkettle
East Linton
Silcote
Hepworth
Ainslie Wood
Leith Spit
Leith
Leith Church (1865)
Bayview Escarpment Provincial Nature Reserve
Centreville
Meaford
Balmy Beach
Shallow Lake
Benallen
Annan
Garryowen
MUNICIPALITY OF MEAFORD
Bayview
Park Head
Cruickshank
Billy Bishop Regional
Woodford
Oxmead
Owen Sound Marine & Rail Museum
Billy Bishop Museum/Tom Thomson Memorial Gallery
GEORGIAN BLUFFS
Springmount
Owen Sound
COUNTY
Jackson
Alvanley
Story Book Park
Bognor Marsh
Elmhedge
Minniehill
Inglis Falls
Grey Roots-Grey County Museum
Rockford
Hoath Head
Bognor
Kilsyth
Squire
Pottawatomi Wetlands
Strathnairn
Blantyre
Sydenham Lowlands
Massie Hills McGill
Walters Falls
Tara
Spey River
Fairmount
Keady
Strathavon
Massie
Rocklyn
Temple Hill
Chatsworth
Keward
Goring
Hemstock Mill
Grimston
Arnott
Bighead Headwaters
Robson Lakes
Connell Lake
Sullivan Forest
Wodehouse
Harkaway
Beaverdale
Lily Oak
Desboro
Marmion
Dobbinton
Holland Centre
Williams Lake
CHATSWORTH
Wodehouse
Lueck Mill
Williamsford

1:250 000

2  1  0    2    4    6    8    10 Kilometres
kilomètres

1:250 000

2  1  0  2  4  6  8  10 Kilometres
*kilomètres*

**Legend**

- Bike On Tours route - paved
- Bike On Tours route - unpaved
- Other bike route or trail - paved
- Other bike route or trail - unpaved

© mapmobility corp.

1:250 000

2 1 0 2 4 6 8 10 Kilometres
kilomètres

1:250 000

2 1 0 2 4 6 8 10 Kilometres
*kilomètres*

**Legend**
Bike On Tours route - paved
Bike On Tours route - unpaved
Other bike route or trail - paved
Other bike route or trail - unpaved

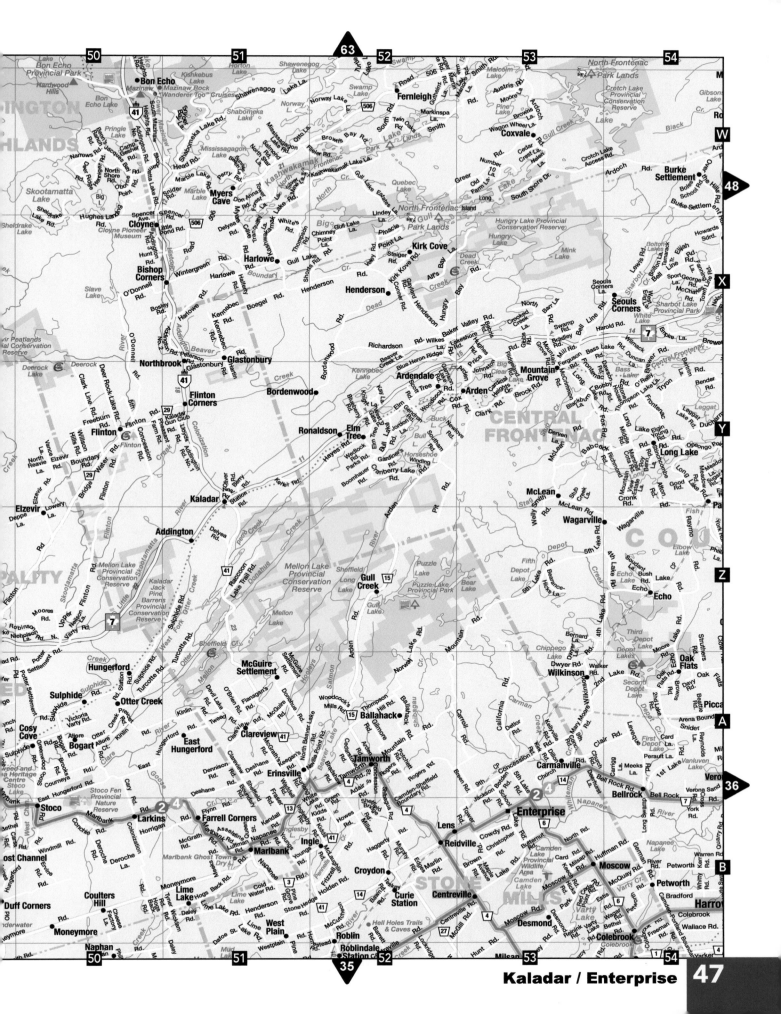

1:250 000

2 1 0 2 4 6 8 10 Kilometres
*kilomètres*

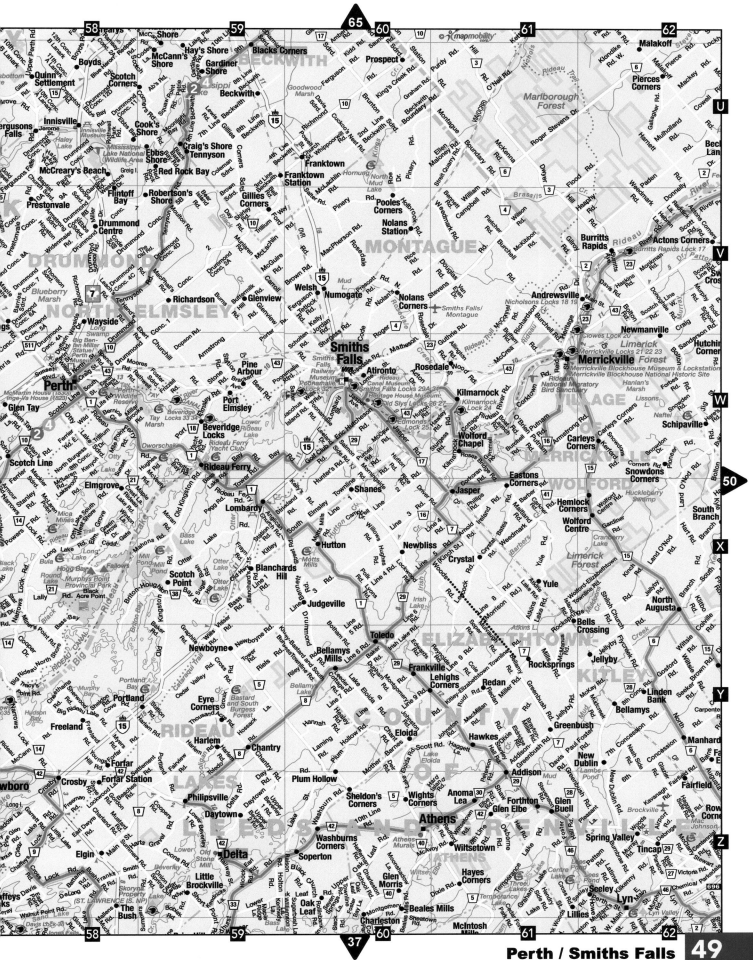

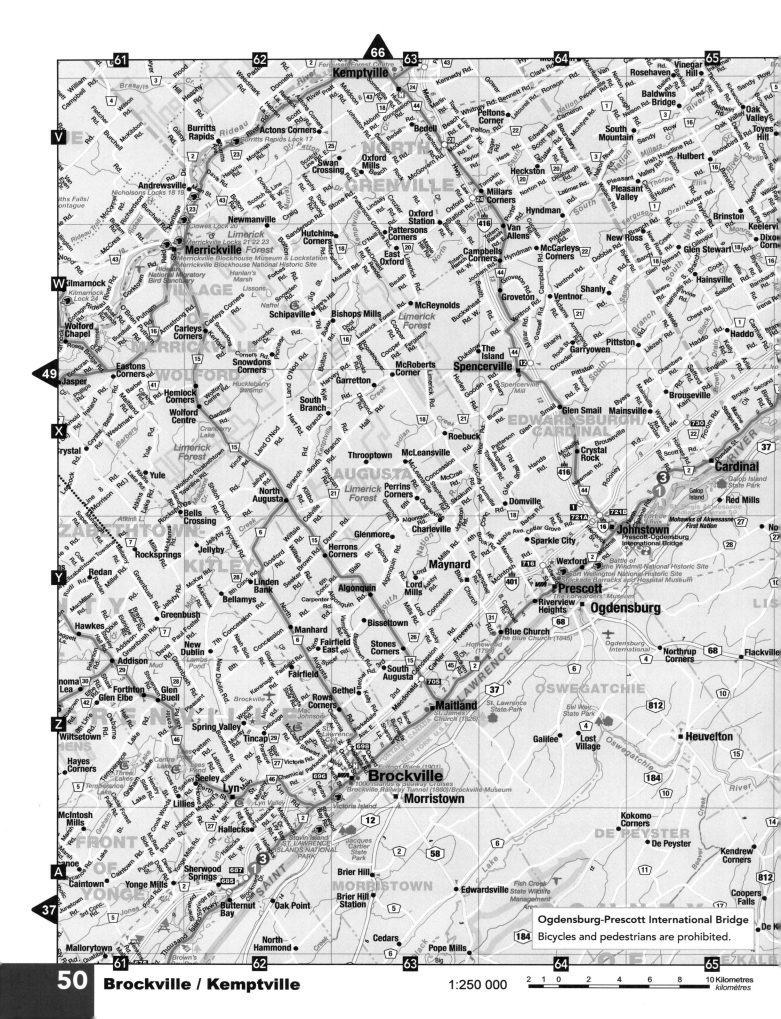

1:250 000

2 1 0 2 4 6 8 10 Kilometres
*kilomètres*

**Ogdensburg-Prescott International Bridge**
Bicycles and pedestrians are prohibited.

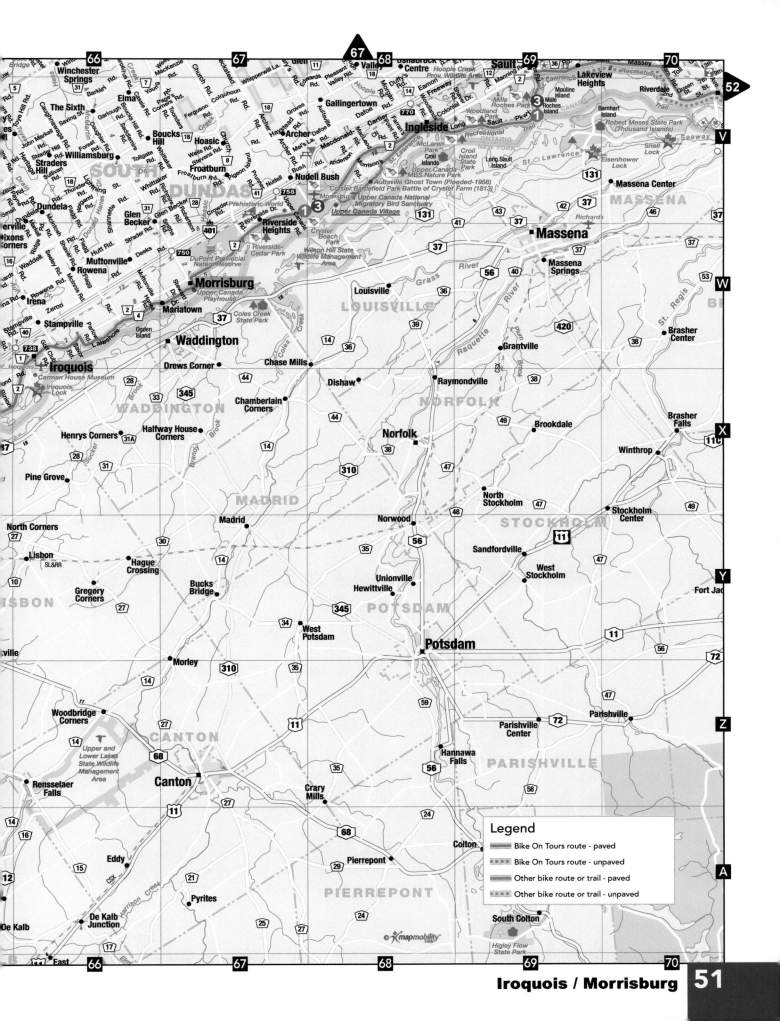

Legend

Bike On Tours route - paved

Bike On Tours route - unpaved

Other bike route or trail - paved

Other bike route or trail - unpaved

© mapmobility corp.

**Legend**

Bike On Tours route - paved

Bike On Tours route - unpaved

Other bike route or trail - paved

Other bike route or trail - unpaved

2  1  0  2  4  6  8  10 Kilometres
*kilomètres*

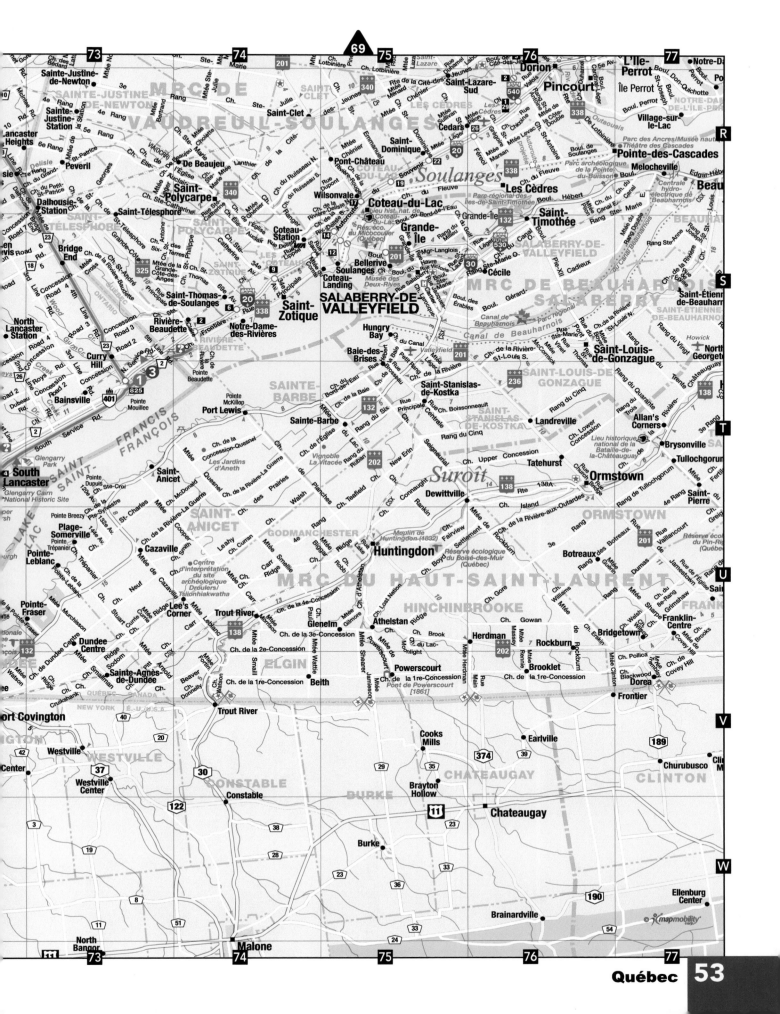

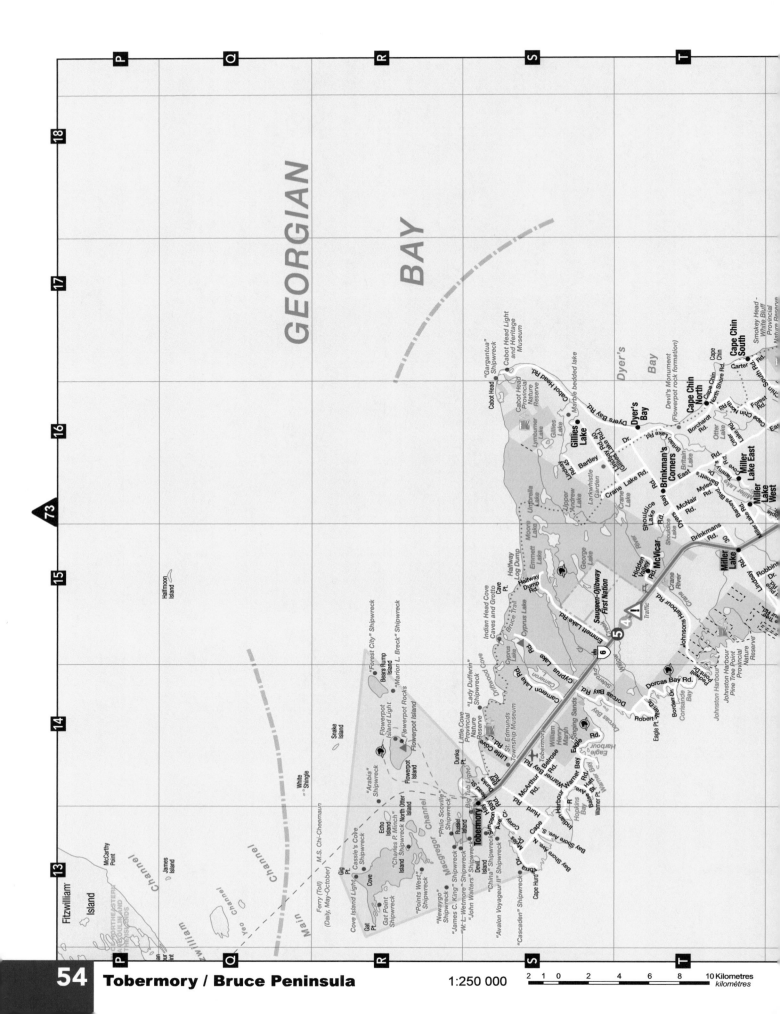

GEORGIAN

BAY

Dyer's

Bay

*"Gargantua"
Shipwreck*

Cabot Head Light
and Heritage
Museum

Cabot Head

Cabot Head
Provincial
Nature
Reserve

Cabot Head Rd.

*Marble bedded lake*

Smokey Head -
White Bluff
Provincial
Nature Reserve

**Cape Chin
South**

Cape Chin
N.

Carter

Chin South Rd.

Forest Rd.

Devil's Monument
*(Flowerpot rock formation)*

Dyers Bay Rd.

**Dyer's
Bay**

**Cape Chin
North**

Cape Chin
North Shore Rd.

Borchardt
Rd.

Otter
Lake
Rd.

Dyer Rd.

*Lymburner*

Gillies
Lake

Dr.

Brittain Lake Rd.

**Gillies
Lake**

Bartley

(Gillies) Lake Rd.

Crane Lake Rd.

**Brinkman's
Corners**

Brittain
Lake

**Miller
Lake East**

**Miller
Lake
West**

Tammy's
Rd.

*Lindsay*

Larkwhistle
Garden

*Upper
Andrew
Lake*

Crane
Lake

Shouldice
Rd.

Myles's
Rd.

Barnes Lake Rd.

*Umbrella
Lake*

McNair
Rd.

Brinkmans
Rd.

30

*Moore
Lake*

*Emmett
Lake*

*George
Lake*

Shouldice
Lakes

**McVicar**

Dyers
Rd.

Crane
River

**Miller
Lake**

Miller Lake Rd.

Kaspui

*Lindsay*

*Halfway
Log Dump*

Halfway
Dump Rd.

Indian Head Cove
Caves and Grotto

Bruce Trail

*Cave
Pt.*

*Cyprus Lake*

**Saugeen-Ojibway
First Nation**

Emmett Lake Rd.

5 4

Traffic

Johnstons Rd.

Hidden
Valley
Rd.

Robbins
Dr.

*Lindsay*

Traffic

Tpa Tra...

*"Lady Dufferin"
Shipwreck*

Little Cove
Provincial
Nature
Reserve

*Driftwood Cove*

Cyprus Lake Rd.

Cameron Lake Rd.

6

Willow

Dorcas Bay Rd.

**Dorcas Bay**

Johnston Harbour -
Pine Tree Point
Provincial
Nature
Reserve

*"Forest City" Shipwreck*

Bears Rump
Island

*"Marion L. Breck" Shipwreck*

*Flowerpot Rocks*

Flowerpot
Island Light

Flowerpot Island

*"Arabia"
Shipwreck*

Flowerpot
Island

Dunks
Pt.

*Little Cove*

St. Edmunds
Township Museum

Cameron Lake Rd.

William
Henry
Marsh

Singing Sands

Eagle
Rd.

Robert

Eagle Pt. Rd.

Borden
Dr.

Corisande
Bay

Dorcas Bay

Johnston Harbour
Point Dr.

Halfmoon
Island

Snake
Island

White
Shingle

M.S. Chi-Cheemaun

*"Philo Scoville"
Shipwreck*

*"Charles P. Minch"
Island Shipwreck*

Otter
Island

**Tobermory**

Little Cove
Rd.

Big Tub Light

Swing
Bay

Hay
Bay

Russel
Island

*"China" Shipwreck*

Cape
Ave. C.

McArthur
Rd.

Belrose
Rd.

Warner Bay Rd.

Warner Bay

Eagle
Bay

Indian
Harbour

Hay Bay Rd.

Hopkins
Bay

Hurd
Harbour

Bayview
St.

Balsam
Rd.

Warner Pt.

Warner
Bay Rd.

*"Newaygo"
Shipwreck*

*"James C. King" Shipwreck*

*"W. L. Wetmore" Shipwreck*

*"John Walters" Shipwreck*

*"Avalon Voyageur II" Shipwreck*

Cove Island Light

*"Points West"
Shipwreck*

Echo
Island

Cassle's Cove
Shipwreck

*"Charles P. Minch"
Island Shipwreck*

Devil

Gat
Pt.

Gig
Pt.

Cove

Gat Point
Shipwreck

Macgregor Channel

Devil

Little Cove
Rd.

Bay Shore Ave. N.

Bay Shore Ave. S.

Cosley
Rd.

Myles
Rd.

Crane S. Rd.

*"Cascaden" Shipwreck*

Cape Hurd

Cape Hurd Dr.

McCarthy
Point

**Fitzwilliam**
**Island**

CAPE HURD
ISLANDS

CABOT/THE NORTHEASTERN
FLOWERPOT
ISLANDS

James
Island

Ferry (Toll)
(Daily; May–October)

Main

Channel

Yeo
Channel

Channel

Fitzwilliam Channel

1:250 000

2  1  0    2    4    6    8    **10 Kilometres**
*kilomètres*

CARLING

McCoy
Islands

North
Limestone
Island

*Limestone Islands
Provincial Nature Reserve*

South Limestone
Island

Elmtree
Island

Mink

Islands

Shebeshekong

*Shebeshekong Rd.*

Dillon

Red Oak Rd.

559

241

237

Shebeshekong

Oak
Islands

Adanac

Brooks
Landing

Dillon

Manes
20 Rd.

Carling

Morrison

Nobel

Murray

Hammel Nobel

Pinetree

Franklin Island
*White Pine
Forest Provincial
Conservation Reserve*

Franklin
Island

Henrietta
Point

Snug
Harbour Rd.

Deep Bay

Fred Dubie
Rd.

Cole
Lake

Big Sound Rd.

Huckleberry
Island

Elizabeth
Island

Red Rock

Snug Harbour
Snug Haven

Back Bay

Kolenko Rd.

Pengally
Rd.

Killbear

*Killbear
Provincial
Park*

Mowat
Island

PARRY

North
Parry

Q

R

S

T

U

V

Pleasant
Island

Linda La.

Beaver
Dams

Harold's
Point

Georgian

Killbear
Point

SOUND

Stockey Centre
Bobby Orr Hall of Fame
Island Queen
Cruises

Rose
Island

Granite
Saddle

Depot
Harbour
*Ghost Town*

Parry
Island

Bateau
Island

Parry Island
*Wasauksing
First Nation*

Waubuno Channel

McLaren
Island

Seven Mile
Narrows

Sandy
Island

Five
Mile

*The Massasa*

**GEORGIAN**

Umbrella
Islands

THE ARCH

*Provincial P*

Sans
Souci
Island

Sans Souci
Fryingpan Island

Copperhead

Wreck
Island

**BAY**

Sharp
Island

Manitou
Dock

Loon
Island

McQuade I.

*GEORGIAN BAY ISLANDS
NATIONAL PARK*

O'Donnell Pt.
Gilford Rocks

Hatch
Is.

*O'Donnell
Provin
Nature Re*

Western

Islands

Bourke Pt.

Pine

Islan

North Watcher I.

*The Watcher*

South Watcher I.

## Legend

— Bike On Tours route - paved

···· Bike On Tours route - unpaved

— Other bike route or trail - paved

···· Other bike route or trail - unpaved

Hope I.

© mapmobility corp.

1:250 000

2 1 0 2 4 6 8 10 Kilometres / kilomètres

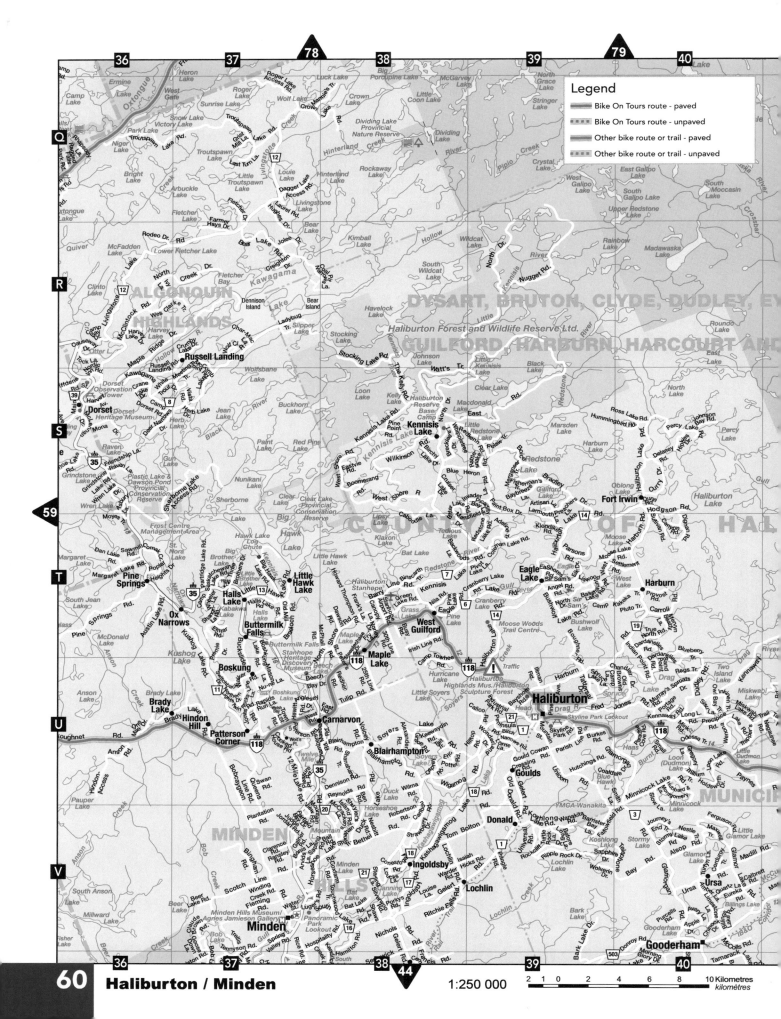

Legend
Bike On Tours route - paved
Bike On Tours route - unpaved
Other bike route or trail - paved
Other bike route or trail - unpaved

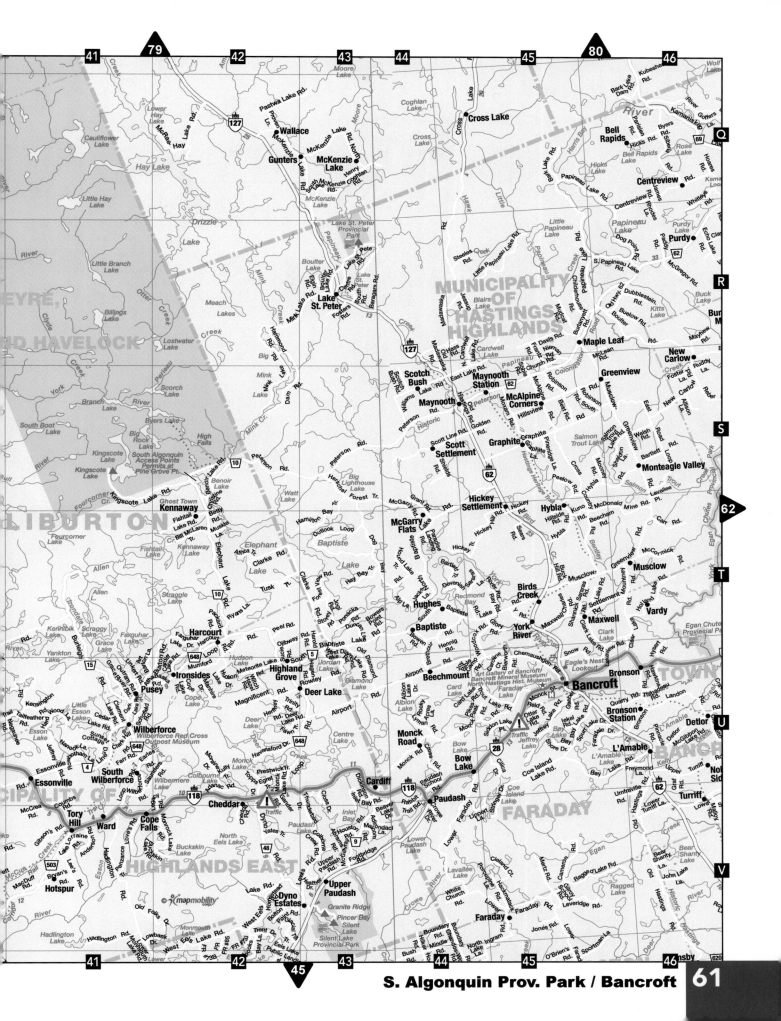

1:250 000

2 1 0 2 4 6 8 10 Kilometres
kilomètres

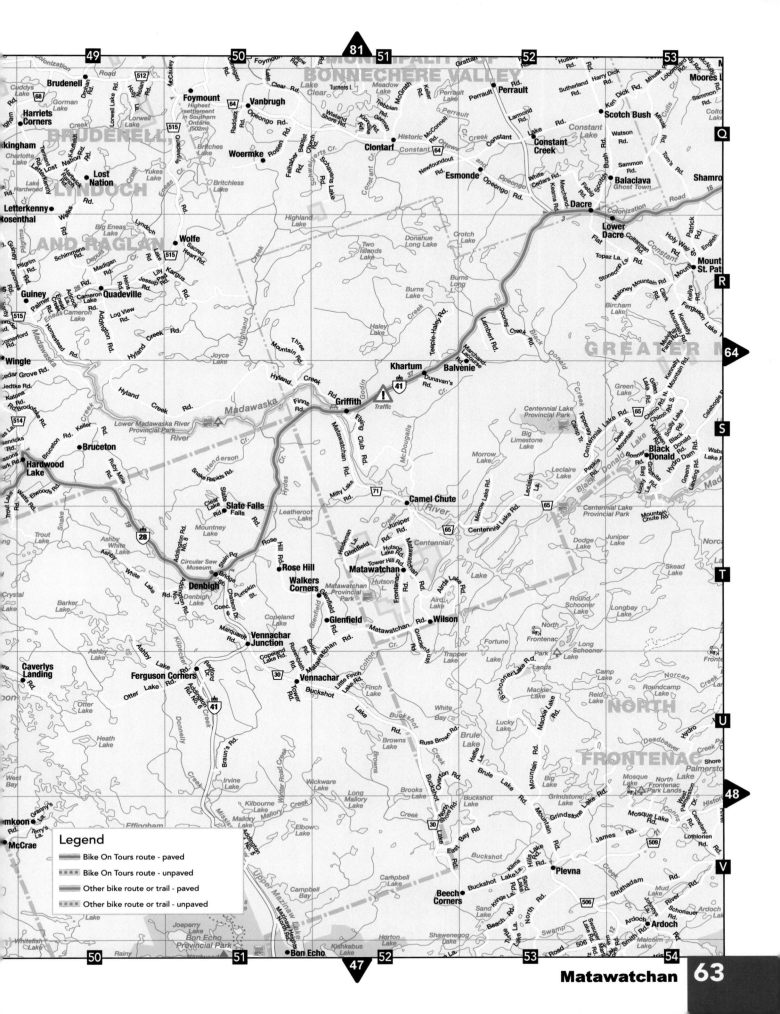

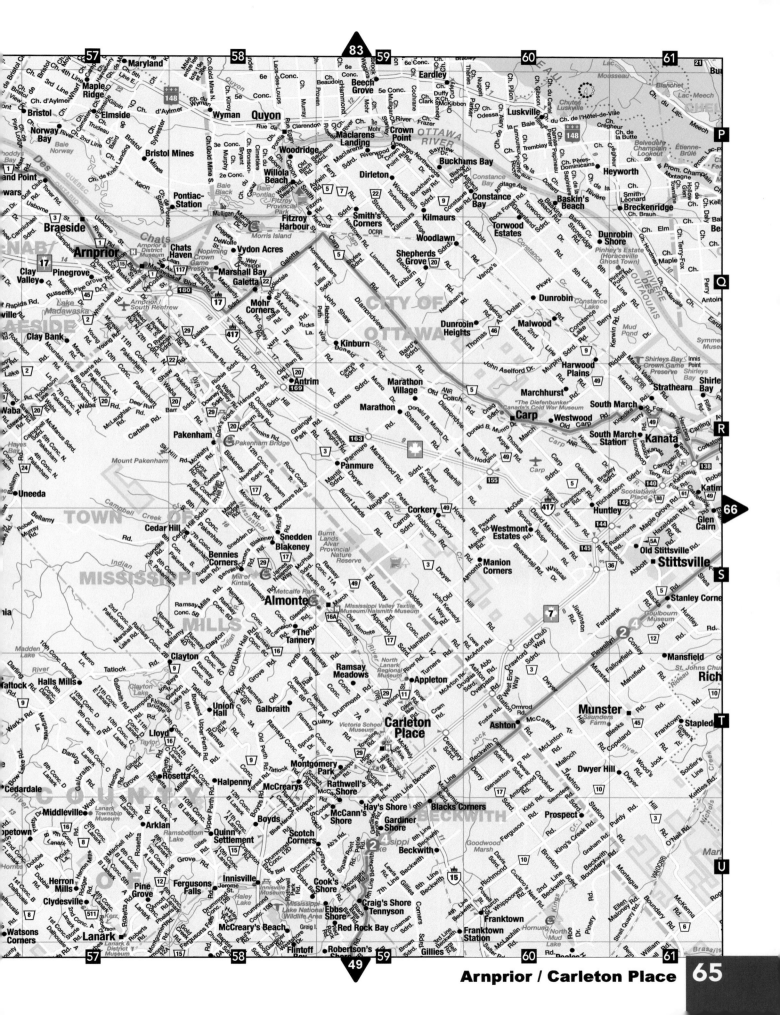

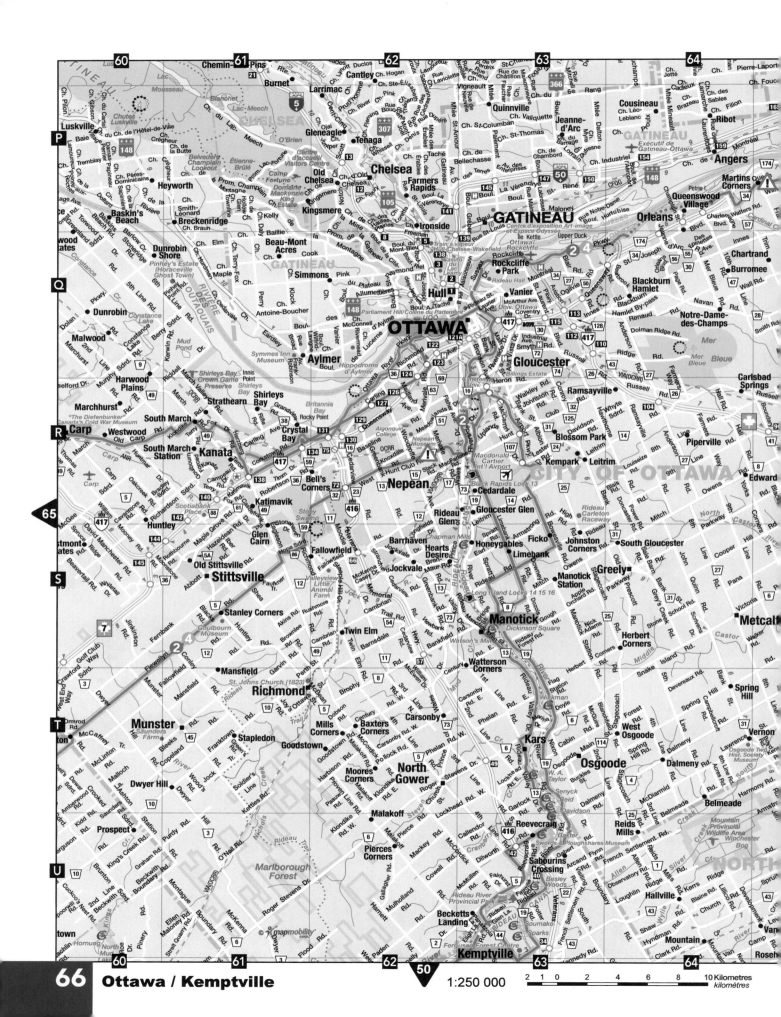

1:250 000

2  1  0    2    4    6    8    10 Kilometres
kilomètres

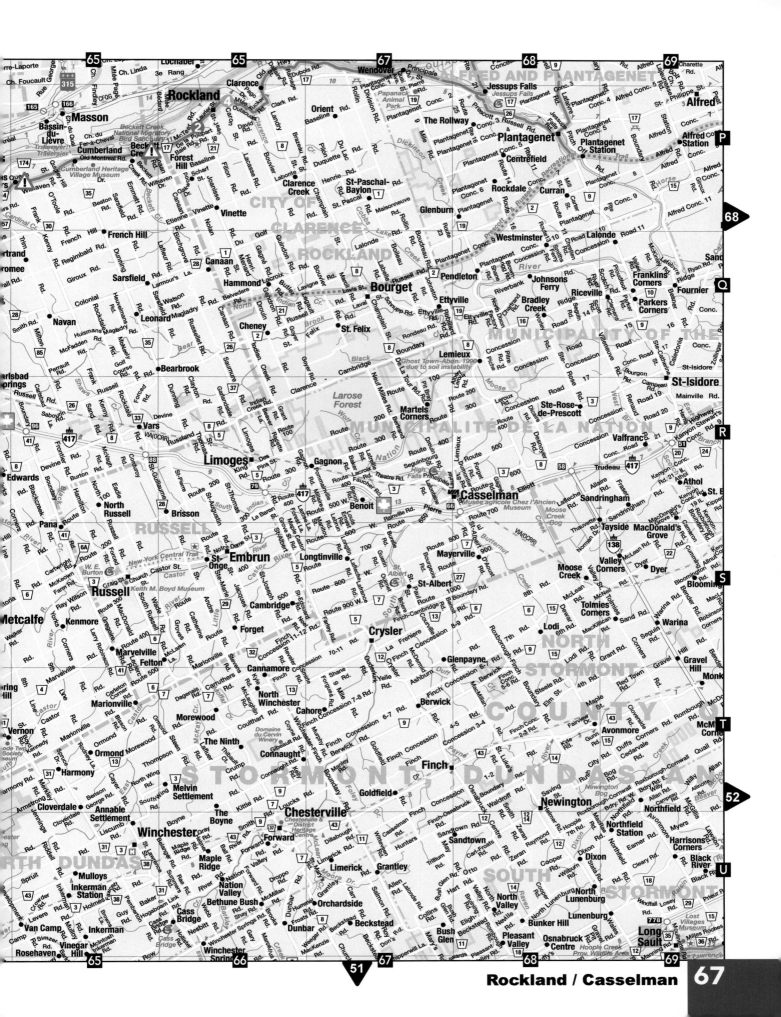

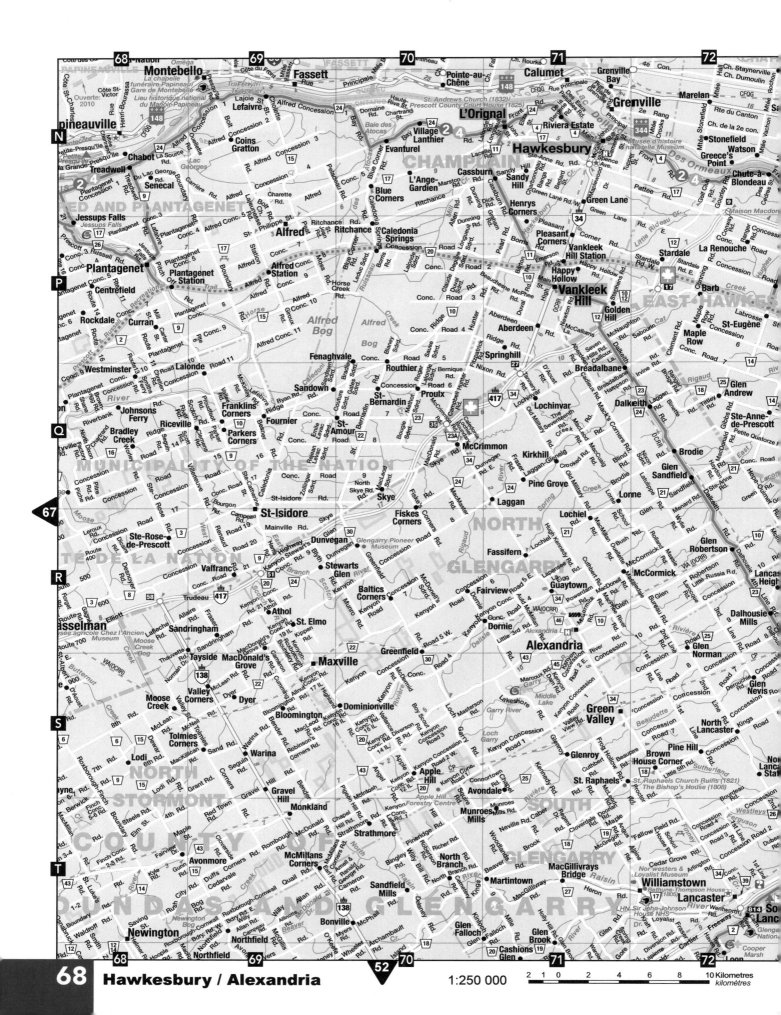

1:250 000

2 1 0 2 4 6 8 10 Kilometres
kilomètres

DRUMMOND
ISLAND

Glen Cove
Glen Point

Monk Point

Robb's
Lake

Thompson Point

Pitman Point

Ross
Point

Robinson Bay

14th Conc.

Tolsma
Bay

Devil's
Horn

Ghost Town

Cockburn
Island
First
Nation

12th    Concession

Tolsmaville (Cockburn Island)

I St.

L St.

COCKBURN

20th

15th

W St.

10th Sideroad

Sdrd.

7th-8th Concession

McCaigs
Hill

Scotch
Block

ISLAND

COCKBURN        ISLAND

Herschell
Island

Little
Kitchener
Island

Kitchener
Island

Wagoose Lake

Sand

Cinder
Point

Mississagi    Strait

False Detour Channel

Wagoose
Bay

Station
Point

Pulpwood
Point

Hindman Bay

Sand Lake

15th Sideroad

Sand Cr.

Ricketts
Harbour

There is no ferry service
to Cockburn Island.
Visitors must arrange
their own transport.

Boom
Point

Sand
Bay

Crescent Island
TOWN OF NORTHEASTERN
MANITOULIN AND THE ISLAN
Boat Harbour

Batture
Island

West
Point

Vidal Island

Arthur
Point

Big
Bay

Meldrum
Bay

Harold
Point

Vidal

Bay

Creasor
Bight

Gravy
Lake

Maggies
Sdrd.

Wasnage

Water St.

Meldrum Bay
Net Shed
Museum

Linda
Lake

Pothole
Lake

Maple
Lake

Totten
Lake

Cemetery
Rd.

Rd.

Burnett
Lake

Mississagi

Lighthouse

Rd.

Kerr
Lake

Easin

Rd.

28

West
Bass
Lake

Young
Lake

Joyce

Wickett
Lake

Falls
Lake

Falls
Lake Rd.

Hog
Lake

540

35th
Sdrd.

Mississagi Lighthouse
Heritage Park & Museum

Carter
Lake

Lily
Lake Rd.

Lily
Lake

Loon
Lake

Dawson

Beaver
Meadow
Lakes

Dorrny Grant Rd.

The Queen Elizabeth
The Queen
Mother M'Nidoo M'Nissing
Provincial Park

Ro

Steevens
Island

Quarry
Bay

Twin
Lakes

Greene
Island

Quarry
Point

TOWN OF NORTHEASTERN
MANITOULIN AND THE ISLANDS

West Belanger Bay

Girouard
Point

East Belanger Bay

Rickley
Point

Burnt Island
Harbour

B

Burnt
Island

Western
Duck
Island

Blake Point

Th
Is

TOWN OF NORTHEASTER
MANITOULIN AND THE ISLA

Middle
Duck
Island

Bluff Point

Desert Poir

Horseshoe
Bay

Duck
Island

Gravel P

ONTARIO
MICHIGAN

© mapmobility
corp.

1:250 000

2 1 0   2   4   6   8   10 Kilometres
kilométres

NORTH CHANNEL

LAKE

HURON

MANITOULIN

Largest Freshwater Island

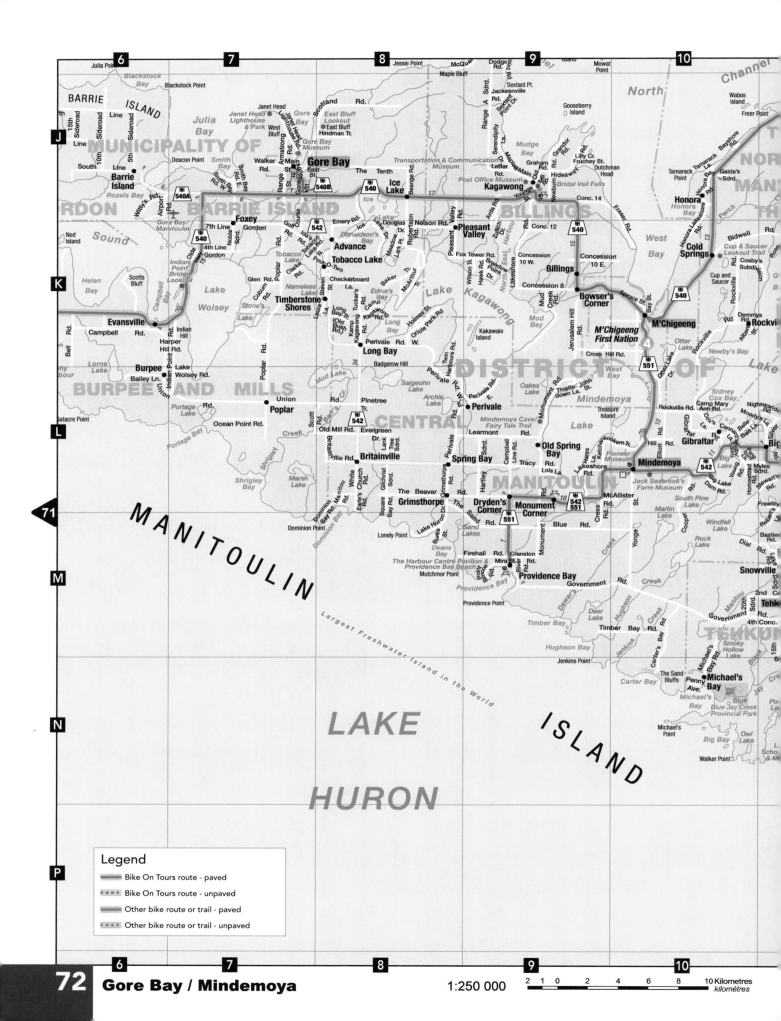

1:250 000

2 1 0  2  4  6  8  10 Kilometres
kilométres

1:250 000

2 1 0     2     4     6     8     10 Kilometres
*kilomètres*

**Legend**
Bike On Tours route - paved
Bike On Tours route - unpaved
Other bike route or trail - paved
Other bike route or trail - unpaved

GEORGIAN BAY

© mapmobility corp.

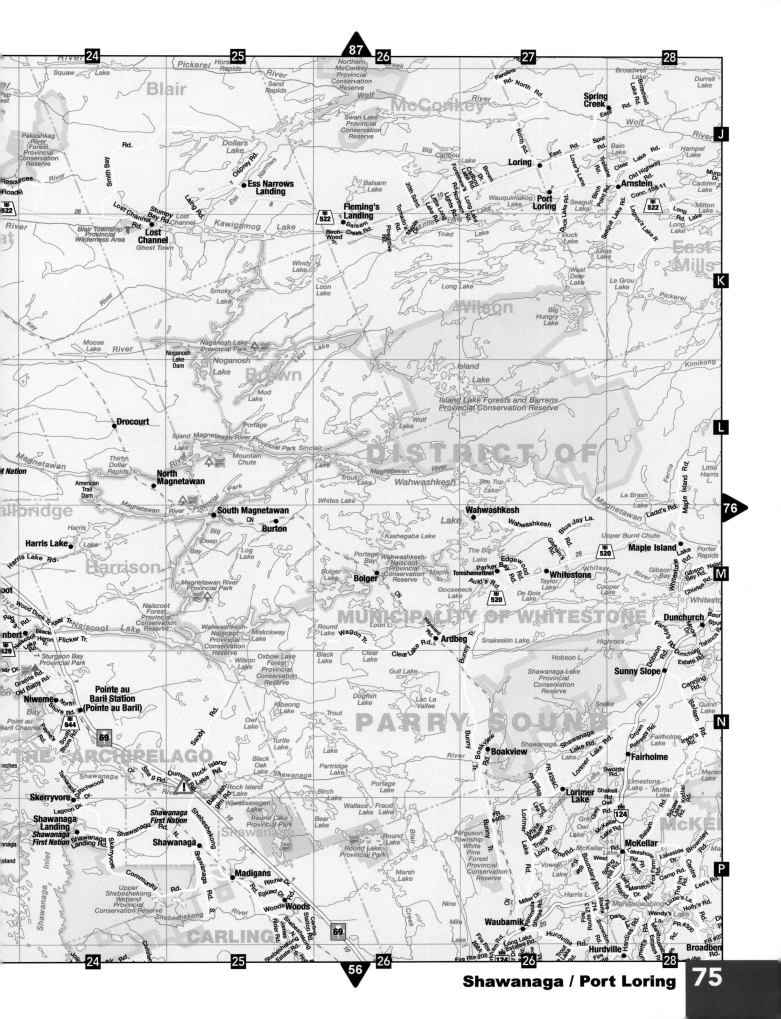

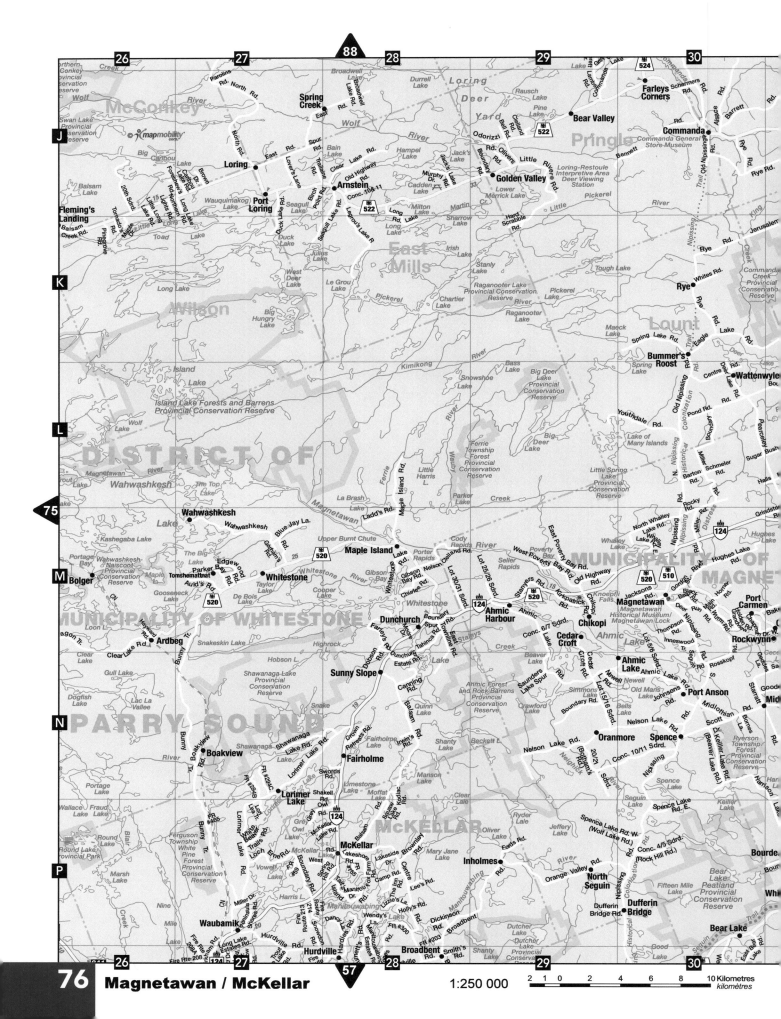

J

McConkey

Wolf

Swan Lake
Provincial
Conservation
Reserve

Balsam
Lake

Fleming's
Landing

Balsam
Creek Rd.

Pinegrove
Rd.

Big
Caribou
Lake

Brown
Lake

Parolins
Rd. North Rd.

Broadwell
Lake

Spring
Creek

East
Rd.

Spur
Rd.

Bain
Lake Rd.

Trailane

Durrell
Lake

Loring

Deer

Yard

Pringle

Rausch
Lake

Cleland
Rd.

Pine
Lake

522

Bell Rd.

Bear Valley

524

Farleys
Corners

Schermers
Rd.

Rd.

Commanda

Commanda General
Store-Museum

Bennett

Alsace
Rd.

Barrett
Rd.

Wolf

River

Loring

Golden Valley

Loring-Restoule
Interpretive Area
Deer Viewing
Station

Trail Old Nipissing

Rye
Rd.

Rye Rd.

Jerusalem

K

Wilson

Long Lake

Island
Lake

Big
Hungry
Lake

Le Grou
Lake

Pickerel

East
Mills

Irish
Lake

Raganooter Lake
Provincial Conservation
Reserve

Pickerel
Lake

Chartier
Lake

Raganooter
Lake

River

Rye

Whites Rd.

Commanda
Creek
Provincial
Conservation
Reserve

Lount

Bummer's
Roost

Spring
Lake

Wattenwyle

L

DISTRICT OF

Island Lake Forests and Barrens
Provincial Conservation Reserve

Wolf
Lake

Magnetawan
River

Trout
Lake

Wahwashkesh

The Top
Lake

Ferrie

Magnetawan

Ladd's Rd.

Maple Island Rd.

Little
Harris
L.

Parker
Lake

Waubuy

Ferrie Township
Forest
Provincial
Conservation
Reserve

Big
Deer
Lake

Snowshoe
Lake

Bass
Lake

Big Deer
Lake
Provincial
Conservation
Reserve

Youtidale
Rd.

Old Nipissing

Colonization Rd.

Little Spring
Lake
Provincial
Conservation
Reserve

Sugar Bush
Rd.

Peacealey Rd.

Grindstone
Lake

Hughes
Lake

◆75◆

M

Bolger

Portage
Bay

Wahwashkesh-
Naiscoot
Provincial
Conservation
Reserve

Maple
Lake

Gooseneck
Lake

Kashegaba Lake

Wahwashkesh

Lake

The Big
Lake

Getham's
Rd.

Parker Bay
Rd.

Edgewood
Rd.

Tomshematnat

Auld's Rd.

520

Blue Jay La.

25

520

Upper Burnt Chute

Maple Island

Whitestone River

Taylor
Lake

De Bois
Lake

Cooper
Lake

Whitestone

Porter
Rapids

Gibson
Bay

Whitestone Lake

Cody
Rapids River

Gibson
Bay Rd.

Chunet
Rd.

Nelson Clelland Rd.

Lot 25/26 Sdrd.

Lot 30/31 Sdrd.

Whitestone

West Poverty Bay
Rd.

East Poverty
Bay

Seller
Rapids

Poverty
Rd.

Stanyers Rd.

15

Old Highway
Rd.

North Whalley
Lake Rd.

Whalley Rd.

Knoepfli
Falls

Knoepfli
Rd.

520

510

Magnetawan
Historical Museum/
Magnetawan Lock

Nipissing Rd.

Miller
Rd.

Rocky
Rd.

124

Hughes Lake
Rd.

MUNICIPALITY OF
MAGNE

Port
Carmen

N

MUNICIPALITY OF WHITESTONE

Loon L.

Hayward
Rd.

Wagon Tr.

Ardbeg

Clear
Lake

Clear Lake Rd.

Bunny Tr.

Snakeskin Lake

Highrock

Hobson L.

Shawanaga Lake
Provincial
Conservation
Reserve

Dunchurch

Farleys Rd.

Spur

Dobson
Rd.

Dunchurch
Estate Rd.

Tahinca Rd.

Sunny Slope

Canning
Rd.

Balsam Rd.

Quinn
Lake

Ahmic
Lake

124

Ahmic
Harbour

Conc. 6/7 Sdrd.

Elm
Townline Rd.

Staleys Rd.

520

Ahmic

Beaver
Lake

Ahmic Forest
and Rock Barrens
Provincial
Conservation
Reserve

Crawford
Lake

Chikopi

Cedar
Croft

Cedar
Croft
Rd.

Saunders
Lake Spur

Simmons
Lake

Boundary Rd.

Bells
Lake

Ahmic
Lake

Ahmic

Old Man's
Rd.

Johnsons
Rd.

Inneswood
Tr.

Lot 15/16 Sdrd.

Newell
Rd.

Newell
L.

Ahmic
Lake

Rosskopt
Rd.

Rockwynn

Port Anson

N

PARRY SOUND

Boakview

Boakview
Rd.

Bunny
Tr.

Shawanaga
River

Portage
Lake

FR #294C

FR #465

Shawanaga Lake Rd.

Lormer Lake Rd.

Crown
Rd.

Fairholme

Fairholme Rd.

Irvin's Rd.

Retreats Rd.

Swords
Rd.

Shanty
Lake

Beckett L.

Manson
Lake

Ahmic Forest
and Rock Barrens

Nelson Lake Rd.

20/21
Sdrd.

Bothams
Rd.

Oranmore

Spence

Conc. 10/11 Sdrd.

Seguin

Spence
Lake

Spence
Lake
Rd. E.

Keiller
Lake

Ryerson Township
Forest
Provincial
Conservation
Reserve

Midl

P

Round Lake
Provincial Park

Round
Lake

Wallace
Fraud
Lake

Marsh
Lake

Blair
Lake

Portage
Lake

Lac La
Vallee

Dogfish
Lake

Gull Lake

Lorimer
Lake

Ferguson Township
White Pine
Forest
Provincial
Conservation
Reserve

Loch Erne Rd.

White Beaver
Trails Rd.

McKellar
Rd.

Greg
Owl Rd.

Balsam
Rd.

124

McKellar

Lakeshore
Rd.

West
Spring
Hill Rd.

Boundary Rd.

Vowell
Lake

Island

McKellar
Lake

Shakell
Rd. OW

Moffat
Lake

Limestone
Lake

Square
Lake

Kodiac
Rd.

McKELLAR

Lakeside
Dr.

Browney
Rd.

The Inn Rd.

Camp Rd.

Lee's Rd.

Mary Jane
Lake

Clear
Lake

Oliver
Lake

Ryder
Lake

Jeffery
Lake

Fords Rd.

Spence Lake Rd. W.
(Wolf Lake Rd.)

Conc. 4/5 Sdrd.
(Rock Hill Rd.)

Inholmes

Orange Valley
Rd.

North
Seguin

Nipissing

Colonization

River

Bear
Lake Peatland
Provincial
Conservation
Reserve

Bourde

Waubamik

CN

Miller Dr.

Nine
Mile

Harris L.

Fire Rte #208

211

Long Lake
Estates Rd.

Graham Rd.

124

Fire Route 213

214

Fire Rte #300

Peninsula
Shoes Rd.

20

Manitouwabing
Lake

Hurdville

Lizzie's La.

Troutville

Wendy's
Rd.

Dancy
Rd.

Hardies Rd.

Holly's Rd.

Dickinson
Rd.

Broadbent

Broadbent
Rd.

Smith's
Rd.

Dutcher
Lake

Dutcher
Lake
Provincial
Conserva

Dufferin
Bridge Rd.

Dufferin
Bridge

Shanty
Lake

Fifteen Mile
Lake

Bear Lake

Good
Lake

Seguin
Trail

Historical

Wh

East Rd.

ⓜ mapmobility corp.

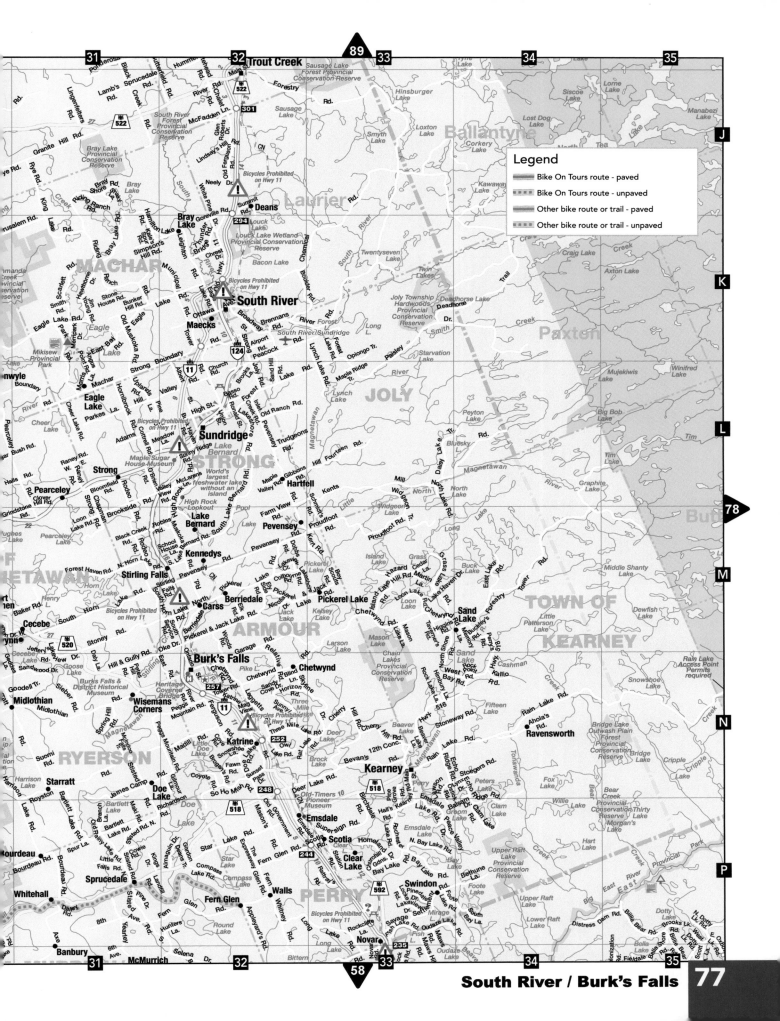

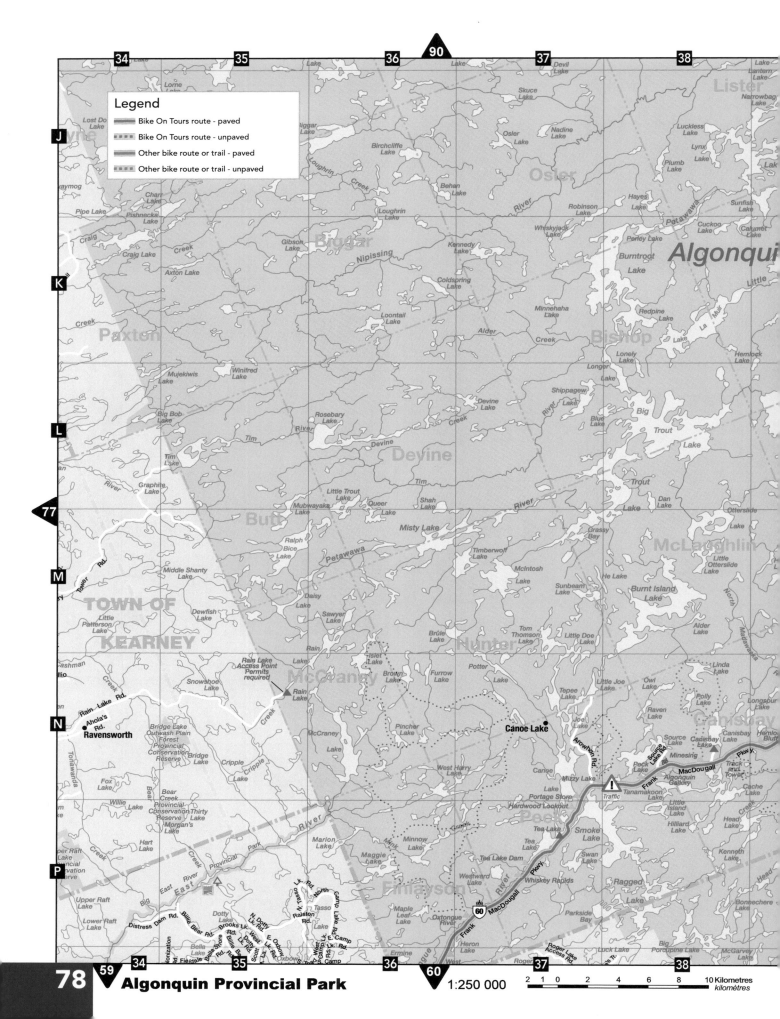

## Legend

- Bike On Tours route - paved
- Bike On Tours route - unpaved
- Other bike route or trail - paved
- Other bike route or trail - unpaved

**Algonquin Provincial Park**     1:250 000     2 1 0    2    4    6    8    10 Kilometres *kilométres*

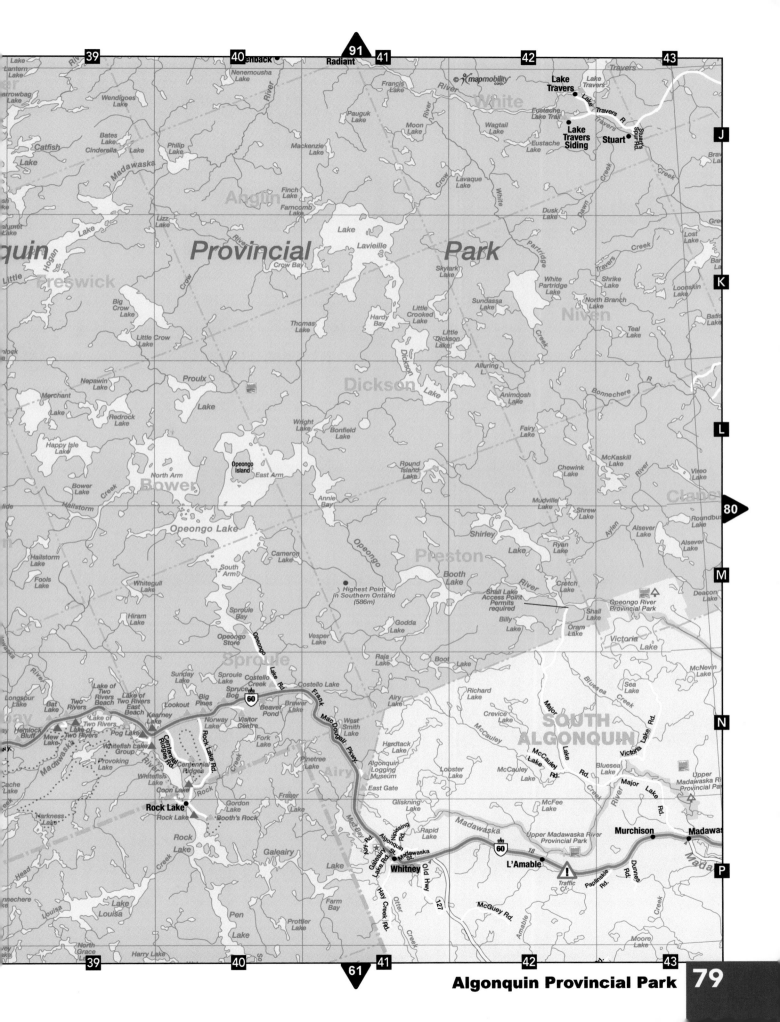

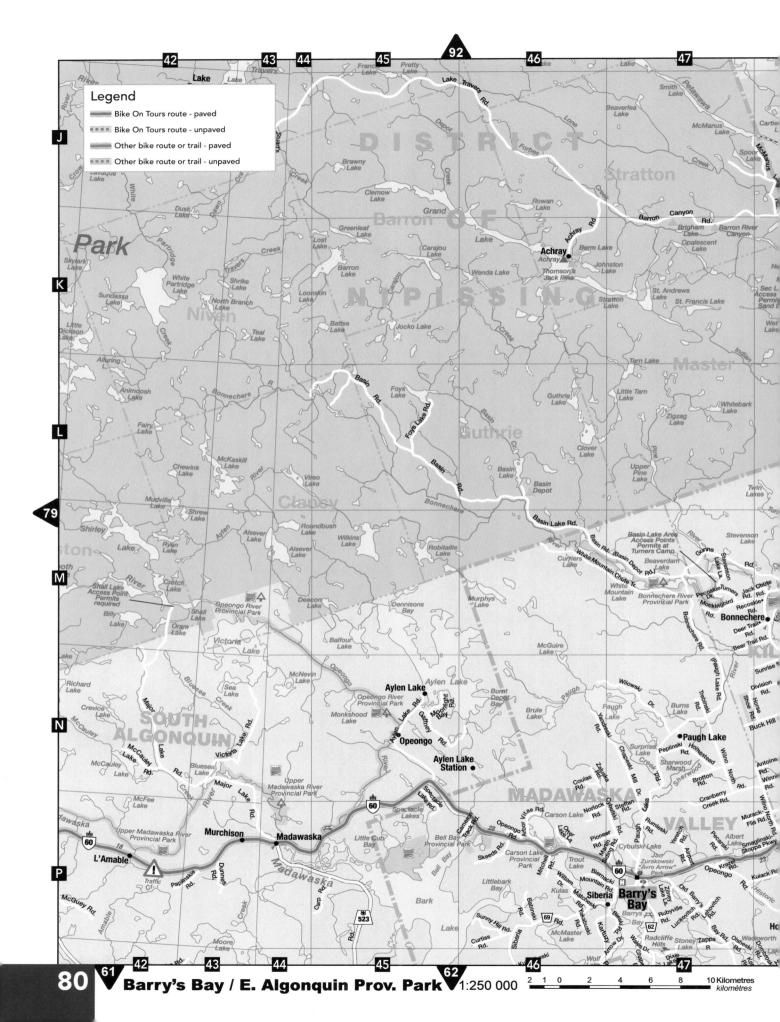

## Legend

- Bike On Tours route - paved
- Bike On Tours route - unpaved
- Other bike route or trail - paved
- Other bike route or trail - unpaved

2 1 0   2   4   6   8   10 Kilometres
kilomètres

1:250 000

2  1  0    2    4    6    8    10 Kilometres
*kilomètres*

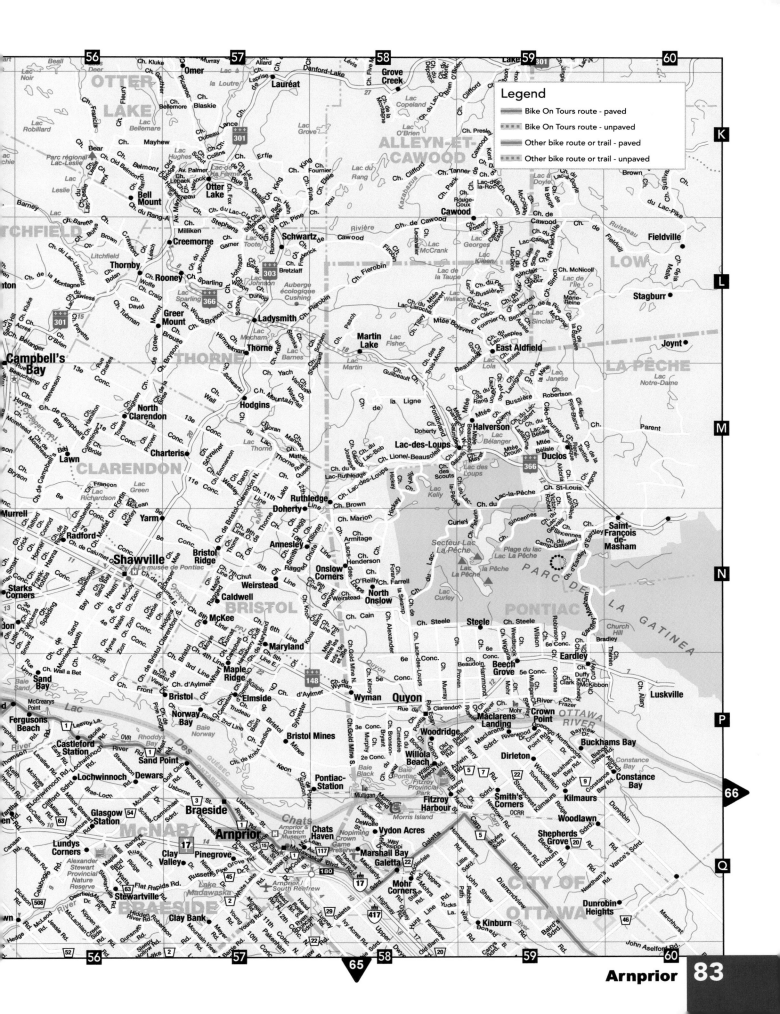

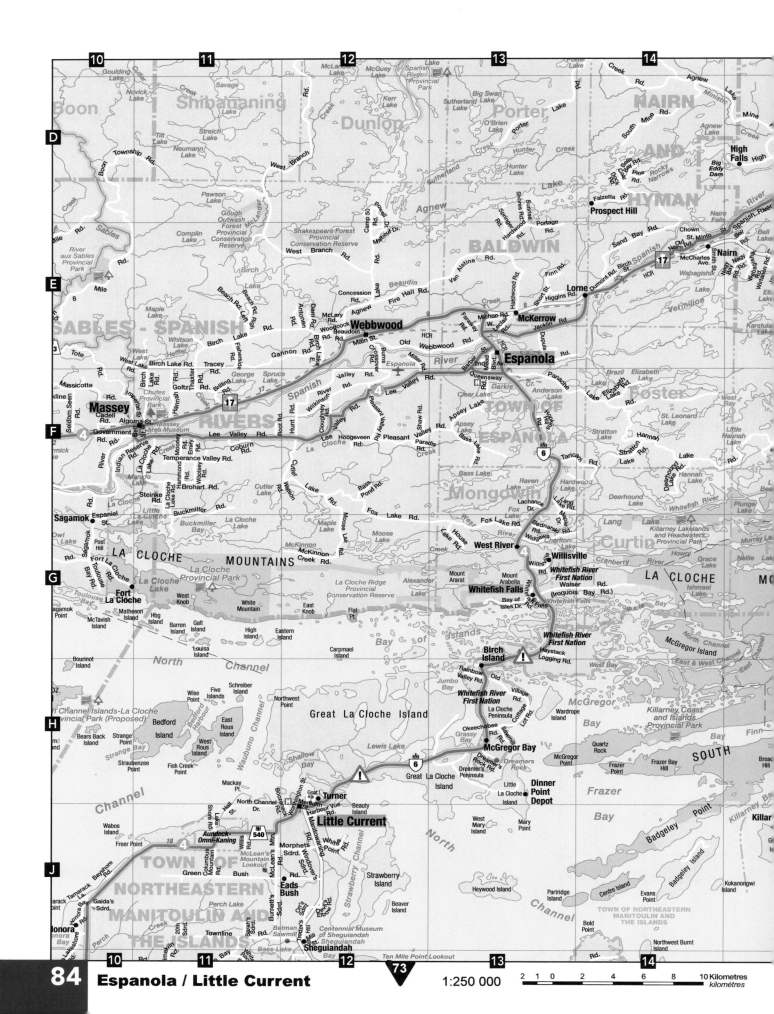

1:250 000

2  1  0  2  4  6  8  10 Kilometres
*kilomètres*

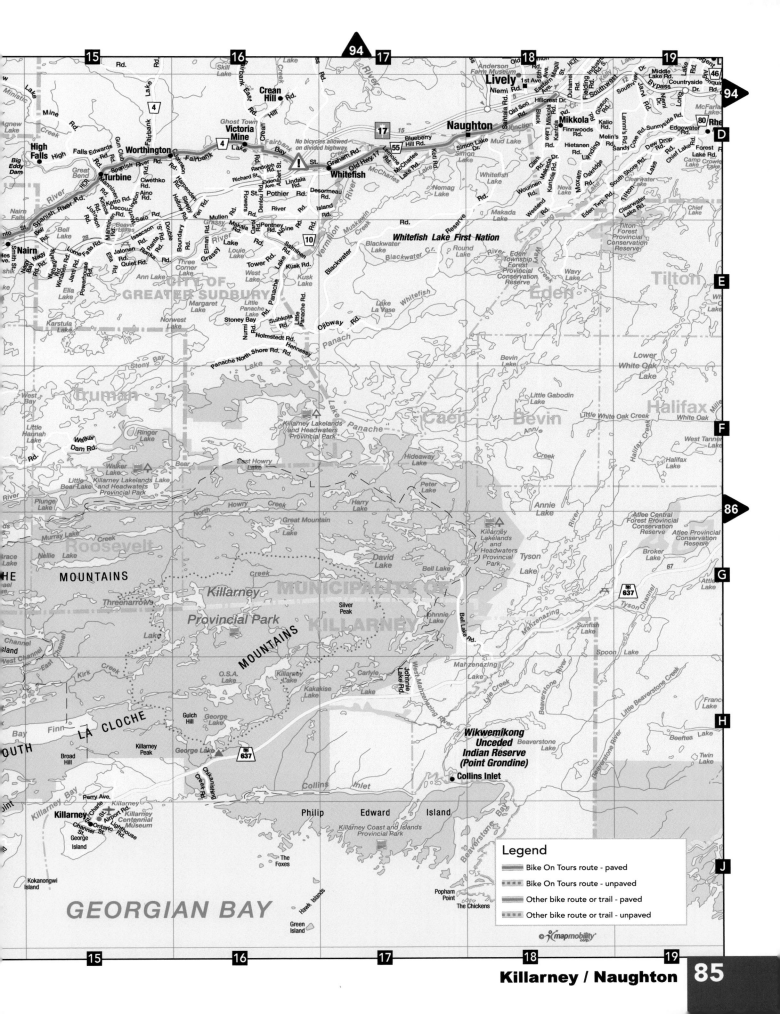

## Sudbury Inset

1:250 000

2 1 0 2 4 6 8 10 Kilometres
kilomètres

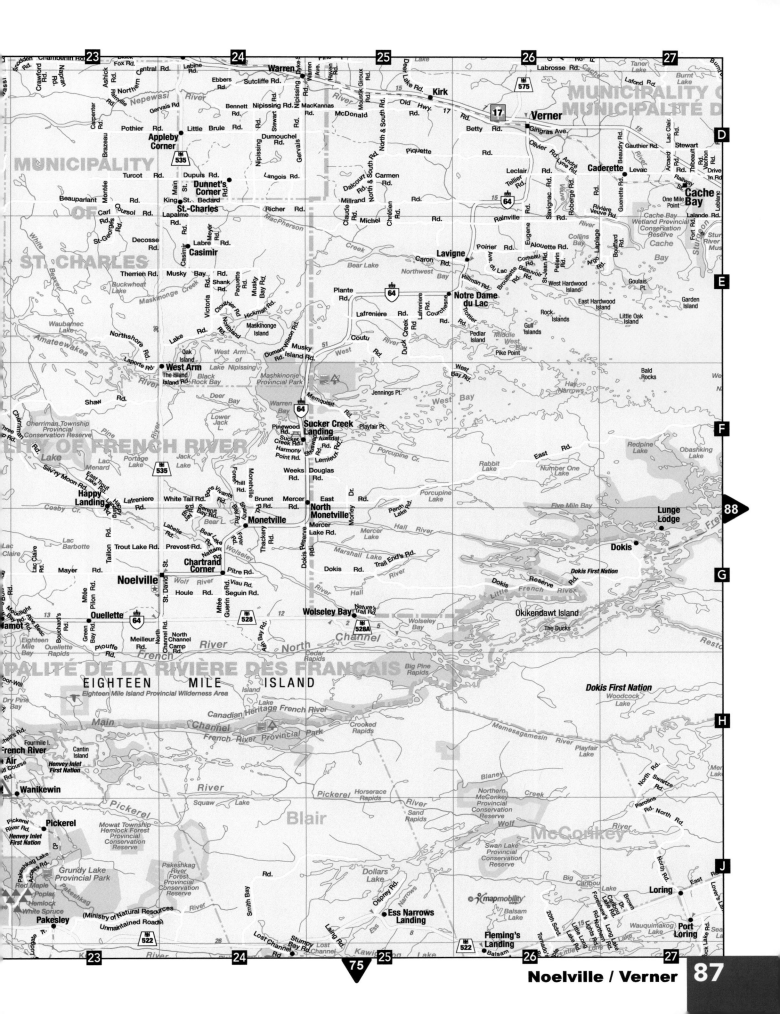

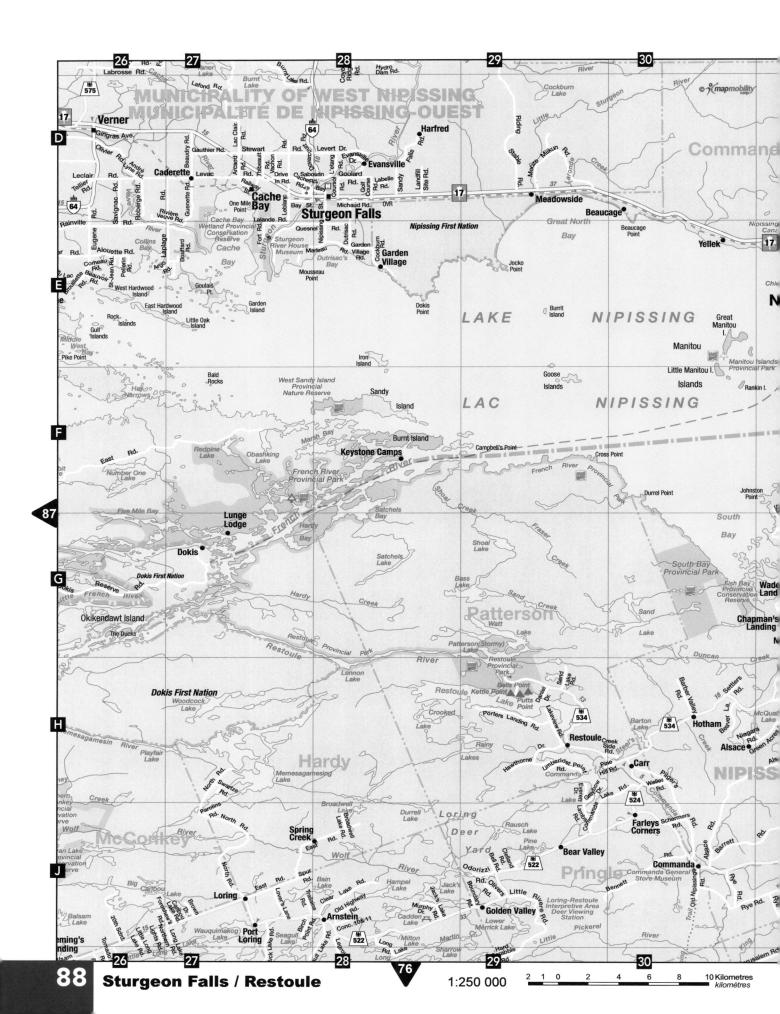

MUNICIPALITY OF WEST NIPISSING
MUNICIPALITÉ DE NIPISSING-OUEST

575

17
D
Verner
Gingras Ave.

Olivier Rd.
André Lane Rd.
Leclair Rd.
Tellier Rd.
64

Rainville

Caderette
Levac
Guenette Rd.
Roberge Rd.
Savignac Rd.
Rivière Veuve Rd.
Laplage Rd.
Comeau Rd.
Pelloin Rd.
Beauvoir Rd.
Eugene Rd.
Alouette Rd.
St-Jean Rd.
Argo Rd.
Bouffard Rd.
West Hardwood Island
E
East Hardwood Island
Goulais Pt.
Garden Island
Little Oak Island
Rock Islands
Gulf Islands
Middle West Bay
Pike Point
Half Narrows
Bald Rocks

Burnt Lake
Labrosse Rd.
Lafond Rd.
Gauthier Rd.
Stewart
Beaudry Rd.
Arcand Rd.
Thibeault Rd.
Rd. Vechon Rd.
Railway
One Mile Point
Cache Bay
Leblanc
Bay St.
Lalande Rd.
Fort Rd.

Burnt Lake Rd.
Coyote Rd.
Hydro Dam Rd.
64
Levert Dr.
Covert Rd.
L'etang
Sabourin
Cache Rd.
Coursol Rd.
Goulard
Evansville Dr.
Evansville
Michaud Rd.
Sturgeon Falls
Quesnel
Marleau
Dutrisac's Rd.
Mousseau Point
Garden Village Rd.
Cockburn Rd.
Garden Village
Dokis Point

Cache Bay Wetland Provincial Conservation Reserve
Sturgeon River House Museum
Sturgeon River

Harfred
Sandy Falls
Golf Course Rd.
Labelle Rd.
Landfill Site Rd.
17

Nipissing First Nation

Riding Rd.
Stable Rd.
Moose Milkun Rd.
Laronde Creek
Cockburn Lake
Little River
Sturgeon River

mapmobility corp.

Commanda
Meadowside
Beaucage
Beaucage Point
Yellek
17

Nipissing Cana

Jocko Point

LAKE NIPISSING
Burrit Island
Goose Islands
Great Manitou I.
Manitou
Little Manitou I.
Islands
Manitou Islands Provincial Park
Rankin I.

LAC NIPISSING

Great North Bay

F
East Rd.
Number One Lake
Redpine Lake
Obashking Lake
French River Provincial Park
Five Mile Bay
Marsh Bay
Sandy Island
West Sandy Island Provincial Nature Reserve
Iron Island
Burnt Island
Keystone Camps
French River
Campbell's Point
Cross Point
French River Provincial Park
Durrel Point
Johnston Point
South Bay

87
Lunge Lodge
Hardy Bay
Satchels Bay
Satchels Lake
Shoal Creek
Shoal Lake
Fraser Creek
G
Dokis
Dokis First Nation
Reserve
French River
Little French River
Okikendawt Island
The Ducks
Restoule
Restoule Provincial Park
Bass Lake
Sand Creek
Sand Lake
Patterson
Watt Lake
South Bay Provincial Park
Fish Bay Provincial Conservation Reserve
Wade Land
Chapman's Landing

Dokis First Nation
Woodcock Lake
Hardy Creek
Lennon Lake
Restoule River
Patterson(Stormy) Lake
Restoule Provincial Park
Bells Point
Putts Point
Sand Lake Rd.
Barber Valley Rd.
18 Settlers
McQual Lake
H
Memesagamesin River
Playfair Lake
Restoule Kettle Point
Daniel Dr.
Porters Landing Rd.
534
Crooked Lake
Lakeview Rd.
Restoule
Creek Side Rd.
Steel's Rd.
Barton Lake
Barton Rd.
534
Hotham
Alsace
Green Acres
Niagara Rd.
Beaver La.

Memesagamesin River
Hardy
Memesagamesing Lake
Rainy Lakes
Hawthorne Dr.
Limberlost Point Rd.
Commanda
Pine Hill Rd.
Carr
Pliger's Rd.
NIPISS
Als

North Rd.
North Swartze Rd.
Parolins Rd.
North Rd.
Broadwell Lake
Broadwell Lake Rd.
Durrell Lake
Loring
Deer
Rausch Lake
Geybow Dr.
Everett Rd.
Lambton Dr.
Commanda Lake
524
Weller Rd.
Farleys Corners
Schamers Rd.

McConkey
Spring Creek
East Rd.
Wolf River
Yard
Pine Lake
522
Chelland Dr.
Bear Valley
Commanda
Commanda General Store-Museum
Pringle
J
Big Caribou Lake
Loring
Spur Rd.
Bain Lake
Lover's Lane
Clear Lake
Hampel Lake
Old Highway
Jack's Lake
Odorizzi Rd.
Bell Rd.
Olivers Rd.
Boundary Rd.
Little River
Golden Valley
Lower Merrick Lake
Loring-Restoule Interpretive Area Deer Viewing Station
Bennett Rd.
Alsace Rd.
Barrett Rd.
Rye Rd.

Balsam Lake
20th Sand.
Northern Lights Rd.
Forehand Rd.
Port Loring
Seagull Lake
Bich Lake
Arnstein
Conc. 108-11
522
Murphy Dr.
Cadden Lake
Milton Rd.
Sharrow Rd.
Martin Cr.
Pickerel River
Hard Rabble Rd.
Trail Old Nipissing
Little River

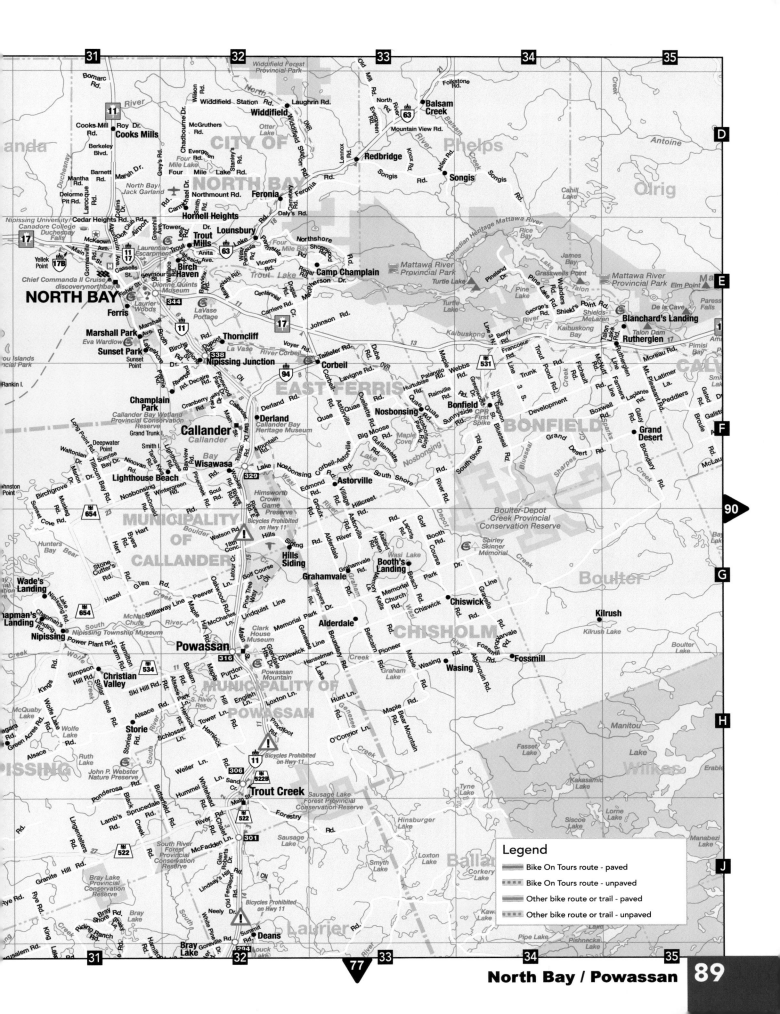

North Bay / Powassan

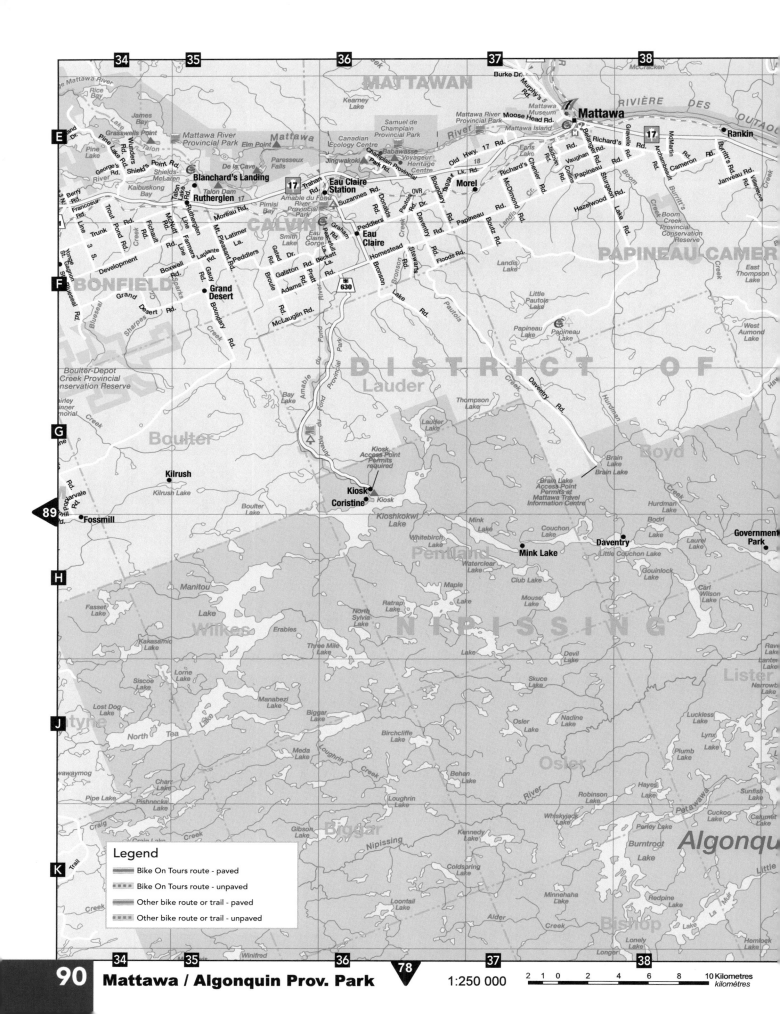

**MATTAWAN**

Burke Dr.
McCracken
Murphy's 5 Rd.
Kearney Lake
Mattawa River Provincial Park
Moose Head Rd.
**Mattawa**
RIVIÈRE DES OUTAOUAIS

Rice Bay
Grasswells Point
James Bay
Mattawa Museum
Mattawa Island
Mattawa
Gravelle Rd.
McMartin

**E**
Pine Lake
Wunders
Talon
Elm Point
Samuel de Champlain Provincial Park
Canadian Ecology Centre
Mattawa River Provincial Park
Mattawa Island
**17**
Burritt's Rd.
**Rankin**

George's River Rd.
Shield's-McLaren
Point Rd.
De la Cave
Paresseux Falls
Babawasse
Champlain Park Provincial Rd. Park
Voyageur Heritage Centre
Earls Lake
Richard's Rd.
Archambault
Cameron Rd.
Janveau Rd.

**Blanchard's Landing**
Kaibuskong Bay
Talon Lake
Talon Dam
**Rutherglen** 17
Pimisi Bay
Jingwakoki
**17**
Trahan Rd.
**Eau Claire Station**
Suzannes
Tague Lk. Rd.
Jadow Rd.
Chenier Rd.
Collins
Vaughan Rd.
Papineau Rd.
Sturgeon
Boom
Hazelwood

Berry Rd.
Francoeur Rd.
Trout Pond Rd.
Trunk
Line 3 S.
McNutt Rd.
Line Farmers Rd.
Laplante Rd.
Moreau Rd.
Mt. Pleasant Rd.
Latimer La.
Peddlers
Smith Lake
Gated Dr.
Amable du Fond
**630**
Eau Claire Gorge
Graham Rd.
Peacefull Rd.
Peddlers
**Eau Claire**
Donalds Rd.
Pautois Rd.
OVR
Daventry Rd.
McDimond Rd.
Papineau Rd.
Boutz Rd.
Landis
Lake
Landis Lake

**F**
**BONFIELD**
Development
Fichault Rd.
Sparks
Boxwell Rd.
Gauy Rd.
Galston Rd.
Broule
Pratt Rd.
Adams Rd.
Beckett La.
Homestead
Bronson
Stewarts Rd.
Floods Rd.
Little Pautois Lake

**Grand Desert**
Grand Desert
Boundary Rd.
McLauglin Rd.
Amable du Fond River
Bay Lake
Lake
Lauder Lake
**PAPINEAU-CAMER**
East Thompson Lake

Blueseal
Sharpes
Creek
Boulter-Depot Creek Provincial Conservation Reserve
Papineau Lake
Papineau Lake
West Aumond Lake

**D I S T R I C T   O F**

**G**
Shirley Dinner Memorial
Creek
Boulter
Kiosk Access Point Permits required
Thompson Lake
Lauder
Lauder Lake
Daventry Rd.
Boyd

**Kilrush**
Kilrush Lake
Boulter Lake
**Kiosk**
**Coristine**
Kiosk
Kioshkokwi Lake
Brain Lake
Brain Lake
Brain Lake Access Point Permits at Mattawa Travel Information Centre
Hurdman Lake
Hurdman Lake

**89**
Pine Poo Narvale Rd.
Rd.
**Fossmill**
Mink Lake
Couchon Lake
Bodri
**Daventry**
Little Couchon Lake
Laurel Lake
**Government Park**

**H**
Manitou
Whitebirch Lake
Waterclear Lake
Maple Lake
Club Lake
Mouse Lake
Gouinlock Lake
Carl Wilson Lake

Fasset Lake
Lake
Pemland
Ratrap Lake
North Sylvia Lake
Devil Lake
Skuce Lake

Kakasamic Lake
Erables
Three Mile Lake
Lake
Nadine Lake
**Lister**
Raw Lake
Lantern Lake

**J**
Siscoe Lake
Lorne Lake
**Wilkes**
Osler Lake
Luckless Lake
Lynx Lake

Lost Dog Lake
Manabezi Lake
Biggar Lake
Birchcliffe Lake
**N I P I S S I N G**
Osler Lake
Plumb Lake

North Tea
Meda Lake
Loughrin
Behan Lake
**Osler**
River
Hayes Lake
Sunfish Lake

Charr Lake
Pipe Lake
Pishnecka Lake
Gibson Lake
**Biggar**
Loughrin Lake
Robinson Lake
Whiskyjack Lake
Perley Lake
Cuckoo Lake
Calumet Lake

Craig
Crain Lake
Creek
Nipissing
Kennedy Lake
Patawawa
Burntroot Lake
**Algonqui**

Coldspring Lake
Minnehaha Lake
Redpine Lake
La M

**K**
Trail

### Legend

━━━ Bike On Tours route - paved
┈┈┈ Bike On Tours route - unpaved
━━━ Other bike route or trail - paved
┈┈┈ Other bike route or trail - unpaved

Loontail Lake
Alder Creek
**Bishop**
Lonely Lake
Longer
Hemlock Lake
Little

**90** **Mattawa / Algonquin Prov. Park**    1:250 000    2 1 0 2 4 6 8 10 Kilometres
kilomètres

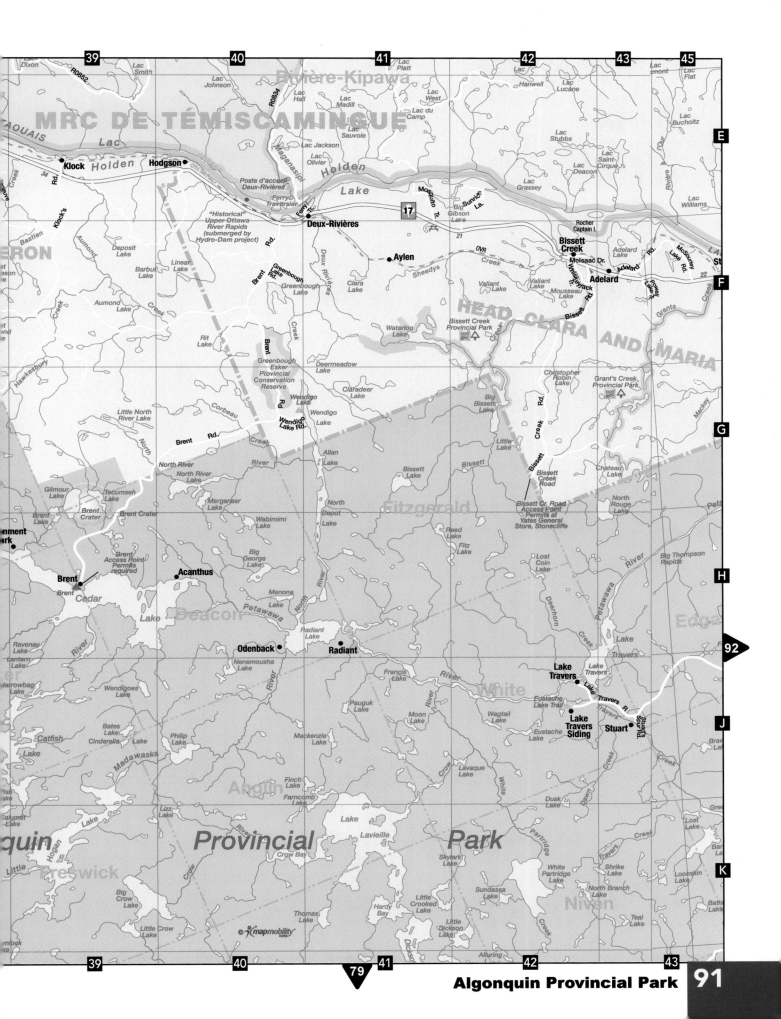

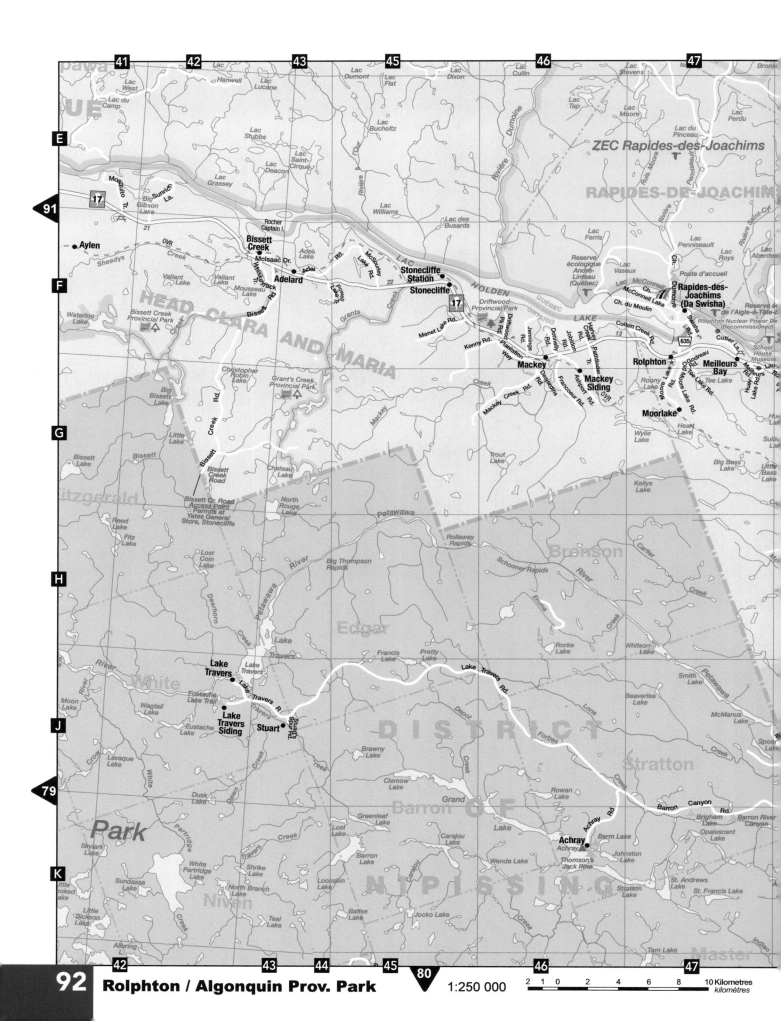

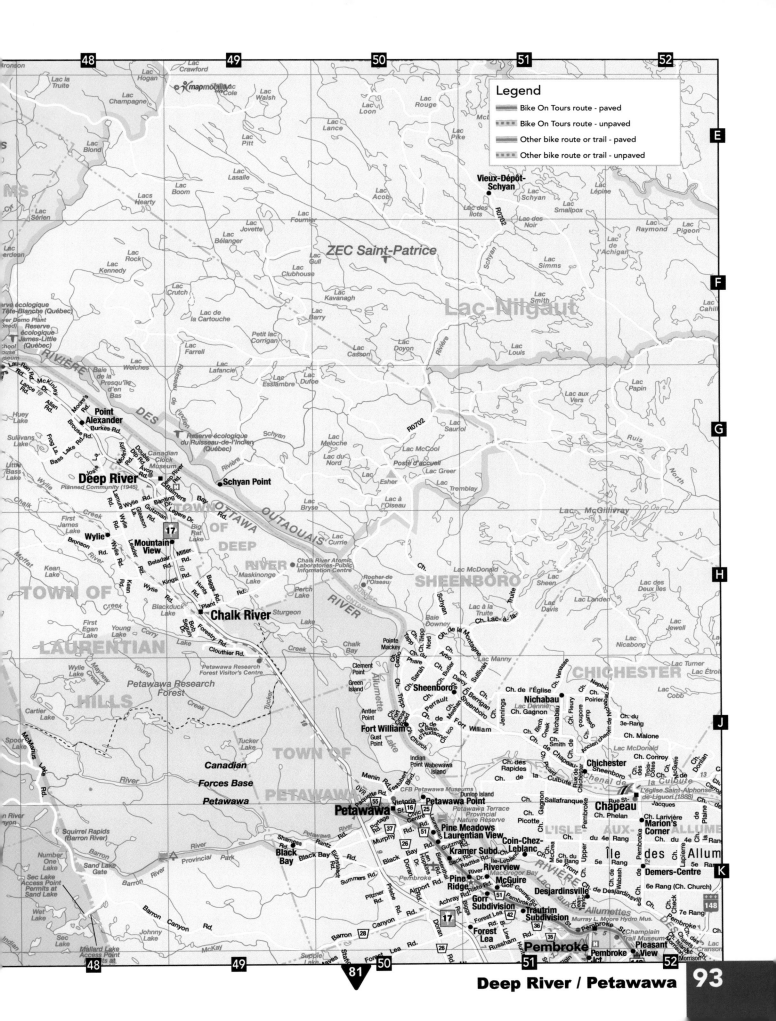

# Routes Across Ontario by Howard Pulver

With the Ontario Bicycle Touring Atlas you have a choice of a number of routes across Ontario. Five of them are described below. Long distance cyclists traveling between the northeastern United States and Michigan or Minnesota have found that bicycling across Ontario eliminates many miles of travel required to go around the Great Lakes.

These routes are described going from west to east, but of course you can follow them in the reverse direction as well, or just tour a section of a route.

Consult the Community Guide in the next section to plan your stops along the way.

## 1 – WATERFRONT ROUTE

**Features:** Go right across Southern Ontario following the shore of Lake Erie, Lake Ontario and the St. Lawrence River.

**Distance:** 1011 km.

**Characteristics:** All paved; via backroads from Windsor to Hamilton, and the Waterfront Trail from Hamilton to Quebec border.

**Description:** This is a scenic waterfront route all the way across Ontario from Windsor to the Quebec border east of Cornwall. The route goes close to Lake Erie, then along Lake Ontario and the St. Lawrence River using the Lake Ontario Waterfront Trail.

**Major Waypoints:** Windsor (Detroit MI) - Leamington/Kingsville (Pelee Island Ferry, Sandusky OH) - Port Dover - Ohsweken – Hamilton – Toronto - Picton - Kingston (Wolfe Island Ferries, Cape Vincent NY) - Cornwall (Massena NY) - Quebec border (continue along Quebec's Route Verte to Montreal)

**Consult these atlas pages to track this route on the maps:** Marked as ❶

| | | |
|---|---|---|
| Map 4 B1 | Windsor | E4 Kingsville |
| Map 5 E5 | Leamington | D8 Port Alma |
| Map 6 C9 | Dealtown | |
| Map 7 Y14 | Eagle | |
| Map 8 W17 | Port Stanley | |
| Map 9 X22 | Jacksonburg | |
| Map 10 V25 | Port Dover | |
| Map 17 S26 | Ohsweken | Q28 Hamilton |
| Map 23 P28 | Aldershot | |

| | | |
|---|---|---|
| Map 24 N29 | Bronte | L32 Toronto |
| Map 25 H37 | Oshawa | |
| Map 32 G40 | Wesleyville | |
| Map 33 F44 | Colborne | |
| Map 34 G49 | Wellington | |
| Map 35 G51 | Picton | E54 Bath |
| Map 36 D56 | Kingston | D57 Pitts Ferry |
| Map 37 A62 | Butternut Bay | |
| Map 50 X65 | Cardinal | |
| Map 51 V68 | Ingleside | |
| Map 52 U71 | Cornwall | T72 South Lancaster |
| Map 53 T73 | Quebec border | |

## 2 – BACKROADS ROUTE

**Features:** Across Southern Ontario generally through the Highway 7 corridor.

**Distance:** 1021 km. from Windsor – 917 km. from Sarnia

**Characteristics:** All paved back roads, except for 20 km. unpaved route from Fergus to Orton.

**Description:** Start from the Bluewater International Bridge in Sarnia or from Riverside Drive in Windsor and bicycle this back road route through the scenic countryside and lakelands of Southern Ontario. Route includes the Thames River valley, Stratford - home of the internationally famous Stratford Festival, Ontario's Mennonite Country, Ontario's last remaining covered bridge, the Trent Canal, many small lakes and quiet countryside to no end. The topography is moderate; quite flat for the first 200 kilometers, rolling through the central 600 kilometers and then quite flat again for the final 200 kilometers from Perth to the Quebec border.

**Major Waypoints:** Windsor (Detroit MI) or Sarnia (Port Huron MI) - Stratford – St. Jacobs – Orangeville – Bradford – Campbellford – Tweed – Perth - Ottawa – Quebec border (Quebec's Route Verte)

**Consult these atlas pages to track this route on the maps:** Marked as ❷

From Windsor:

| | | |
|---|---|---|
| Map 4 B1 | Windsor | |
| Map 5 B6 | Lighthouse Cove | |
| Map 6 A9 | Chatham | X9 Dawn Mills |
| Map 7 W10 | Shetland | |

From Sarnia:

| | |
|---|---|
| Map 12 T7 | Sarnia |

These routes meet at:

| | |
|---|---|
| Map 13 T14 | Strathroy |
| Map 14 R16 | Birr |
| Map 15 Q18 | St. Marys |

| Map 21 P27 | Stratford | L21 Linwood |
|---|---|---|
| Map 22 M22 | St. Jacobs | K24 Fergus |
| Map 23 J25 | Orton | |
| Map 29 H26 | Orangeville | F29 Tottenham |
| Map 30 E31 | Bradford | E32 Sharon |
| Map 31 F36 | Purple Hill | |
| Map 32 E40 | Millbrook | |
| Map 33 C45 | Campbellford | |
| Map 34 C46 | Pethericks Corners | |
| Map 46 A49 | Tweed | |
| Map 47 B53 | Enterprise | |
| Map 36 A54 | Verona, Godfrey | |
| Map 48 Y57 | Westport | |
| Map 49 W58 | Perth | U59 Blacks Corners |
| Map 65 S61 | Stanley Corners | |
| Map 66 Q63 | Ottawa | P64 Orleans |
| Map 67 P68 | Jessups Falls | |
| Map 68 N72 | Chute a Blondeau | |
| Map 69 N73 | Pointe Fortune, Carillon ferry, Quebec border | |

## 3 – CENTRAL ONTARIO ROUTE

**Features:** Across Southern Ontario generally through the area where Highways 401, 402 and 403 are located.

**Distance:** 936 km

**Characteristics:** All paved back roads from Windsor or Sarnia to Hamilton; Waterfront Trail from Hamilton to Quebec border.

**Description:** This is a countryside route from Sarnia or Windsor that goes quite directly east toward Toronto including the Thames River valley, lush scenic farmland, the Native Canadian Six Nations Territory and historic Ancaster. From Hamilton to the east the route uses the Lake Ontario Waterfront Trail, close to Lake Ontario and the St. Lawrence.

**Major Waypoints:** Windsor (Detroit MI) or Sarnia (Port Huron MI) – London – Ohsweken – Hamilton - - Toronto - Picton - Kingston - Cornwall (Massena NY) - Quebec border (Quebec's Route Verte to Montreal)

**Consult these atlas pages to track this route on the maps:** Marked as ❸

From Windsor:
| Map 4 B1 | Windsor | |
|---|---|---|
| Map 5 B6 | Lighthouse Cove | |
| Map 6 A9 | Chatham | X9 Dawn Mills |
| Map 7 W10 | Shetland | |

From Sarnia:
| Map 12 T7 | Sarnia |
|---|---|

These routes meet at:

| Map 13 T14 | Strathroy | |
|---|---|---|
| Map 14 U16 | Lambeth, London | |
| Map 15 T20 | Mount Elgin | |
| Map 16 S24 | Scotland | |
| Map 17 S26 | Ohsweken | Q28 Hamilton |
| Map 23 P28 | Aldershot | |
| Map 24 N29 | Bronte | L32 Toronto |
| Map 25 H37 | Oshawa | |
| Map 32 G40 | Wesleyville | |
| Map 33 F44 | Colborne | |
| Map 34 G49 | Wellington | |
| Map 35 G51 | Picton | E54 Bath |
| Map 36 D56 | Kingston | D57 Pitts Ferry |
| Map 37 A62 | Butternut Bay | |
| Map 50 X65 | Cardinal | |
| Map 51 V68 | Ingleside | |
| Map 52 U71 | Cornwall | T72 South Lancaster |
| Map 53 T73 | Quebec border | |

## 4 – TRANS-CANADA ROUTE

**Features:** Across Ontario from the Manitoba border to the Quebec border through Southern Ontario.

**Distance:** 2423 km. from Manitoba border - 1243 km. from Sault Ste. Marie.

**Characteristics:** All paved. Main roads from Manitoba border to Manitoulin Island. Back roads from Manitoulin Island to Quebec border

**Description:** Bicycle across Ontario from Manitoba, Quebec and United States border crossings from Minnesota and Michigan, connecting with Quebec's Route Verte and American Cycling Association Routes. Explore the northern edge of Southern Ontario.

**Major Waypoints:** Kenora – Fort Frances (International Falls MN) - Thunder Bay (Grand Portage MN) – Sault Ste. Marie (Sault Ste. Marie MI) – Manitoulin Island (ferry) – Owen Sound – Collingwood – Bradford – Campbellford – Tweed – Perth – Ottawa – Quebec border (Quebec's Route Verte

**Consult these atlas pages to track this route on the maps:** Marked as ❹

| Map 2 | Manitoba border | |
|---|---|---|
| | Kenora | Fort Frances |
| | Thunder Bay | White River |
| | Sault Ste Marie | Massey |

To avoid traffic on the TransCanada Highway
From Sault Ste. Marie:
East on Road 17 (Trunk Road) to Road 638 at Echo Bay
Left to go East on Road 638 to Gordon Lake Road
Right to go South on Gordon Lake Road to Highway 17 at

Portlock
Left to continue East on Highway 17

Alternate Route From Sault Ste Marie
East on Road 17 (Trunk Road) and pass Echo Bay to Bar River Road
Left to go East on Bar River Road to Government Road
Right to go South and East on Government Road to Road 638
Right to go South on Road 638 to Highway 17 at Portlock
Left to continue East on Highway 17

From Bruce Mines:
North on Road 638 pass Bruce Station to Cloudslee Road
Right to go East on Cloudslee Road and continure on Ansonia Road to Little Rapids Road
Right to go South on Little Rapids Road to Road 129
Left to go East on Road 129 to Station Road
Right to go south on Station Road to Highway 17

| | | |
|---|---|---|
| Map 84 J12 | Little Current | |
| Map 73 J12 | Little Current | |
| Map 72 L10 | Mindemoya | |
| Map 73 N11 | South Baymouth  (Note: toll ferry crossing to Tobermory) | |
| Map 54 X18 | Wiarton | |
| Map 39 Z19 | Owen Sound | A21 Walters Falls |
| Map 40 A25 | Collingwood | |
| Map 41 A26 | Batteaux | |
| Map 29 F29 | Beeton | |
| Map 30 E31 | Bradford | E32 Sharon |
| Map 31 F36 | Purple Hill | |
| Map 32 E40 | Millbrook | |
| Map 33 C45 | Campbellford | |
| Map 34 C46 | Pethericks Corners | |
| Map 46 A49 | Tweed | |
| Map 47 B53 | Enterprise | |
| Map 36 A54 | Verona, Godfrey | |
| Map 48 Y57 | Westport | |
| Map 49 W58 | Perth | U59 Blacks Corners |
| Map 65 S61 | Stanley Corners | |
| Map 66 Q63 | Ottawa | P64 Orleans |
| Map 67 P68 | Jessups Falls | |
| Map 68 N72 | Chute a Blondeau | |
| Map 69 N73 | Pointe Fortune, Carillon ferry, Quebec border | |

## 5 – HURON TRAIL ROUTE

**Features:**  Near the shore of the Detroit River, St. Clair River, Lake St. Clair and Lake Huron.

**Distance:**  557 kilometers

**Characteristics:** All Paved Except For 6 kilometers south of Grand Bend.

**Description:** Enjoy this waterfront route between Windsor and Tobermorey.  Watch the ships on the Detroit River and St. Clair River as you bicycle along. Visit the scenic and historic port towns and lighthouses.

**Major Waypoints:** Windsor (Detroit MI) or Sarnia (Port Huron MI) – Goderich – Kincardine – Port Elgin – Wiarton – Owen Sound – Tobermory (Manitoulin Island ferry)

**Consult these atlas pages to track this route on the maps:** Marked as ❺

| From Windsor: | | |
|---|---|---|
| Map 4 B1 | Windsor | |
| Map 5 B6 | Lighthouse Cove | |
| Map 6 W6 | Sombra | |
| Map 12 T7 | Sarnia | S9 Errol |
| Map 13 Q13 | Corbett | |
| Map 20 P13 | Dashwood | J13 Goderich |
| Map 26 E13 | Kincardine | C38 Inverhuron |
| Map 38 B16 | Port Elgin | X18 Wiarton |
| Map 39 Z19 | Owen Sound | |
| Map 55 S13 | Tobermory [Manitoulin Is. Ferry] | |

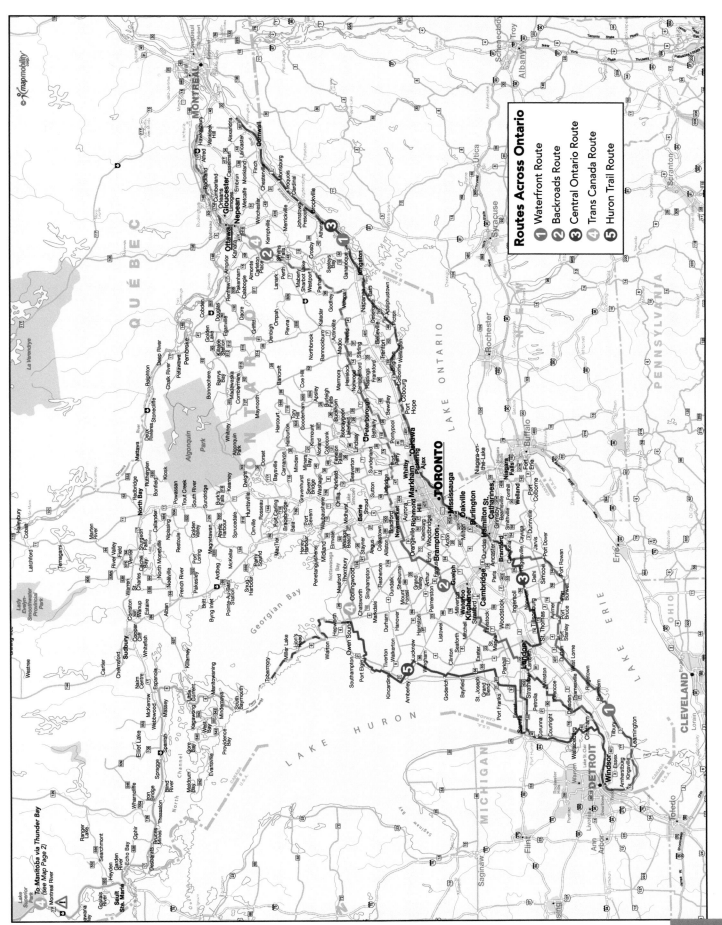

Routes Across Ontario

**Routes Across Ontario**

# Community Guide

## How to use this index

Community name — Grid reference — Community type

**Amherstview** 36 D55: Village

Community amenities

Amenity details

322 Amherst Drive
Amherstview ON  K7N 1S9
www.lennox-addington.on.ca
Tel: (613) 389 6006

This community guide lists communities along the routes which have useful amenities. Some of these amenities are then detailed, including address, website & phone numbers when available.

Beside each community name is their map page and grid reference. To find the grid reference 36 D55, for example, turn to map page 36, locate row D and column 55, and scan through the grid until you find the community. Indexed communities have been highlighted on the maps.

## Legend of Symbols

- Conservation/Park/Zoo
- Bike shop
- Grocery Store
- Convenience Store
- Information
- Restaurant
- Library
- Accommodation Partner
- Accommodation
- Camping
- Event/Attraction
- Casino
- Brewery
- Winery
- Art/Theatre/Culture
- Historic Site
- Services

## Community Index

**Aamjiwnaang First Nation** 12 U7
GPS 42.92368,-82.45195
Annual Pow-Wow in late June
www.aamjiwnaang.ca

**Adolphustown** 35 F52: Hamlet
GPS 44.06307,-77.00686
UEL Heritage Centre & Park
54 Adolphustown Park Road
Box 112  RR#1 Bath ON  K0H 1G0
www.uel.ca
Tel: (877) 384-1784 (613) 373 2196

**Ailsa Craig** 14 R14:  Town
GPS 43.14693,-81.53308

Ailsa Craig Public Library
147 Main Street
Ailsa Craig  ON  N0M 1A0
www.middlesex.library.on.ca/branch/ailsacraig.asp
Tel (519) 293 3441

**Ajax** 25 H35  GPS 43.85075,-79.02109: City

Before The Mast B&B
1144 Shoal Point Road
Ajax ON  L1S 1E2
www.beforethemast.ca  Tel: (905) 683 4830

Maple Shores Bed & Breakfast
485 Maple Avenue   Ajax ON  L1S 1E4
www.mapleshores.com
Tel: (905) 683 3809

Northern Cycle
889 Westney Road South  Ajax 0N L1S 3M4
www.northerncycle.com
Tel. (877) 220 7336  (905) 619-8875

**Alderville First Nation** 33 D43

GPS 44.18122,-78.06747:  Village

First Nation Pow Wow,  July
www.aldervillefirstnation.ca

**Algoma Mills** 2  GPS 46.18493,-82.81948
Village

**Algonquin** 50 Y63  GPS 44.70941,-75.67383
Village

**Alliston** 29 E28  GPS 44.15421,-79.86812: Town

Stevenson Farms Historical Bed & Breakfast
5923 King Street North   Alliston ON  L9R 1V3
www.stevensonfarms.com   Tel: (705) 438 0844

Gramma's House Bed & Breakfast
146 Victoria Street East  Alliston ON  L9R 1K6
www.bbcanada.com/3931.html
Tel: (705) 434 4632  (905) 868-7834

Red Pine Motor Inn restaurant
497 Victoria Street East  Alliston ON  L9R 1T9
www.redpineinn.com
Tel: (800) 328 1404  (705) 435 4381

Earl Rowe Provincial Park
2 km west, on Highway 89
Tel: (705) 435 4331
Reservations- www.ontarioparks.com
Tel: (888) 668 7275

17 Victoria Street
Alliston ON L9R 1V6
www.ntpl.ca   Tel: (705) 435 5651

**Alton** 29 H26  GPS 43.85847,-80.06530:  Village

Millcroft Inn restaurant
55 John Street   Alton ON  L0N 1A0
www.millcroft.com
Tel: (800) 383 3976  (519) 941 8111

**Ameliasburg** 34 F48  GPS 44.05912,-77.43614:
Village

Ameliasburg Museum
www.pecounty.on.ca/government/rec_parks_
culture/rec_culture/museums/ameliasburgh.
php

Roblin Lake and Conservation Area

**Amherstburg** 4 D1  GPS 42.10187,-83.10892
Historic town on the Detroit River; Kings Navy
Yard Park

Gordon House and Park House Museum,
Dalhousie Street;  historic 1796 Fort Malden
on Laird Street
Shores of Erie International Wine Festival in
September
www.soewinefestival.com

D'Angelo Estate Winery
55141 Concession 5 RR4 Amherstburg
www.dangelowinery.com   Tel: (519) 736 7959

Sanson Estate Winery
9238 Walker Road
Amherstburg ON  N0R 1J0
www.sansonestatewinery.com
Tel: (519) 726 9609

Pier 41 Bed & Breakfast
GPS 42.055967, -83.115193

41 Mickle Drive
Amherstburg ON  N9V 1V3
www.pier41bb.com
Tel. (519) 737 9187

Bondy House Bed & Breakfast
199 Dalhousie Street
Amherstburg ON  N9V 1W5
www.bbcanada.com/bondyhousebnb
Tel: (519) 736 9433

Caldwell's Grant
269 Dalhousie Street
Amherstburg ON  N9V 1W8
www.caldwellsgrant.com
Tel: (519) 736 2100

Ducks On The Roof
1430 Front Road South
Amherstburg ON  N9V 3K1
www.ducksontheroof.com
Tel: (519) 736 0044

232 Sandwich Street South
Amherstburg ON  N9V 2A4
www.essexcountylibrary.ca
Tel: (519) 736 4632

**Amherstview** 36 D55  GPS 44.21900,-76.64188:
Village

322 Amherst Drive
Amherstview ON  K7N 1S9
www.lennox-addington.on.ca
Tel: (613) 389 6006

**Ancaster** 17 Q27  GPS 43.22502,-79.97737
Historic Ancaster dating from 1795 is now part
of Hamilton

Online Cycling Map  www.myhamilton.
ca/myhamilton/CityandGovernment/
CityDepartments/PublicWorks/
TrafficEngineeringAndOperations/Cycling

Hamilton Tourism
www.tourismhamilton.com

Ridgemoor Bed & Breakfast
902 Shaver Road Ancaster ON  L9G 3K9
www.ridgemoor.ca
Tel: (905) 648 0116

Old Mill Restaurant
historic 548 Old Dundas Road
off Wilson Street East,  Ancaster ON
www.ancasteroldmill.com
Tel: (905) 648 1827

Ancaster Cycle Ltd.
365 Wilson Street East Ancaster ON
www.ancastercycle.ca   Tel: (905) 648 2288

300 Wilson Street East
Ancaster ON  L9G 2B9
www.inform.hamilton.ca/record/HAM0547
Tel: (905) 648 6911

**Angus** 29 C28  GPS 44.32145,-79.88728: Town

Angus Public Library
18 King Street  Angus ON  L0M 1B2
www.essa.library.on.ca/index.htm
Tel: (705) 424 6531

**Arkona** 13 S12  GPS 43.07436,-81.83414
Village in fruit growing area

Rock Glen Conservation Area waterfall and

museum with Devonian fossils and Native
Canadian artifacts

Rock Glen Motel
7502 Arkona Road, Arkona ON
www.rockglenmotel.com
Tel: (519) 828 3838

16 Smith Street
Arkona ON  N0M 1B0
www.lclmg.org  Tel: (519) 828 3406

## Arnprior 65 Q57 GPS 45.43563,-76.35837: Town

Ottawa Valley Tourist Association
9 International Drive
Pembroke ON  K8A 6W5
www.ottawavalley.org
Tel: (800) 757 6580  (613) 732 4364

Kirkman House Bed & Breakfast
294 John Street North
Arnprior ON  K7S 2P6
www.bbcanada.com/3742.html
Tel: (613) 623 5890

Arnprior Quality Inn
70 Madawaska Boulevard
Arnprior ON  K7S 1S5
www.arnpriorqualityinn.com
Tel: (877) 700 5637  (613) 623 7991

Arnprior Public Library
21 Madawaska Street
Arnprior ON  K7S 1R6
www.arnprior.library.on.ca
Tel: (613) 623 2279

## Ashton 65 T60 GPS 45.15710,-76.03225:

## Athens 49 Z60 GPS 44.62545,-75.95344: Town

See the history of the town, pictured in thirteen
murals.

## Atikokan 2 GPS 48.75923,-91.59287: Town

Atikokan Hotel  restaurant
400 Front Street  Box 1448
Atikokan ON  P0T 1C0
www.atikokanhotel.com
Tel: (807) 597 2533

Burns Street B&B
127 Burns Street  Box 662
Atikokan ON  P0T 1C0
Tel: (807) 597 4353

Quetico Provincial Park
Atikokan ON  P0T 1C0
Tel: (807) 597 2735

Dawson Trail Campground
French Lake, 40 kilometers east
Reservations: www.ontarioparks.com
Tel: (888) 668 7275

## Aurora 30 G31 GPS 43.99973,-79.46746: City

Rec Cycle n' Sports
15483 Yonge Street
Aurora ON  L4G 1P3
www.recsports.ca  Tel: (905) 841 5757

15145 Yonge Street
Aurora ON  L4G 1M1
www.library.aurora.on.ca
Tel: (905) 727 9493

## Ayr 16 Q23 GPS 43.28565,-80.45000: Town on Nith River

The Swan and the Peacock Bed & Breakfast
1140 Swan Street R.R.#3 Ayr, Ontario N0B 1E0
www.theswanandthepeacock.ca
Tel: (519) 632 5058

92 Stanley Street  Ayr ON  N0B 1E0
www.rwl.library.on.ca  Tel: (519) 632 7298

## Bamberg 22 M21 GPS 43.48930,-80.68909: Hamlet in Mennonite farming area

## Bancroft 61 U45 GPS 45.05654,-77.85335: Town

Tourist Information: www.bancroftontario.com

Dreamer's Rock Bed & Breakfast
RR#4 Bancroft ON  K0L 1C0
www.dreamersrockbandb.com
Tel: (613) 332 2350

Bancroft Motor Inn

528 Hastings Street North
RR#1 Bancroft ON  K0L 1C0
www.bancroftmotorinn.com
Tel: (888) 219 4900  (613) 332 4900

Best Western Sword Motor Inn
146 Hastings Street North
Bancroft ON  K0L 1C0
www.bestwesternontario.com/hotels/best-
western-sword-motor-inn
Tel: (800) 780 7234  (613) 332 2474

Trips and Trail Adventure Outfitting
258 Hastings Street North
RR#2 Bancroft ON  K0L 1C0
tripsandtrails.ca
Tel: (613) 332 1969

Bancroft Public Library
14 Flint Street  Box 127
Bancroft ON  K0L 1C0
www.bancroftpubliclibrary.ca
Tel: (613) 332 3380

## Barrie 42 B30 GPS 44.38930,-79.68632: City on Lake Simcoe

Tourist Information: Tourism Barrie
205 Lakeshore Drive
Barrie ON  L4N 7Y9
www.tourismbarrie.com
Tel: (800) 668 9100  (705) 739 9444

Richmond Manor Bed & Breakfast
16 Blake Street Barrie ON  L4M 1J6
www.bbcanada.com/1145.html
Tel: (705) 726 7103

Best Western Royal Oak Inn
35 Hart Drive  Barrie ON
www.bestwesternontario.com/hotels/best-
western-royal-oak-inn
Tel: (800) 780 7234 ( (705) 721 4848

Comfort Inn Barrie
75 Hart Drive  Barrie ON
www.comfortinnbarrie.com
Tel: (877) 424 6423  (705) 722 3600

Mountain Equipment Coop
61 Bryne Drive Barrie ON  L4N 8V8
www.mec.ca  Tel: (705) 792 4675

Bikeland
49 Anne Street South  Barrie ON L4N 2E1
www.bikeland.ca  Tel: (705) 726 7372

Barrie Public Library
60 Worsley Street  Barrie ON  L4M 1L6
www.library.barrie.on.ca/main.html
Tel: (705) 728 1010

## Barrow Bay 55 V17 GPS 44.96003,-81.22703 Village

## Barry's Bay 80 P47 GPS 45.48819,-77.67849

Fortune's Madawaska Valley Inn
19854 Hwy. 60
Barry's Bay, Ontario K0J 1B0
www.madawaskavalleyinn.com
Tel: (800) 363 2758  (613) 756 9014

Barry's Bay Public Library
19474 Opeongo Line
P.O. Box 970 Barry's Bay ON  K0J 1B0
/library.barrys-bay.ca/
Tel: (613) 756-2000

## Batchawana Bay 96 K13 GPS 46.93948,-84.59061: Village

Pancake Bay Provincial Park
Box 61
Batchawana Bay ON  P0S 1A0
Tel: (705) 882 2209
Reservations- www.ontarioparks.com
Tel: (888) 668 7275

## Bath 36 E54 GPS 44.18304,-76.77526: Village

1859 Layer Cake Hall Museum

Bergeron Estate Winery
9656 Loyalist Parkway  Bath ON K0H 1G0
www.bergeronestatewinery.com
Tel: (613) 373 0181

Bayshore Bed & Breakfast
Bath ON  K0H 1G0
www.bbcanada.com/bayshorebb

Tel: (613) 352 5889

Loyalist Golf & Country Club
1 Loyalist Blvd, Bath ON
www.loyalistcc.com
Tel: (613) 352 5152

197 Davy Street
(located in the Layer Cake Hall)
Bath ON  K0H 1G0
www.lennox-addington.on.ca
Tel: (613) 352 5600

## Battersea 36 B57 GPS 44.43217,-76.38345: Village, convenience store

## Bayfield 20 L13 GPS 43.56138,-81.69643
Charming historic village with attractive shops,
galleries, marina and beaches on Lake Huron

Fresh and smoked fish on the north pier -
north side of Bayfield River

Bayfield Fall Fair mid August at Bayfield arena
on James Street
www.bayfieldfallfair.ca

Folmar Windmill, wind driven saw and grist
mill north of Bayfield just off Road 13

The Little Inn restaurant
Main Street  Box 100
Bayfield ON N0M 1G0
www.littleinn.com
Tel: (800) 565 1832  (519) 565 2611

Albion Hotel restaurant
1 Main Street  Box 114
Bayfield ON  N0M 1G0
www.thealbionhotel.com  Tel: (519) 565 2641

The Red Pump restaurant
21 Main Street  Box 40  Bayfield ON N0M 1G0
www.theredpumpinn.com
Tel: (519) 565 2576

Main Street Bayfield ON  N0M 1G0
www.huroncounty.ca/library
Tel: (519) 565 2886

## Beamsville 18 R31 GPS 43.16583,-79.47634 Town

Silver Birches by-the-Lake Bed and Breakfast
4902 Mountainview Road
Beamsville ON  L0R 1B3
www.silverbirchesbythelake.com
Tel: (905) 563 9479

Grapeview Guesthouse on the Vinyard
4163 Merritt Road Beamsville ON  L0R 1B1
www.bbcanada.com/grapeview
(905) 563-5077

August Restaurant
5204 King Street West  Beamsville ON
www.augustrestaurant.ca
Tel: (905) 563 0200

Peninsula Ridge Winery Restaurant
5600 King Street West
Beamsville ON
www.peninsularidge.com
Tel: (905) 563 0900

Mountainview Cycle & Sports Inc
4282 Mountainview Road South
Beamsville ON L0R 1B0
www.mountainviewcycle.ca
Tel: (905) 563 8585

4996 Beam Street
Beamsville ON  L0R 1B0
www.lincoln.library.on.ca
Tel: (905) 563 7014

## Beeton 30 F29 GPS 44.07882,-79.78498: Town

42 Main Street West
Beeton ON  L0G 1A0
www.ntpl.ca
Tel: (905) 729 3726

## Belfountain 23 J27 GPS 43.79388,-80.01394: Village, park

## Belle River 4 B4 GPS 42.29306,-82.70632: Town on Lake St. Clair

Stone Garden B&B
582 Notre Dame Street
Belle River ON  N0R 1A0
www.bbcanada.com/4831.html

Tel: (519) 728 1587
304 Rourke Line Road
RR#3 Belle River ON  N0R 1A0
www.essexcountylibrary.ca
Tel: (519) 727 4253

**Belleville** 34 E49 GPS 44.16105,-77.38190:  City, attractive parks on the Bay of Quinte

⭐ **Waterfront Festival and Ethnic Festival** in mid July

⭐ **Farmers Market** at City Hall; Tuesday, Thursday and Saturday

**Glanmore House museum and restored Victorian mansion**
257 Bridge Street East
www.glanmore.org/glanmoreind.html
Tel: (613) 962 2329

**Ramada Inn restaurant**
11 Bay Bridge Road
Belleville ON  K8N 4Z1
www.bellevilleramada.com
Tel: (800) 420 3555  (613) 968 3411

**Holiday Inn Express**
291 North Front Street Belleville ON K8P 3C3
www.hiexpress.com/hotels/us/en/belleville/xvvon/hoteldetail Tel: (613) 962 1200

**Inn by the Rose Garden Bed & Breakfast**
144 Bridge Street East
Belleville ON  N8N 1M7
innbytherosegarden.on.ca/
Tel: (613) 969 2894

**L'Auberge de France**
304 Front Street  Belleville ON  K8N 2Y6
www.aubergedefrance.ca Tel: (613) 966 2433

**Capers Restaurant**
272 Front Street Belleville ON
www.capers.ca Tel: (613) 968 7979

**The Boathouse Restaurant**
32 Front Street
Belleville, ON K8N 2Y3
www.boathouselure.ca/web
Tel: (613) 969 2211

**Dougs Bicycle Sales & Service**
159 College Street West
Belleville ON
Tel: (613) 966 9161

254 Pinnacle Street
Belleville ON  K8N 3B1
www.bellevillelibrary.com
Tel: (613) 968 6731

**Belmont** 9 U18 GPS 42.88064,-81.08735:  Village

**Benmiller** 20 K14 GPS 43.72844,-81.64078: Restored mills and houses in the Maitland River valley form a luxurious resort

**Benmiller Inn  historic restaurant**
81175 Benmiller Road
RR#4 Goderich  ON  N7A 3Y1
www.benmiller.on.ca
Tel: (800) 265 1711  (519) 524 2191

**Falls Reserve Conservation Area**
Benmiller
Tel: (877) 325 5722  (519) 524 6429

**Big Bay** 39 X19 GPS 44.79158,-80.94727:

**MaiTribe Gallery B&B**
504143 Grey Road 1, Big Bay ON
www.bbcanada.com/maitribe
Tel: (519) 534 4603

**Big Chute** 41 W30 GPS 44.88680,-79.66727: Village

⭐ **Trent Severn Waterway**
Marine Railway Lock 44
Group camping at most lock stations with prior approval
www.pc.gc.ca/eng/lhn-nhs/on/trentsevern/visit/visit6.aspx
Tel: (888) 773 8888 (705) 750 4900

**Birr** 14 R16 GPS 43.11903,-81.33316: Village

**Black River** 35 G51 GPS 43.96811,-77.03476: Village

**Black River Cheese Factory**

913 County Road 13
Milford ON  K0K 2P0
www.pec.on.ca/blackrivercheese
Tel: (888) 252 5787  (613) 476 2575

**Blacks Corners** 49 U59  65 T59
GPS  45.11824,-76.11568:

**Blenheim** 7 B10 GPS 42.33519,-81.99770: Town in fruit growing area

⭐ **RM Auctions**
Classic Car Exhibit
One Classic Car Drive
Blenheim ON  N0P 1A0
www.rmauctions.com
Tel: (877) 523 2684  (519) 452 9024

**Queens Motel**
9194 Talbot Trail RR 1
Blenheim ON  N0P 1A0
Tel: (519) 676 5477

**Jack's Family Restaurant**
67 Talbot Street West
Blenheim ON  N0P 1A0
Tel: (519) 676-5050

16 George Street
Blenheim ON  N0P 1A0
www.chatham-kent.ca/community+services/library/Library.htm
Tel: (519) 676 3174

**Blessington** 35 D50 GPS 44.25553,-77.30186: Village

**Blind River** 2 GPS 46.18769,-82.96038:  Town

**Timber Village Museum**
Tel: (705) 356 7544

**Regional Tourist Information Centre,** east end of town
Tel: (800) 563 8719

**Auberge Eldo Inn**
1 White Road Box 156
Blind River ON  P0R 1B0
www.eldoinn.on.ca
Tel: (800) 798 3536  (705) 356 2255

**Old Mill Motel**
Highway 17 and Woodward Avenue
Blind River ON
www.oldmillmotel.ca
Tel: (800) 871 0842  (705) 356 2274

**A Taste of Home Bed & Breakfast**
29 Fullerton Street
Blind River ON  P0R 1B0
www.bbcanada.com/989.html
Tel: (705) 356 7165

**MacIver's Mississauga Motel and Camp**
Box 502
Highway 17 West
Blind River ON  P0R 1B0
www.brchamber.ca/macivers
Tel: (877) 573 1078  (705) 356 7411

**Bloomfield** 35 G50 GPS 43.98549,-77.23418: Village

**Angeline's Inn & Spa restaurant**
433 Main Street  Box 16
Bloomfield ON  K0K 1G0
www.angelinesinn-spa.com
Tel: (877) 391 3301  (613) 393 3301

**Renlea House Bed & Breakfast**
420 Main Street
Bloomfield ON  K0K 1G0
www.bbcanada.com/538.html
Tel: (800) 490 7666  (613) 393 1846

**Cornelius White House Bed & Breakfast**
8 Wellington Street
Bloomfield ON  K0K 1G0
www.bbcanada.com/558.html
Tel: (866) 854 2282  (613) 393 2282

**Bloomfield Cycle bicycle rental**
225 Main Street
Bloomfield ON
www.torontocyclist.com/bbc/
Tel: (613) 393 1060

300 Main Street
Bloomfield ON
www.peclibrary.org  Tel: (613) 393 3400

**Bobcageon** 44 F60 GPS 44.54521, -78.541514

**Bobgageon Inn Restaurant & Waterfront Patio**
31 Main Street Bobcageon ON  K0M 1A0
www.bobcaygeoninn.com
Tel: (800) 900 4248  (705) 738 5433

**Kawartha Lakes Public Library**
21 Canal Street Bobcaygeon ON  K0M 1A0
www.city.kawarthalakes.on.ca/residents/library-services/hours-and-locations
Tel: (705) 738 2088

**Bowmanville** 32 G-H38
GPS 43.91383,-78.68847:  Town

**Tourist Information:** Tourism Clarington
181 Liberty Street South
Bowmanville ON  L1C 3Z2
www.claringtontourism.net
Tel: (800) 563 1195  (905) 623 4356

**Howard Johnson Hotel**
143 Duke Street at Liberty Street
Bowmanville ON  L1C 2W4
www.howardjohnsonbowmanville.com
Tel: (800) 406 1411  (905) 623 8500

**Darlington Provincial Park**
1600 Darlington Beach Road
Bowmanville ON  L1C 3K3
Tel: (905) 436 2036
Reservations - www.ontarioparks.com
Tel: (888) 668 7275

**Bowmanville Sports Shop**
58 King Street West  Bowmanville ON
www.bowmanvillesportshop.com
Tel. (905) 623 0322

**Bracebridge** 59 U5 GPS 45.05558,-79.28863: Town

**Century House Bed and Breakfast**
155 Dill Street
Bracebridge ON  P1L 1E5
www.bbmuskoka.com/centuryhouse
Tel: (705) 645 9903

**The Monastery B&B**
15 Sadler Drive
Bracebridge ON  P1L 1K5
www.bbmuskoka.com/themonastery
Tel: (705) 646-0871

**Muskoka Riverside Inn**
300 Ecclestone Drive
Bracebridge ON  P1L 1G5
www.bracebridge.com/riverside
Tel: (705) 645 8775 (800) 461 4474

**Wellington Motel**
265 Wellington Street
Bracebridge ON
www.wellingtonmotel.com
Tel: (800) 212 2280  (705) 645 2238

**Ecclestone Cycling Company**
230 Ecclestone Drive
Bracebridge ON  P1L 1G4
www.ecclestonecycle.com
Tel: (705) 645 1166

**Bracebridge Public Library**
94 Manitoba Street
Bracebridge ON  P1 L2B5
www.bracebridge.library.on.ca
Tel: (705) 645 4171

**Bradford** 30 E-F30 GPS 44.11455,-79.56366: Town

**Brampton** 24 K29 GPS 43.68431,-79.75873: City

**Best Western Brampton**
30 Clark Boulevard
Brampton ON  L6W 1X3
www.bestwesternontario.com/hotels/best-western-brampton
Tel: (800) 780 7234  (905) 454 1300

**Comfort Inn**
5 Rutherford Road South
Brampton ON  L6W 3J3
www.choicehotels.ca/en/brampton-hotel-comfort-ontario-cn256-en
Tel: (877) 424 6423 (905) 452 0600

**Residence & Conference Centre – Brampton**

7897 McLaughlin Road
Brampton ON  N6Y 5H9
www.stayrcc.com/default/profile/25
Tel: (905) 874 4393  (877) 225 8664

**The Cyclepath Brampton**
60 Main Street North
Brampton ON  L6V 1N6
www.cyclepathbrampton.com
Tel: (905) 457 4481

**Brampton Public Library**
65 Queen Street East
Brampton ON  L6W 3L6
www.bramlib.on.ca
Tel: (905) 793 4636

## Brantford  16 R24 GPS 43.14136,-80.26174
Historic city on the Grand River

**Tourist Information** – Brantford
www.visitbrantford.ca
Tel: (800) 265 6299
Brant County
www.brant.ca  Tel: (888) 250 2296

**Glenhyrst Art Gallery of Brant**
22 Ava Road
www.glenhyrst.ca Tel: (519) 756 5932

**Sanderson Centre for the Performing Arts**
88 Dalhousie Street
www.sandersoncentre.ca
Tel: (800) 265 0710  (519) 758 8090

**Brantford International Jazz Festival**
September with concerts all year
www.brantfordjazzfestival.com

**The Canadian Military Heritage Museum and
Vintage Motorcycle Museum**
347 Greenwich Street
www.cmhmhq.ca
Tel: (519) 759 1313

**Woodland Cultural Centre native culture
museum**
184 Mohawk Street
www.woodland-centre.on.ca
Tel: (519) 759 2650

**Kanata reconstructed 1600's Iroquoian village
and Her Majesty's Royal Chapel of the
Mohawks**
291 Mohawk Street
www.mohawkchapel.ca
Tel: (519) 756 0240

**Brantford Riverfest** on Victoria Day weekend
and International Villages Festival in early July

**Brantford Charity Casino**
40 ICOMM Drive
Tel: (888) 694 6946

**Bell Homestead  museum** house where
Alexander Graham Bell grew up, picnic area,
restaurant
94 Tutela Heights Road
Brantford ON
www.bellhomestead.ca
Tel: (519) 756 6220

**Be My Guest Bed & Breakfast**
538 Mount Pleasant Road RR#2
Brantford ON  N3T 5L5
www.bbcanada.com/3933.html
Tel. (519) 753-6922

**Quality Inn & Suites**
664 Colborne Street East
Brantford  ON  N3S 3P8
www.qualityinn.com/hotel-brantford-canada-
CN870
Tel: (877) 424 6423  (519) 758 9999

**John Peel**
48 Dalhousie Street
Brantford ON
johnpeelrestaurant.ca Tel: (519) 753 7337

**Warmington's Bistro**
42 George Street Brantford ON N3T 2Y1
Tel.  (519) 770-4941

**The Bicycle Shop**
228 Clarence Street
Brantford ON
www.thebicycleshopbrantford.ca
Tel: (519) 752 2414

173 Colborne Street
Brantford ON  N3T 2G8
www.brantford.library.on.ca
Tel: (519) 756 2220

## Bridgenorth  44 G40 GPS 44.38497,-78.38608

## Brighton  33 F45  34 F46 GPS 44.04247,-77.73562
Town in apple growing area

**Proctor House Museum**
96 Young Street Brighton ON  K0K 1H0
www.proctorhousemuseum.ca
Tel: (613) 475 2144

**Presqu'ile Beach Motel**
GPS 44.03769,-77.74917
243 Main StreetW
RR4 Brighton ON  K0K 1H0
www.ruralroutes.com/presquilebeachmotel
Tel: (877) 769 6153  (613) 475 1010

**The Cider House Bed & Breakfast**
GPS 44.0391088, -77.7356195
74 Prince Edward Street
Box 1138  Brighton ON   K0K 1H0
www.ciderhouse.ca
Tel: (613) 475 5087

**Presqu'ile Provincial Park**
RR#3 Brighton ON  K0K 1H0
Tel: (613) 475 2204
Reservations - www.ontarioparks.com
Tel: (888) 668 7275

**The Gables**
14 Division Street  Brighton ON
www.thegablesrestaurant.net
Tel: (613) 475 5565

**Dougalls on the Bay**
75 Harbour Street, P.O. Box 762
www.ruralroutes.com/dougalls
Tel: (613) 475 4142

35 Alice Street  Brighton ON
www.brighton.library.on.ca
Tel: (613) 475 2511

## Brockville  50 Z62-63 GPS :44.59039,-75.68301:
Historic city on St Lawrence River founded in 1784

**Historic railway tunnel;** Brockville Museum
Henry Street

**Fulford House 1900's Edwardian mansion**
287 King Street East Brockville ON
www.heritagefdn.on.ca/userfiles/HTML/nts
Tel: (613) 498 3003

**Best Western White House Inn**
1843 Road 2  Brockville ON  K6V 5T1
bestwesternontario.com/hotels/best-western-
white-house-inn
Tel: (800) 780 7234  (613) 345 1622

**St Lawrence College - Residence Services**
60 Magedoma Bloulevard
Brockville ON  K6V 7N7
www.sl.on.ca/residence/
SummerAccomodations.htm
Tel: (613) 345 0452, ext. 3000

**St Lawrence Park**
Road 2 Brockville ON
Tel: (613) 345 1341

**Brockberry Café & Suites**
64 King Street East  PO Box 808
Brockville ON K6V SW1
www.brockberry.com  Tel: (613) 498 2692

**The Mill Restaurant**
123 Water Street  Brockville ON
www.themillrestaurant.ca Tel: (613) 345 7098

**Dave Jones Sports**
65 King Street West
Tel: (613) 345 5574

23 Buell Street
Brockville ON
www. brockvillelibrary.ca
Tel: (613) 342 3936

## Bruce Mines  2 GPS 46.30021,-83.79414
Village

**Bruce Mines Museum** in 1894 Presbyterian
Church and Simpson's Shaft copper mine

**Bavarian Inn  restaurant**
9181 Highway 17
Bruce Mines ON  P0R 1C0
www.bavarianinnbrucemines.com
Tel: (705) 785 3447

**Bruce Mines Tourist Park**
Williams Street
(off Highway 17 at Highway 638)
Bruce Mines ON   Tel: (705) 785 3099

## Burford  16 S23 GPS 43.10309,-80.43003:  Town

**County of Brant Public Library** – Burford Branch
24 Park Ave Box 267
Burford ON  N0E 1A0
www.brant.library.on.ca Tel: (519) 449 5371

## Burgessville  16 S22 GPS 43.02401,-80.65197:
Town

**Oxford County Library** – Burgessville Branch
604 Main Street South
Burgessville ON  N0J 1C0
www.ocl.net  Tel: (519) 424 2404

## Burlington  18 P29 GPS 43.32618,-79.79854
City

**Tourist Information:** Tourism Burlington
414 Locust Street just north of Lakeshore Road.
www.tourismburlington.com
Tel: (877) 499 9989  (905) 634 5594

**Wilkie House Bed & Breakfast**
1211 Sable Drive
Burlington ON  L7S 2J7
www.canvisit.com/wilkiehouse
Tel: (866) 233 2632  (905) 637 5553

**Waterfront Hotel – Downtown**
2020 Lakeshore Road
Burlington ON L7R 4G8
www.thewaterfrontdowntown.com
Tel: (905) 681-5400

**Pepperwood Bistro**
1455 Lakeshore Road
Burlington ON  L7S 2J1
www.pepperwood.on.ca/index2.html
Tel: (905) 333 6999

**Spencers at the Waterfront**
1340 Lakeshore Road
Burlington ON  L7S 1B1
www.spencers.ca Tel: (905) 633 7494

**Waterfront Trail Leisure Company café
bicycle rentals**
2049 Pine Street  Burlington ON  L7R 1E9
waterfronttrailleisure.com
Tel: (905) 633 9852  (877) 338 9852

**Brant Cycle And Sports Limited**
892 Brant Street
Burlington ON  L7R 2J5
www.brantcycle.ca  Tel:(905) 637 3737

**Mountain Equipment Co-Op**
1030 Brant Street Burlington ON
www.mec.ca  Tel: (888) 8470  (905) 333 8559

2331 New Street
Burlington ON
www.bpl.on.ca  Tel: (905) 639 3611

## Burritts Rapids  50 V62  GPS 44.98345,-75.79860:

**Rideau Canal**
Lock 17, group camping with prior approval
www.pc.gc.ca/lhn-nhs/on/rideau/index.aspx
Tel: (888) 773 8888  (613) 283 5170

## Caledon East  29 H28 GPS 43.87526,-79.85994:
Village

## Caledonia  17 S28 GPS 43.07356,-79.95072:  Town

**Haldimand County Library** – Caledonia Branch
100 Haddington Street, Unit 2
www.haldimandcounty.on.ca
Tel: (905) 765 2634

## Cambridge  22 NP24 GPS 43.36141,-80.31533:  City

**Cambridge Butterfly Conservatory**
2500 Kossuth Road
Cambridge ON
www.cambridgebutterfly.com
Tel: (519) 653 1234

**Cambridge Galleries**
1 North Square
Cambridge ON
www.cambridgegalleries.ca
Tel: (519) 621 0460

**Cambridge Farmers Market**
40 Dickson Street at Ainslie Street
Saturday and Wednesday
www.cambridgefarmersmarket.ca

**Southworks Outlets & Antiques**
64 Grand Avenue South

Cambridge ON  N1S 2L8
www.southworks.ca   Tel: (519) 740 0380

🛏 **Best Western Cambridge Hotel**
730 Hespeler Road
Cambridge ON  N3H 5L8
bestwesternontario.com/hotels/best-western-cambridge-hotel
Tel: (800) 780 7234  (519) 623 4600

🛏 **Comfort Inn**
220 Holiday Inn Drive
Cambridge ON
www.choicehotels.ca/en/cambridge-hotel-comfort-ontario-CN260-en?cid=1371119
Tel: (877) 424 6423  (519) 658 1100

🍴 **Cambridge Mill**
130 Water Street
North Cambridge ON N1R 1P1
www.cambridgemill.ca Tel:( 519) 624 1828

🍴 **Blackshop Restaurant**
595 Hespeler Road
Cambridge ON  N1R 6J3
www.blackshop.ca
Tel: (519) 621 4180

🍴 **Melville Café**
7 Melville Street
Cambridge ON  N1S 2H4
www.melvillecafe.ca
Tel (519) 624 3984

🚲 **Hub Bicycle Shop**
22 Queen Street West
Cambridge ON
www.hubbicycleshop.com
Tel: (888) 250 8838  (519) 249 1473

📚 **Queen's Square**
1 North Square Cambridge ON
www.cambridgelibraries.ca
Tel: (519) 621 0460

**Campbellford** 34 C45 GPS 44.30921,-77.79749:
Town on the Trent Severn Waterway, at Lock
13 Group camping at most lock stations with
prior approval
www.pc.gc.ca/eng/lhn-nhs/on/trentsevern/visit/visit6.aspx
Tel: (888) 773 8888 (705) 750 4900
gigantic two dollar coin, Healey Falls and
footbridge

🍴📚💢🏛🏕📷📚⭐

🎭 **Westben Arts Festival Theatre** music program
just north on Road 30
www.westben.on.ca
Tel: (887) 883 5777  (705) 653 5508

⭐ **World's Finest Chocolate Canada Company**
103 Second Street Campbellford ON L0L 1L0
www. worldsfinest.ca  Tel: (800) 461 1957

🏭 **Church Key Brewing Company**
Pethericks Corners 1678 County Rd#38
Campbellford ON  K0L 1L0
www.churchkeybrewing.com
Tel: (877) 314 2337  (705) 653 9950

⭐ **Empire Cheese & Butter Co-op**
County Road 8 RR#5
Campbellford 5 kilometers east
www.empirecheese.ca
Tel: (705) 653 3187  (800) 461 6480

🛏 **Grand Victoria House B&B**
258 Grand Road, Box 520
Campbellford ON  K0L 1L0
www.bbcanada.com/2769.html
Tel: (877) 592 7282  (705) 632 0587

🛏 **King and Knight Bed & Breakfast**
188 Queen Street  Box 310
Campbellford ON  K0L 1L0
www.kingandknightbedandbreakfast.com
Tel: (800) 434 0378  (705) 632 1441

🛏 **Campbellford River Inn**
352 Front Street
Campbellford ON  K0L 1L0
www.riverinn.on.ca/
Tel: (800) 984 6665 (705) 653 1771

🏕 **Ferris Provincial Park**
Road 8 (Centre Street) Box 1409
Campbellford ON  K0L 1L0
Tel: (705) 653 3575
Reservations www.ontarioparks.com
Tel: (888) 668 7275

🍴 **Capers Casual Dining**
28 Bridge Street West
Campbellford ON
www.capersrestaurant.ca  Tel: (705) 653 5262

🍴 **Rubbs Barbecue Bistro**
18 Bridge Street West

Campbellford ON
www.rubbsbbq.ca   Tel: (705) 632 0227

🛏 98 Bridge Street East
Campbellford ON  K0L 1L0
www.trenthillslibrary.ca/campbellford
Tel: (705) 653 3611

**Cardiff** 61 V39 GPS 44.99251,-78.09247:
🍴🛏🍴🚲📚

📚 **Haliburton County Public Library**
Monck Road Cardiff ON  K0L1M0
www.haliburtonlibrary.ca Tel: (613) 339 2712

**Cardinal** 50 X65 GPS 44.78731,-75.38481:
Village
🛏📚

📚 618 Kings 2 Highway  Cardinal ON
www.edwardsburghcardinal.ca/index.php/city-hall/departments/cityhall_library-facilities/
Tel: (613) 657 3822

**Carp** 65 R60 GPS 45.35004,-76.04258: Town
🍴🛏🍴🚲📷📚

📚 **Ottawa Library – Carp Branch**
www.biblioottawalibrary.ca
Tel: (613) 839 5412

🏛 **Diefenbunker, Canada's Cold War Museum**
3911 Carp Road  Carp ON  K0A 1L0
www.diefenbunker.ca
Tel: (800) 409 1965  (613) 839 0007

**Castleton** 33 E44 GPS 44.09270,-77.93811:
Village
🛏

**Cataract** 23 J27 GPS 43.82338,-80.02304: Hamlet
Forks of the Credit Provincial Park  scenic,
Cataract Falls and mill ruins, hiking trails

**Cayuga** 18 T28:  Town
🍴🛏

🛏 **Carrousel Red & Breakfast**
51 Winnett Street North
Cayuga ON  N0A 1E0
www.carrouselbb.ca  Tel: (905) 772-5348

🛏 **Broecheler Inn 4648**
Talbot Road West, Highway 3 RR#4 Cayuga
www.broechelerinn.com  Tel: (905) 772 5362

🍴 **Twisted Lemon Restaurant**
3 Norton Street West
Cayuga, ON N0A 1E0
www.twistedlemon.ca  Tel:  (905) 772 6636

**Cedar Springs** 7 C10 GPS 42.28163,-82.03217:
Village
🍴🛏📷

🍷 **Smith & Wilson Estate Wines**
8368 Water St., RR1 Blenheim ON  N0P 1A0
www.smithandwilsonestatewines.ca
Tel: (519) 676 5867

**Centreville** 47 B53 GPS 44.40665,-76.90439:
Village
🛏

**Chatham** 6 A8-9 GPS 42.40444,-82.18958: City
on the Thames River
🍴🛏ℹ🎬📷🍴🏕🚲📚

ℹ **Tourist Information – Chatham Kent**
www.cktourism.com
Tel: (800) 561 6125

🎬 **Chatham Capitol Theatre**
238 King Street West
chathamcapitoltheatre.com
Tel: (519) 358 7079

🏛 **Chatham Cultural Centre and
Milner Heritage House**
75 William Street North
www.theculturalcentre.com
Tel: (866) 807 7770  (519) 354 8338

🛏 **Comfort Inn** GPS 42.38074,-82.21476
1100 Richmond Street
Chatham ON  N7M 5J5
www.choicehotels.ca/hotels/hotel?hotel=CN262
Tel: (877) 424 6423  (519) 352 5500

🛏 **The Duchess of Wellington Bed & Breakfast**
320 Wellington Street West
Chatham ON N7M 1K1
www.theduchessofwellington.com
Tel: (877) 424 6423  (519) 352 5500

🛏🍴 **Retro Suites & Chilled Cork Restaurant**
2 King Street West

Chatham ON  N7M 1C6
www.retrosuites.com
Tel: (866) 617 3876 (519) 351 5885

🚲 **Chatham Outdoor Power & Pedal**
134 Inshes Avenue
Chatham ON  N7M 2Y9
www.chathamopp.com  Tel: (519) 354 3990

📚 120 Queen Street
Chatham ON  N7M 2G6
www.chatham-kent.ca/community+services/library/library.htm
Tel: (519) 354 2940

**Cheltenham** 23 J-K28 GPS 43.76665,-79.92518:
Village, store
🛏🛏

🛏 **Top of the Hill Bed & Breakfast** - historic
14318 Creditview Road
Cheltenham ON L7C 1N4
www.thetopofthehillbb.ca
Tel: (905) 838 3790

**Chepstow** 27 E17 GPS 44.15438,-81.27425: Village
🛏

**Cherry Valley** 35 G50 GPS 43.93585,-77.15443: Village
🛏

**Chesley** 27 C18 GPS 44.30223,-81.08803: Town;
nearby Amish Mennonite farming community
🍴🛏

**Chippewa** 19 S35 GPS 43.05000,-79.05000: Village
🍴🛏

**Clarksburg** 40 A23 GPS 44.54538,-80.46170: Town
🛏

**Clinton** 20 L14 GPS 43.61767,-81.53970: Town
🛏⭐🛏🍴

⭐ **Clinton Pluckinfest**
July 1 weekend

🛏 **The Parker House Motel**
77575 London Road  RR#5
Clinton ON  N0M 1L0
www.parkerhousemotel.com
Tel: (519) 482 3469

🍴 **Bartliff's Bakery Restaurant**
46 Albert Street
PO Box 1506 Clinton ON
Tel: (519) 482 9727

🍴 **Dinner Bell Restaurant**
272 Huron Street P.O. Box 1712
Clinton ON  N0M 1L0
www.dinnerbell.ca Tel: (519) 482 1119

**Cobden** 82 N53 GPS 45.62707,-76.87998:  Town
🛏🍴🛏🚲

🛏🍴 **17 West Motel Bar & Grill**
9 Pembroke Street
Cobden ON  K0J 1K0
Tel: (613) 646 2091

📚 **Cobden Public Library**
P.O. Box 152 Cobden ON  K0J 1K0
Tel: (613) 646 7592

**Cobourg** 33 G42 GPS 43.95961,-78.16778:
Historic town on Lake Ontario, beach
ℹ⭐🛏🍴🏕🚲📚

ℹ **Tourist Information – Northumberland Tourism**
Visitor centre at Marie Dressler House
212 King Street West
www.northumberlandtourism.com
Tel: (800) 354 7050  (905) 372 014

⭐ **Waterfront Festival** July 1 weekend
160 Victoria Hall courtroom,
concert hall and art gallery at
55 King Street West
www.concerthallatvictoriahall.com
Tel: (905) 372 2210

🛏🍴 **Best Western Cobourg Inn**
930 Burnham Street
Cobourg ON  K9A 2X9
bestwesternontario.com/cobourg-hotels
Tel: (905) 372 2105

🛏🍴 **Woodlawn Terrace Inn restaurant**
420 Division Street
Cobourg ON
www.woodlawninn.com
Tel: (800) 573 5003  (905) 372 2235

🛏 **Essex House Bed & Breakfast**
351 George Street
Cobourg ON K9A 3M2

www.essexbb.net
Tel: (.905) .377.3922

North Side Grill
92 King Street West
Cobourg ON K9A 2M3
thenorthside.ca Tel: (905) 377 9709

Matterhorn Restaurant
95 King Street West
Cobourg ON
www.matterhorn.ca Tel: (905) 372 5231

Victoria Park Campground
138 Division Street
Cobourg ON K9A 3P3
www.cobourg.ca/victoria-park-camp-ground.html
Tel: (905) 373 7321

The Bike Shop
1040 Division Street Cobourg ON K9A 5Y5
www.tbs-cobourg.ca Tel: (905) 372-1788

Sommerville's
84 King Street West
Tel: (905) 372 7031

200 Ontario Street
Cobourg ON K9A 5P4
www.cobourg.library.on.ca
Tel: (905) 372 9271

**Colborne** 33 F44 GPS 44.00559,-77.88576:
Town, landmark Big Apple

Big Apple
RR#5 Colborne ON west of Road 25 and
south of Highway 401
www.visitcramahe.ca/cramahe/
tourism/apple.asp Tel: (905) 355 2574

Loughbreeze Bay B&B
GPS 43.987317 -77.869120105
Victoria Beach Road Colborne ON K0K 1S0
www.loughbreezebay.com Tel: (905) 355 1487

6 King Street West
Colborne ON
Tel: (905) 355 3722

**Colchester** 4 F2 GPS 41.98655,-82.92961:
Village

John Park Homestead
restored 1850 house on the lake
www.erca.org/conservation/area.john_r_park_
homestead.cfm
Tel: (519) 738 2029

**Colebrook** 35 36 B54 GPS 44.38571,-76.77109:
Village, convenience store

**Collingwood** 40 A25 GPS 44.49989,-80.21682:
Attractive regional centre, Harbourview Park
and beach

Tourist Information – South Georgian Bay
Collingwood & Area
www.visitsouthgeorgianbay.ca
Tel: (888) 227 8667 (705) 445 7722

Holiday Inn Express
4 Balsam Street Collingwood ON L9Y 3J4
www.hiexpress.com
Tel: (877) 660 8550 (705) 444-2144

Thurso House Bed & Breakfast
167 Pine Street
Collingwood ON L9Y 2P1
www.thursohouse.com
Tel: (705) 445 7117

Azzurra
100 Pine Street Collingwood ON L9Y
www.azzurra.ca Tel: (705) 445 7771

Cafe Chartreuse
70 Hurontario Street
Collingwood ON L9Y 2L6
www.cafechartreuse.com
Tel: (705) 444 0099

Little Ed's Ski and Bike Shop
15 Balsam Street
Collingwood ON
www.littleeds.com Tel: (705) 444 5488

100 Second Street
Collingwood ON L9Y 1E5
www.collingwoodpubliclibrary.ca
Tel: (705) 445 1571

**Collins Bay** 36 D55: Village

**Conestogo** 22 M23 GPS 44.23954,-76.61453:
Village in Mennonite farming area

**Consecon** 34 G47 GPS 43.99142,-77.52149:
Village, North Beach Provincial Park south off
Road 33, day use sand beach on Lake Ontario

211 Road 29
Consecon ON
www.peclibrary.org
Tel: (613) 392 1106

**Copenhagen** 9 W19 GPS 42.67436,-80.98434:

**Corbett** 13 Q13 GPS 43.24720,-81.68884:

**Cornwall** 52 U70 GPS 45.02844,-74.73569: City

Ontario Travel Information Centre
Seaway International Bridge
903 Brookdale Avenue
Cornwall ON K6J 4P3
www.ontariotravel.net
Tel: (613) 933 2420 (800) 668 2746

Tourist Information - Cornwall & Seaway Valley
www.visit.cornwall.on.ca
Tel: (800) 937 4748 (613) 938 4748

Cornwall Community Museum
160 Water Street West Cornwall ON K6J 1A3
www.visit.cornwall.on.ca/herit04.htm
Tel: (613) 936 0280

Lighthouse Landing Bed & Breakfast
18177 Road 2
RR#1 Cornwall ON K6H 5R5
www.lighthouse-landing.com
Tel: (877) 501 2508 (613) 931 2508

Best Western Cornwall
1515 Vincent Massey Drive
Cornwall, ON K6H 5R6
www.bestwesterncornwall.com
Tel: (613) 932 0451

Comfort Inn
1755 Vincent Massey Drive
Cornwall ON K6H 5R6
www.choicehotels.com
Tel: (877) 424 6423 (613) 937 0111

St. Lawrence College – Residence Services
2 Belmont Street
Cornwall ON K6H 4Z1
www.sl.on.ca/residence/
SummerAccomodations.htm
Tel: (613) 933-6080 ext. 2558

Fusion Grill
109 Pitt Street
Cornwall ON K6J 3P5
Tel: (613) 932-8286

Moustache Joe's Cafe
105 Pitt Street
Cornwall ON K6J 3P5
www.moustachejoescafe.ca Tel: (613) 937 0700

Bicycle World
150 Pitt Street
Cornwall ON N6J 3P4
www.bicycleworld.com
Tel: (866) 216 6668 (613) 932 2750

45 Second Street East
Cornwall ON K6H 5V1
www.library.cornwall.on.ca Tel: (613) 932 4796

**Corunna** 12 U7 GPS 42.88552,-82.42561:
Village

1838 St. Joseph's Roman Catholic Church

**Courtland** 10 and 16 V22 GPS 42.840407-
80.632582: Village

Courtland Antique and Collectible
Warehouse tea room
283 Main Street Courtland ON
www.courtlandantiquewarehouse.com
Tel: (519) 842 9011

**Courtright** 12 V6 GPS 42.81656,-82.47093:
Village

**Craigleith** 40 A24 GPS 44.56112,-80.44739:
Hamlet near Blue Mountain Ski Resort

Blue Mountain Resort restaurant
Blue Mountain Road
RR3 Collingwood ON L9Y 3Z2
www.bluemountain.ca Tel: (705) 455 0231

Craigleith Provincial Park
RR#3 Collingwood ON L9Y 3Z2
Tel: (705) 445 4467
Reservations-www.ontarioparks.com
Tel: (888) 668 7275

Squire John's
Highway 26 Craigleith ON
www.squirejohns.com Tel: (705) 445 1130

**Creemore** 29 C26 GPS 44.33044,-80.10857:
Unique village with microbrewery

Creemore Springs Brewery
139 Mill Street Creemore ON L0M 1G0
www.creemoresprings.com/live
Tel: (800) 267 2240 (705) 466 2240

Blacksmith House Bed & Breakfast
7 Caroline Street West
Box 130 Creemore ON L0M 1G0
www.blacksmithhouse.ca Tel: (705) 466 3373

Angel House Bed & Breakfast
3 Nelson Street
Creemore ON L0M 1G0
www.angelhouse.ca
Tel: (705) 466 6505 (877) 842 4438

**Crofton** 34 F49 GPS 44.06736,-77.31697: Hamlet

**Crosshill**: 22 M21 GPS 43.55651,-80.61390:
Village

**Crystal Beach** 19 U35 GPS 42.86363,-79.03427:
Resort town

Crystal Beach Motel
122 Ridgeway Road
Box 1261 Crystal Beach ON L0S 1B0
www.crystalbeachmotel.com
Tel: (905) 894 1750

**Damascus** 28 H23 GPS 43.91471,-80.48172:
Hamlet

Pritty Place Bed & Breakfast
GPS 43.91471,-80.48172
8924 Road 16 Damascus
RR#4 Kenilworth ON N0G 2E0
www.bbcanada.com/3092.html
Tel: (519) 848 3598

**Dashwood** 20 P13 GPS 43.34607,-81.63452:
Village

**Dealtown** 6 C9 GPS 42.26461,-82.04796: Village

**Delta** 49 Z59 GPS 44.60935,-76.12289: Village
with historic 1810 mill

Denaut Mansion Country Inn Bed & Breakfast
5 Mathew Street
Delta ON K0E 1G0
www.denautmansion.com
Tel: (877) 788 0388 (613) 928 2588

**Demorestville** 35 F50 GPS 44.09253,-77.20802:
Hamlet, picnic area at Demoresville Dam
Conservation Area

**Denbigh** 63 T50 GPS 45.14279,-77.26554

Swiss Inn Motel and Restaurant
Hwy 41
Denbigh ON K0H 1L0
www.swissinn.ca
Tel: (800) 844 0284 (613) 333 2221

**Desbarats** 2 GPS 46.34407,-83.92423: Village

**Deseronto** 35 D51 GPS 44.19458,-77.04929:
Town on the shore of the Bay of Quinte, Native
gift shops just north on Highway 49; historic
Mohawk landing site and Christ Church
Mohawk Chapel

🏨🍴🛏️🏞️

🏨 **Town's Edge Bed & Breakfast**
GPS 44.1904831, -77.0596391
73 Main Street
Deseronto ON  K0K 1X0
www.bbcanada.com/townsedgebb
Tel: (613) 396 6389

🍴 **The O'Connor House**
369 Main Street Deseronto ON K0K 1X0
www.theoconnorhouse.com
Tel: (613) 396 1888

📚 358 Main Street
Deseronto ON  K0K 1X0
www.deserontopubliclibrary.ca
Tel: (613) 396 2744

**Dorchester** 9 T18 GPS 42.98908,-81.04889:
Town

🛏️🍴🏨 **Fifth Wheel Travel Centre**
RR 2  3305 Dorchester Road
Dorchester ON
www.5thwheel.com/dorchester.html
Tel: (519) 268 7319

**Dresden** 6 X9 GPS 42.58951,-82.17964:  Town

🍴🏨🔥📚

🔥 **Uncle Tom's Cabin** historic home of Rev. Josiah
Henson, a slave for 41 years in the southern
United States and one of the models for
Harriet Beecher Stowe's "Uncle Tom's Cabin"
29251 Uncle Tom's Road
www.uncletomscabin.org
Tel: (519) 683 2978

📚 187 Brown Street
Dresden ON  N0P 1M0
www.chatham-kent.ca/community+ services/
library/Library.htm
Tel: (519) 683 4922

**Drumbo** 16 Q23 GPS 43.23675,-80.55288:
Town

🍴🏨

**Dunnville** 18 U30 GPS 42.90436,-79.61987:
Town on Grand River

🍴🔥🏨ℹ️🏞️🛏️📚🏨

ℹ️ **Tourist Information** – Dunnville and
Haldimand County
www.tourismhaldimand.com
Tel: (800) 863 9607

🏨 **Waltham's Way Bed & Breakfast**
GPS 42.90446,-79.61470
308 Alder Street East
Dunnville ON  N1A 1E3
www.bbcanada.com/walthamsway
Tel:(905) 774 6174

🛏️ **Lalor Estate Inn**
241 Broad Street West Dunnville ON  N1A 1S8
www.bbcanada.com/lalorestateinn
Tel: (905) 774 5438

🏞️ **Byng Island Conservation Area**
4969 Road 20
Dunnville ON  N1A 2W3
Tel: (905) 774 5755
Reservations- www.grandriver.ca
Tel: (866) 668 2267

🏞️ **Rock Point Provincial Park**
beach on Lake Erie;
Box 158
Dunnville ON  N1A 2X5
Tel: (905) 774 6642
Reservations- www.ontarioparks.com
Tel: (888) 668 7275

🍴 **Bob's Place**
121 Lock Street East
Dunnville ON  N1A 1J6
Tel: (905) 774 7463

🍴 **Grand Island Bar-B-Q**
7336 Rainham Road
P.O. Box 72 Dunnville ON  N1A 2X1
www.villageonthegrand.com
Tel: (905) 774 6051

📚 **Dunnville Public Library**
317 Chestnut Street
Dunnville ON
www.haldimandcounty.on.ca/residents.aspx?id=258

&ekmensel=c580fa7b_32_524_btnlink
Tel: (905) 318 3272

**Dutton** 8 W15 GPS 42.66620,-81.49950:  Town

🍴🏨📚

📚 236 Shackleton Street
Dutton ON  N0L 1J0
www.library.elgin-county.on.ca
Tel: (519) 762 2780

**Eagle** 8 Y14 GPS 42.56775,-81.56250: Hamlet

**Echo Bay** 2 GPS 46.48493,-84.07005:

🍴🏨

**Eganville** 81 P51  82 P51  GPS 45.53329,-77.11235

🏨📚🍴🛏️📚

🏨 **Pine Tree Motel**
Highway 41 and 60
RR#6 Eganville ON  K0J 1T0
www.pinetreemotel.ca
Tel: (800) 517 9382  (613) 628 2832

📚 **Bonnechere Union Public Library**
RR#3 74A Maple Grove
Eganville ON  K0J 1T0
Tel: (613) 628 2400

**Elmira** 22 L22 GPS 43.59865,-80.55872:  Town
in the heart of Mennonite country

🍴🏨🚲📚

📚 65 Arthur Street South
Elmira ON  N3B 2M6
www.rwl.library.on.ca  Tel: (519) 669 5477

**Elora** 22 K23 GPS 43.68158,-80.42975: Scenic
town with shops, antique mall, mill restored as
an inn overlooking the Elora Gorge

🏨🍴🏨🚲⭐🏞️📚📚

⭐ **Hike the Elora Gorge** by crossing the footbridge
and going right (south) along the river

⭐ **Elora Festival**, music festival mid-July to early
August www.elorafestival.com
Tel: (888) 747 7550  (519) 846 0331

🏨 **Tynavon Bed & Breakfast**
84 Mill Street East
Box 1024 Elora ON  N0B 1S0
www.tynavon.ca
Tel: (866) 334 3305  (519) 846 6695

🏨 **The Sem Wissler House B&B**
17 George Street Elora ON  N0B 1S0
www.bbcanada.com/semwissler
Tel: (519) 846-2130

🍴 **Elora Mill Country Inn restaurant**,
(closed for renovations)
historic 1870 flour mill
77 Mill Street West
Elora ON  N0B 1S0
www.eloramill.com
Tel: (866) 713 5672  (519) 846 9118

🏞️ **Elora Gorge Conservation Area**  scenic river
valley, swimming (pond)
7400 Road 21  Box 356
Elora ON  N0B 1S0
Tel: (519) 846 9742
Reservations- www.grandriver.ca
Tel: (866) 668 2267

🍴 **Cork Restaurant**
146 Metcalf Street, Elora ON  N0B 1S0
www.eloracork.com  Tel: (519) 846 8880

🍴 **East Mill Restaurant**
14 Mill Street East, Elora ON  N0B 1S0
www.eastmill.ca
Tel: (519) 846 2015

🚲 **Salem Cyclery**
115 Geddes Street
Elora ON
www.salemcycleryelora.com
Tel: (519) 846 8446

📚 144 Geddes Street
Box 280  Elora ON  N0B 1S0
www.county.wellington.on.ca
Tel: (519) 846 0190

**Emeryville** 4 B4 GPS 42.29763,-82.76021:

📚

**Embro** 15 R20 GPS 43.15611,-80.90123: Village

📚

**Emo** 2 GPS 48.63254,-93.83885:  Town

📚🍴🏨

🍴 **Emo Inn restaurant**
Highway 11  Box 598

Emo ON  P0W 1C0
www.emoinn.com
Tel: (807) 482 2272

**Empire Corners** 18 S29
GPS 43.02398,-79.89189:  Village

📚

**Enterprise** 47 B53 GPS 44.46257,-76.87797:

📚📚

📚 2861 Road 14
Enterprise ON  K0K 1Z0
www.lennox-addington.on.ca
Tel: (613) 358 2058

**Espanola** 84 E13 GPS 46.25677,-81.76423:  Town

🏨🍴🏨🛏️📚🏨📚

🏨 **Mill House Bed & Breakfast**
GPS 46.26576,-81.77166
114 Sheppard Street
Espanola Ont. P5E 1A1
www.bbcanada.com/8787.html
Tel: (866) 659 0932  (705) 869 4515

🛏️ **Pinewood Motor Inn restaurant**
GPS 46.2574504, -81.76424
Box 1578, 378 Centre Street
Espanola ON  P0P 1C0
Tel: (705) 869 3460  (800) 361 3460

📚 245 Avery Drive
Espanola ON  P5E 1S4
Tel: (705) 869 2940

**Eugenia** 28 C23 GPS 44.31230,-80.52567: Village,
picnic area & walkway to Eugenia Falls

📚🏨

**Everett** 29 E27 GPS 44.19123,-79.93888: Village

📚🍴

**Fairground** 10 X22 GPS 42.63497,-80.65956: Village

📚🍴

**Fenwick** 19 S32  GPS 43.02616,-79.35745:
Town, convenience store, restaurant

📚🍴

**Fergus** 22 K24 GPS 43.70544,-80.37814:  Town
on Grand River

🍴🏨⭐🏞️📚

🏨 🍴 **Breadalbane Inn restaurant**
487 St. Andrew Street West
Fergus ON
www.breadalbaneinn.com
Tel: (519) 843 4770  (888) 842 2825

🏨 **Stonehurst Bed & Breakfast**
265 St. David Street South
Fergus ON  N1M 2L6
www.stonehurstbb.com
Tel: (519) 843 8800

📚 190 St. Andrew Street West
Fergus ON  N1M 1N5
www.county.wellington.on.ca
Tel: (519) 843 1180

**Fingal** 8 W16 GPS 42.71325,-81.31187:  Village

📚

**Flesherton** 28 D22 GPS 44.26123,-80.54986: Town

📚🏨📚📚🍴

🏨 🍴 **Munshaw Village Inn restaurant**
1 Toronto Street
Flesherton ON  N0C 1E0
www.bbcanada.com/4058.html
Tel: (888) 209 6222  (519) 924 2282

📚 10 Elizabeth Street
Flesherton ON  N0C 1E0
www.greyhighlandspubliclibrary.com
Tel: (519) 924 2241

**Floradale** 22 L22 GPS 43.63489,-80.58008:
Village in Mennonite farming country

📚

**Fonthill** 19 S33  GPS 43.04409,-79.28182:  Town,
convenience store, grocery store, restaurants

📚📚🍴

**Forest** 13 S10 GPS 43.09797,-81.99934:  Town

📚🍴📚🛏️📚📚⭐

🔥 **Forest Lambton Museum**
8 Main Street North Forest ON
www.lambtononline.com/forest_lambton
Tel: (519) 786 3239

**Forest Golf & Country Hotel restaurant**
102 Main Street South
Forest ON N0N 1J0
www.golfforest.com
Tel: (800) 265 0214 (519) 786 2397

**Western Ontario Steam Threshers Reunion**
Forest Fair Grounds, late August
www.steamthresher.com

**Forest Fall Fair**, late September
www.forestfair.ca

**Through Windows Past Bed & Breakfast**
64 King Street West
Forest ON
www.throughwindowspast.ca
Tel: (519) 786 5070

61 King Street West
Forest ON N0N 1J0
www.lclmg.org
Tel: (519) 786 5152

**Formosa** 27 F17 GPS 44.06701,-81.21409: Village

**Brick Brewing Company** now operates the historic 1870 Formosa Springs Brewery

**Fort Erie** 19 U36 GPS 42.90197,-78.97420: City

**Fort Erie – Buffalo, New York USA Bicycle Crossing**
Bicycles are permitted on the Peace Bridge. Crossing to Buffalo bicycle or walk on the south sidewalk from Mather Park. Crossing to Fort Erie use the north sidewalk from Busti Avenue. www.peacebridge.com
Tel: (905) 871 1608 (716) 884 6744

**Ontario Travel Information Centre**
Peace Bridge in the Ontario Welcome Centre
350 Bertie Street, Unit 1 L2A 6S6
www.ontariotravel.net
Tel: (905) 871 3505 (800) 668 2746

**Historical Railroad Museum** on Central Avenue
www.museum.forterie.ca/railroad.html
Tel: (905) 871 1412

**Friendship Trail Bed & Breakfast**
128 Kraft Road
Fort Erie ON L2A 4M5
www.friendshiptrailbandb.ca
Tel: (905) 871 1424

**Clarion Hotel and Conference Centre restaurant**
1485 Garrison Road
Fort Erie ON L2A 1P8
www.clarionhotel.com/hotel-fort_erie-canada-CN965
Tel: (877) 424 6423 (905) 871 8333

**Comfort Inn**
1 Hospitality Drive
Fort Erie L2A 6G1
www.choicehotels.com
Tel: (877) 424 6423 (905) 871 8500

**Frenchmans Creek Park**
1047 Niagara Boulevard
Fort Erie ON
Tel: (905) 871 4449

**Windmill Point Park**
2409 Dominion Road
Ridgeway ON L0S 1N0
www.windmillpointpark.com
Tel: (800) 977 8888 (905) 894 2809

**Steve's Place Bicycles & Repair** bicycle rental
181 Niagara Boulevard
Fort Erie ON
www.cycleman.com
Tel: (905) 871 7517

136 Gilmore Road
Fort Erie ON L2A 2M1
www.forterie.library.on.ca
Tel: (905) 871 2546

**Fort Frances** 2 GPS 48.61001,-93.39111: Town on shores of Rainy Lake and Rainy River

**Bridge to International Falls, Minnesota,**
Ontario Travel Information Centre Fort Frances International Bridge 400 Central Avenue P9A 1X8 www.ontariotravel.net
Tel: (807) 274 7566 (800) 668 2746

**La Place Rendez-Vous restaurant**
1201 Idylwild Drive East
Fort Frances ON

www.rendezvoushotel.com
Tel: (800) 544 9435 (807) 274 9811

**Super 8 Motel**
810 King's Highway
Fort Frances ON
www.super8.com
Tel: (800) 800 8000 (807) 274 4945

363 Church Street
Fort Frances ON P9A 1C9
library.fort-frances.com
Tel: (807) 274 9879

**Foxboro** 34 D48 GPS 44.25125,-77.43913: Former village now part of Belleville

**Frankford** 34 D47 GPS 44.20112,-77.59635:

**Town at Trent Canal Lock 6** Group camping at most lock stations with prior approval
www.pc.gc.ca/eng/lhn-nhs/on/trentsevern/visit/visit6.aspx
Tel: (888) 773 8888 (705) 750 4900

**Frankville** 49 Y60 GPS 44.72096,-75.96107:

**Gananoque** 37 C59 GPS 44.32848,-76.16426: Gateway town to the 1000 Islands, Scenic boat tours and 1000 Islands Historic Village on Water Street

**Tourist Information:** 1000 Islands Gananoque Chamber of Commerce
10 King Street East Gananoque ON
www.1000islandsgananoque.com
Tel: (800) 561 1595 (613) 382 3250

**Thousand Islands Playhouse**
185 South Street Gananoque ON
www.1000islandsplayhouse.com
866 382 7020 (613) 382 7020

**Sleepy Hollow Bed & Breakfast**
GPS 44.32601,-76.16622
95 King Street West
Gananoque ON K7G 2G2
www.sleepyhollowbb.ca
Tel: (866) 426 7422 (613) 382 4377

**Islandview Inn**
GPS 44.3244346, -76.1626757
195 Market Street
Gananoque ON K7G 2M6
www.islandviewinnbb.com
Tel: (613) 382 2745

**Beaver Hall Bed & Breakfast**
75 King Street West
Gananoque ON K7G 2G2
www.beaverhallbedandbreakfast.com
Tel: (613) 382 4590

**Athlone Inn restaurant**
250 King Street West
Gananoque ON K7G 2G6
www.athloneinn.ca
Tel: (888) 382 7122 (613) 382 3822

**Gananoque Inn restaurant**
550 Stone Street South
Gananoque ON K7G 2A8
www.gananoqueinn.com
Tel: (888) 565 3101 (613) 382 2165

**TI Cycle**
711 King Street East, Unit 7
Gananoque ON K7G 1H4
www.ti-cycle.com Tel: (613) 382 5144

100 Park Street
Gananoque ON K7G 2Y5
Tel: (613) 382 2436

**Garden Hill** 32 F40 GPS 44.05762,-78.40256: Village;

**1869 Dorothy's Historic House Museum**
Road 9 west of Road 10 in Garden Hill
www.porthopehistorical.ca/museum.htm

**Woodland Gardens Bed & Breakfast**
GPS 44.05762,-78.40256 8250
Woodland Avenue Box 7 Garden Hill
www.bbcanada.com/woodlandgardens
Tel: (905) 797 2799

**Garden River First Nation** 2
GPS 46.55206,-84.18150: Village

**Georgetown** 23 K-L28 GPS 43.65001,-79.89888: Town

**Downtown Farmers Market**

Saturday mornings on Main Street south of Guelph Street
www.downtowngeorgetown.com/directory/farmers-market-co-georgetown-bia

**Best Western Inn On the Hill**
GPS 43.6490616, -79.8801106
365 Guelph Street
Georgetown ON L7G 4B6
www.bestwesternontario.com/georgetown-hotels
Tel: (800) 780 7234 (905) 877 6986

**Main Street Inn Bed & Breakfast**
126 Main Street South
Georgetown ON L7G 3E6
www.bbcanada.com/9452.html
Tel: (905) 702 5411

**The Cellar**
78 Main Street South
Georgetown ON
www.cellarrestaurant.com
Tel: (905) 873 7402

**Ollie's Cycle & Ski**
30 Main Street South
Georgetown ON
www.olliescycle.com Tel: (905) 873 2441

9 Church Street
Georgetown ON L7G 2A3
www.library.hhpl.on.ca
Tel: (905) 873 2681

**Glencoe** 7 W13 GPS 42.74855,-81.71080:

**Middlesex County Library** – Glencoe Branch
178 McKellar Street
Glencoe ON N0L 1M0
www.middlesex.library.on.ca/branch/glencoe.asp
Tel: (519) 287 2735

**Glen Morris** 16 Q24 17 Q25
GPS 43.27594,-80.34362: Village on Grand River

**Glen Ross** 34 D47 GPS 44.26475,-77.59695: Convenience store

**Hamlet at Trent Canal Lock 7**
Group camping at most lock stations with prior approval
www.pc.gc.ca/eng/lhn-nhs/on/trentsevern/visit/visit6.aspx
Tel: (888) 773 8888 (705) 750 4900

**Glen Williams** 23 K28 GPS 43.68447,-79.93013: Village, arts andcrafts studios

**Glencairn** 29 C27 GPS 44.30072,-80.01719: Village

**Glenora** 35 F51 GPS 44.04071,-77.05811:

**Glenora** - Adolphustown Ferry free continuous half hour service – fifteen minute crossing Leaves Glenora on the hour and half-hour Leaves Adolphustown on the quarter-to and quarter-past
www.mto.gov.on.ca/english/traveller/ferry

**Goderich** 20 K13 GPS 43.74264,-81.70776: Recovering from a tornado in August 2011, octagonal street pattern centered on the town square, lighthouse, beaches

**Tourist Information** –
Goderich and Huron County
www.ontarioswestcoast.com
Tel: (800) 280 7637

**Historic Gaol**
181 Victoria Street North, flea market on Sunday

**Huron County Museum**
110 North Street north of the square and Marine Museum at harbour
www.huroncounty.ca/museum

**Farmers Market**, Saturdays 8 AM to 1 PM south side of the square

**Goderich Festival of Arts and Crafts** on the square, second weekend in July.

**Celtic Roots Festival**, early August
www.celticfestival.ca

**Menesetung Bridge** across the Maitland River from North Harbour Road

**Colborne Bed & Breakfast**
GPS 43.74503,-81.71359

72 Colborne Street
Goderich ON
www.colbornebandb.com
Tel: (800) 390 4612

**Hotel Bedford historic restaurant**
92 The Square
Goderich ON  N7A 1M7
www.hotelbedford.on.ca   Tel: (519) 524 7337

**Point Farms Provincial Park**
north on Highway 21
RR#3 Goderich ON  N7A 3X9
Tel: (519) 524 7124
Reservations- www.ontarioparks.com
Tel: (888) 668 7275

**Bailey's Restaurant**
120 The Square
Goderich ON  N7A 1M8
Tel: (519) 524 5166

**Thyme On Twenty One**
80 Hamilton Street
Goderich ON  N7A 1P9
www.thymeon21.com
Tel: (519) 524 4171

**Goderich Cyclery bicycle rental**
622 Pentland Avenue
Goderich ON
Tel: (519) 524 4720

52 Montreal Street
Goderich ON
www.huroncounty.ca/library/index.php
Tel: (519) 524 9261

**Godfrey** 36 A55 GPS 44.54311,-76.67906:

**Gore Bay** 71 J7 GPS 45.91657,-82.46608:

**The Queen's Inn**
19 Water Street, Box 677
Gore Bay ON  P0P 1H0
www.thequeensinn.ca
Tel: (705) 282 0665

**Gore Bay Union Public Library**
15 Water Street,  P.O. Box 225
Gore Bay ON  P0P 1H0
www.gorebay.ca   Tel: (705) 282 2221

**Gores Landing** 33 E41-42
GPS 44.11920,-78.23249: Cottage village

**Tourist Information:** www.ricelakecanada.com

**The Victoria Inn  restaurant**
GPS 44.12407,-78.22266
Gores Landing ON  K0K 2E0
www.thevictoriainn.ca
Tel: (905) 342 3261

**Aye Lighthouse Bed & Breakfast**
5303B Traill Road. North RR#1
Grafton ON  K0K 2E0
www.ayelighthouse.info
Tel: (905) 342 5570

**Grafton** 33 G43 GPS 43.99238,-78.02431:
Historic village; 1819 Barnum House

**Shelter Valley Folk Festival  early Setember**
Vernonville Road north of Highway 2
www.sheltervalley.com

**Grafton Village Inn restaurant** - historic
10830 Road 2
Grafton ON  K0K 2G0
www.graftonvillageinn.ca
Tel: (905) 349 3024

**Grand Bend** 20 P12-13 GPS 43.31247,-81.75653:
Lively summer resort community

**Huron Country Playhouse**
RR#1 Grand Bend 3 kilometers east on
Highway 81 at B Line
www.draytonentertainment.com
Tel: (855) 372 9866 (519) 238 6000

**Multi-use Rotary Trail** along Highway 21 from
Grand Bend to Pinery Provincial Park

**Oakwood Inn golf and tennis resort, restaurant**
Ontario Street North Box 400
Grand Bend ON  N0M 4T0
www.oakwoodinnresort.com
Tel: (800) 387 2324

**Pine Dale Motor Inn**
107 Ontario Street South Box 191

Grand Bend ON  N0M 4T0
www.pinedale.on.ca
Tel: (888) 838 7463 (519) 238 2231

**Pinery Provincial Park**
oak savannah forest and sand beach on Lake
Huron, canoeing, bicycling
RR#2 Grand Bend ON  N0M 1T0
Tel: (519) 243 2220
Reservations- www.ontarioparks.com
Tel: (888) 668 7275

**FINE A Restaurant**
42 Ontario Street South  Grand Bend ON
www.finearestaurant.com
Tel: (519) 238 6224

**Schoolhouse Restaurant**
19-81 Crescent Street
Grand Bend ON
www.schoolhouserestaurant.ca
Tel: (519) 238 5515

15 Gill Street
Grand Bend ON  N0M 1T0
www.lclmg.org   Tel: (519) 238 2067

**Grande Pointe** 6 A7 GPS 42.44145,-82.35558:
French Canadian village

**Gravenhurst** 58 V32 GPS 44.92084,-79.37370:

**Tourist Information:  Muskoka Tourism**
Information Centres : Kilworthy - Highway 11 North
of Severn Bridge and Port Severn - Highway 400
www.discovermuskoka.ca
Tel: (800) 267 9700

**Blaincroft Bed & Breakfast**
180 Hughson Street
Gravenhurst ON  P1P 1H2
www.bbmuskoka.com/blaincroft
Tel: (705) 684 8994

**The Inn on the Bay Bed & Breakfast**
291 Bay Street
Gravenhurst ON  P1P 1H1
www.innonbay.com
Tel: (800) 493 0235  (705) 681 0258

**Howard Johnson Inn**
1165 Muskoka Road South
Gravenhurst ON  P1P 1K6
www.hojo.com
Tel: (800) 406 1411 (705) 687 7707

**Gravenhurst Public Library**
180 Sharpe Street West
Gravenhurst ON  P1P 1J1
www.surenet.net/~glib
Tel: (705) 687 3382

**Grimsby** 18 Q31 GPS 43.19902,-79.58552:
Town in wine producing area

**Gateway Niagara Visitor Centre** – QEW at
Casablanca Boulevard at South Service Road
convenience store, restaurant

**Kittling Ridge Wines & Spirits**
297 South Service Road
Grimsby ON
www.kittlingridge.com
Tel: (800) 694 6798  (905) 945 9225

**Doran House Bed & Breakfast**
470 Main Street West
Grimsby ON
www3.sympatico.ca/doranhouse
Tel: (905) 309 1312

**Vinifera Inn Bed & Breakfast**
245 Main Street East
Grimsby ON
www.viniferainn.ca
Tel: (905) 309 8873

**Casablanca Winery Inn  restaurant**
4 Windward Drive
Grimsby ON
www.casablancawineryinn.com
Tel: (877) 446 5746  (905) 309 7171

**Home Hardware**
35 Main Street West  Grimsby
Tel: (905) 945 2034

18 Carnegie Lane
www.town.grimsby.on.ca/Library
Tel: (905) 945 5142

**Guelph** 23 M25 GPS 43.54730,-80.24414: City

**Tourist Information:**  Guelph and Wellington

County Tourism Services
59 Carden Street
Guelph ON  N1H 3A1
www.visitguelphwellington.ca
Tel: (800) 334 4519

**London House B&B**
80 London Road West
Guelph ON  N1H 2B7
www.londonhouse.ca
Tel: (877) 836 6874 (519) 824 6874

**Lyon's Den Bed & Breakfast**
18 University Avenue East
Guelph ON  N1G 1M9
www.bbcanada.com/3260.html
Tel: (519) 821 2556

**Days Inn Guelph**
785 Gordon Street
Guelph ON
www.daysinnguelph.ca
Tel: (800) 329 7466  (519) 822 9112

**Best Western Royal Brock Hotel & Conference
Centre**
716 Gordon Street  Guelph ON
www.bestwesternontario.com/hotels/best-
western-royal-brock-hotel-and-conference-
centre
Tel: (800) 780 7234  (519) 836 1240

**Artisanale Cafe & Bistro**
37 Quebec Street
Guelph ON  N1H 2T1
artisanale.ca
Tel: (519) 821 3359

**Diana's Downtown**
141 Wyndham Street North
Guelph ON
www.dianadowntown.com
Tel: (519) 836 3460

**Braun's IS Bicycles**
43 Cork Street East
Guelph ON  N1H 2W7
www.brauns.com   Tel: (226) 706 2498

**Guelph Public Library**
100 Norfolk Street
Guelph ON  N1H 4J6
www.library.guelph.on.ca
Tel: (519) 824 6220

**Haliburton** 60 V39 GPS 45.04670,-78.50880:

**Tourist Information:**
Haliburton Tourism Association
P.O. Box 485  Haliburton ON  K0M 1S0
www.haliburton-tourism.com

**Country Charm Bed and Breakfast**
152 Mountain Street
Haliburton ON  K0M 1S0
www.countrycharmbb.ca/index.htm
Tel: (705) 457 8821 (866) 457 8821

**Heritage House Bed & Breakfast**
33- 35 Pine Street PO Box 1076
Haliburton ON  K0M 1S0
www.bbcanada.com/10967.html
Tel: (705) 457 2522

**Haliburton County Public Library**
739 Mountain Street
Haliburton ON
www.haliburton.canlib.ca  Tel: (705) 457 2241

**Hamilton** 17 Q28  18 Q29
GPS 43.26099,-79.88845: City

**Online Cycling Map** www.hamilton.
ca/CityDepartments/PublicWorks/
TrafficEngineeringAndOperations/Cycling

**Hamilton Tourism** -
www.tourismhamilton.com

**Dundurn National Historic Site** -
castle and military museum
610 York Boulevard
Hamilton ON
www.hamilton.ca/CultureandRecreation/
Arts_Culture_And_Museums/
HamiltonCivicMuseums/Dundurn/
Tel: (905) 546 2872

**Royal Botanical Gardens**
680 Plains Road West
Burlington ON
www.rbg.ca        Tel: (905) 527 1158

**HMCS Haida**- Famous warship from
WWII and the Korean War
658 Catherine Street

North Pier 9 Hamilton ON
www.pc.gc.ca/eng/lhn-nhs/on/haida/index.aspx
Tel: (905) 526 0911
Hamilton Waterfront Trust
www.hamiltonwaterfront.com

**Whitehern Historic House & Garden**
41 Jackson Street West
Hamilton ON
www.whitehern.ca   Tel: (905) 546 2018

**Art Gallery of Hamilton**
123 King Street West
Hamilton ON
www.artgalleryofhamilton.com
Tel: (905) 527 6610

**Hamilton Farmers Market**
Tuesday, Thursday, Friday, Saturday
55 York Boulevard  Hamilton ON
www.hamilton.ca/CultureandRecreation/
Arts_Culture_And_Museums/
HamiltonFarmersMarket

**Admiral Inn**
149 Dundurn Street North
Hamilton ON  L8R 3M1
www.admiralinn.com
Tel: (866) 236 4662  (905) 529 2311

**Visitors Inn**
649 Main Street West
Hamilton ON  L8S 1A2
www.visitorsinn.com
Tel: (800) 387 4620  (905) 529 6979

**55 York Boulevard**
Hamilton ON  L8N 4E4
www.myhamilton.ca/public-library
Tel: (905) 546 3200

**Hanover** 27 E19 GPS 44.15237,-81.02582:
Attractive town first settled in 1849

**Travelers Inn Hanover**
244 7th Avenue
Hanover ON  N4N 2H1
www.tih.ca
Tel: (800) 801 8398   (519) 364 1911

**Alternative Health Spa Bed & Breakfast**
GPS 44.1543233, -81.0273261
540 10th Avenue Hanover ON  N4N 2P4
www.bbcanada.com/4723.html
Tel: (877) 868 8883  (519) 364 0466

**Queen's Bush Pub**
451 10th Street  Hanover ON
www.queensbushpub.com  Tel: (519) 364 6666

**The Grey Rose** Restaurant and Suites
319 10th Street
Hanover ON  www.greyrose.ca
Tel: (877) 473 9767   (519) 364 2600

**Wheelfast The Bicycle Shoppe**
292 10th Street Hanover ON N4N 1P2
www.wheelfast.ca   519 372 7022

**Harrow** 4E2 GPS 42.03552,-82.91791:  Town

**Canadian Transportation Museum and
Heritage Village**
history of Essex County in 14 buildings and
historical vehicles from 1800 to 1994
Road 23 6155 Arner Townline
PO Box 221 Harrow ON  N0R 1G0
www.ctmhv.com  Tel: (519) 776 6909

**Colio Winery**
1 Colio Drive PO Box 372
Harrow ON  N0R 1G0
www.coliowines.com
Tel: (800) 265 1322  (519) 738 2241

**Muscedere Vinyards**
7457 County Road 18, RR4
Harrow  ON NOR 1G0
muscederevineyards.com  Tel: (519) 965 1075

**Harrowsmith** 36 B55 GPS 44.40499,-76.66557:
Village

**Harwood** 33 E42 GPS 4.13751,-78.18044:  Village

**Golden Beach Resort**
GPS 44.1276928, -78.1029508
7100 County Road 18, RR#2
Roseneath ON  K0K 2X0
www.goldenbeachresort.com
Tel: (800) 263 7781  (905) 342 5366

**Clearstone Lodge Bed & Breakfast**
7300A County Rd. #18  RR#2
Roseneath ON

www.clearstonelodge.com
Tel: (905) 342 9470

**Hastings** 33 C44 GPS 44.51915,-77.78066:

**Town** at Lock 18 on Trent Severn Waterway
Group camping at most lock stations with
prior approval
www.pc.gc.ca/eng/lhn-nhs/on/trentsevern/
visit/visit6.aspx
Tel: (888) 773 8888 (705) 750 4900

**Hastings House Bed & Breakfast**
PO BOX 425 - 109 Front St West
Hastings ON  K0L 1Y0
www.bbcanada.com/11411.html
Tel: (705) 696-2045

**Annie's Bed & Breakfast**
1453 Concession 6
RR#3 Hastings ON  K0L 1Y0
www.bbcanada.com/5355.html
Tel: (705) 696 2552

**Birdsall Beach Trailer Park**
1170 Birdsall Line
RR#3 Hastings ON K0L 1Y0
www.birdsallbeach.ca   Tel: (705) 696 2116

**6 Albert Street East**
www.trenthillslibrary.ca/hastings/index.html
Tel: (705) 696 2111

**Hawkesbury** 68 N71 GPS 45.60790,-74.61414:
French Canadian town on the Ottawa River

**Ontario Travel Information Centre**
777 Highway 417
RR#1  Chute a Blondeau K0B 1B0
www.ontariotravel.net
Tel: (613) 674 2000  (800) 668 2746

**Best Western L'Heritage**
1575 Tupper Street  Hawkesbury ON  K6A 3T5
www.bestwesternontario.com/hawkesbury-
hotels  Tel: (800) 780 7234  (613) 632 5941

**Netheldale Bed & Breakfast**
577 Green Lane Road East
Hawkesbury ON  K6A 2R2
www.netherdale.com        Tel: (613) 632 8881

**Camping Domaine Chartrand**
2775 Chartrand Road
Lefaivre ON K0B 1J0
www.campingdomainechartrand.com
Tel: (613) 679 2687

**550 Higginson Street**
Hawkesbury ON  K6A 1H1
www.bibliotheque.hawkesbury.on.ca
Tel: (613) 632 0106

**Hensall** 20 N15 GPS 43.43417,-81.50208:  Town

**Huron County Library – Hensall Branch**
108 King Street
Hensall ON
www.huroncounty.ca/library
Tel: (519) 262-2445

**Highgate** 7 Y12 GPS 42.49947,-81.81441: Village

**Hillier** 34 G48 GPS 43.974362,-77.455967:
Hamlet

**Hillier Creek Estates Winery**
46 Stapleton Road  Hillier ON
off Highway 33 north of Hillier
www.hillierestates.com
Tel:  (613) 399 1900

**Hoards** 3 34 C46 GPS 44.29510,-77.66441:
Village, convenience store, restaurant

**Hockley** 29 F27 GPS 44.03750,-79.94682:
Hamlet

**Holland Landing** 30 F31 GPS 44.10463,-79.49236:

**Holmesville** 20 L14 GPS 43.64576,-81.60370:
Village

**Holt** 30 E32 GPS 44.12367,-79.34395:

**Hope Bay** 39 W18 GPS 44.90598,-81.16699:

**Hope Bay Campgrounds**
2 Hope Bay Road
Wiarton ON  N0H 2T0
www.hopebaycampground.com
Tel: (519) 534 1208

**Howe Island** 37 D58 36 D57
GPS 44.28896,-76.23688:  Cottages and farms,
no stores

**County Ferry Service** - On demand, 24 hours/
day - (613) 542 4959 (613) 548 9400.
www.mto.gov.on.ca/english/traveller/ferry
Howe Island Ferry Road [Road 22], south of
Road 2 at end of Joyceville Road
Frontenac Islands Township Ferry Service -
On demand 6:30 AM to 1 PM Schedule varies.
municipality.frontenacislands.on.ca/?q=ferries
Tel.: (613) 542 0550
Howe Island Ferry Road [Road 37] south of
Road 2, 3 kilometers east of Gananoque

**Huntsville** 59 R33 GPS 45.32657,-79.21800:

**Tourist Information:**
Huntsville/Lake of Bays Chamber of Commerce
8 West Street North
Huntsville ON P1H 2B6
www.huntsvillelakeofbays.on.ca
Tel: (705) 789 4771

**Algonquin Retreat B&B**
7 Forestview Drive
Huntsville ON  P1H 1G2
bbcanada.com/aretreat
Tel: (705) 789 4115

**Comfort Inn**
86 King William Street
Huntsville ON
www.choicehotels.ca/en/huntsville-hotel-
comfort-ontario-CN269-en?cid=1782632
Tel: (877) 424 6423   (705) 789 1701

**King William Inn**
23 King William Street
Huntsville ON  P1H 1G4
www.kingwilliaminn.com
Tel: (888) 995 9169   (705) 789 9661

**Spencer's Tall Trees Restaurant**
87 Main Street West
Huntsville ON  P1H 1X1
www.spencerstalltrees.com
Tel.: (705) 789-9769

**The Cottage Bar and Grill**
7 John Street
Huntsville ON  P1H 1H2
www.huntsvillecottage.com
Tel: (705) 789 6842

**Muskoka Bicycle Pro Shop  bicycle rental**
63 Main Street East
Huntsville ON  P1H 2B8
www.mbps.ca
Tel:  705 789 8344

**Ingleside** 51 V68 GPS 44.99579,-74.98685:
Village

**Island View Motel**
Road 2  Box 341
Ingleside ON K0C 1M0
Tel: (613) 537 2642

**Farran Park**
Road 2 Ingleside ON
www.southstormont.ca/tourism/farrans.html
Tel: (613) 537 8600

**Ingersoll** 15 S20 GPS 43.03811,-80.88385:

**Comfort Inn & Suites**
RR#4  20 Samnah Cres
Ingersoll ON
www.choicehotels.com
Tel: (877) 424 6423   (519) 425 1100

**Elm Hurst Inn & Country Spa  restaurant**
415 Harris Street
Ingersoll ON  N5C 3K1
www.elmhurstinn.com
Tel: (800) 561 5321 (519) 485 5321

**Ingersoll Public Library**
The Town Centre  130 Oxford Street
Ingersoll ON  N5C 2V5
www.ocl.net/locations/ingersoll
Tel: (519) 485 2505

**Inglewood** 23 J27-28 GPS 43.80455,-79.93584: Village

**Caledon Hills Cycling**
15640 McLaughlin Road
Inglewood ON  L0N 1K0
www.caledonhillscycling.com
Tel: (866) 838 1698  (905) 838 1698

**Innerkip** 16 Q21 GPS 43.20964,-80.69666:  Village

**Inverhuron** 26 C14 GPS 44.27765,-81.57349: Hamlet

**The Philosopher's Wool Company** - wool yarn and garments on Albert Road just north of Inverhuron
www.philosopherswool.com
Tel: (519) 368 5354

**Inverhuron Provincial Park**
19 Jordon Road
RR#2  Tiverton ON  N0G 2T0
Tel: (519) 368 1959
Reservations- www.ontarioparks.com
Tel: (888) 668 7275

**Ipperwash Beach** 13 Q11
GPS 43.21393,-81.96144: Resort area, extensive sandy beach with shallow shoreline

**The Village Inn Motel & Diner**
7424 Lakeshore Road, Highway 21
Ravenswood ON
Tel: (519) 243 3535

**Carolinian Forest Campground**
9589 Ipperwash Road
RR#2 Forest ON  N0N 1J0
Tel: (519) 243 2253

**Iron Bridge** 2 GPS 46.27860,-83.21959: Village, log museum

**Red Top Motor Inn**
114 Highway 17 East,  Box 427
Iron Bridge ON  P0R 1H0
www.redtopmotorinn.com
Tel: (877) 843 2100  (705) 843 2100

**Viking Tent and Trailer Park**
Box 310 RR#2
Iron Bridge ON  P0R 1H0
Tel: (705) 843 2834

**Iroquois** 51 W-X66 GPS 44.85172,-75.31518: Village

**Ivy Lea** 37 C60 GPS 44.36816,-75.99003: Village
Thousand Islands International Bridge see Hill Island - Bicycles are prohibited on Highway 137 between the bridge and the Thousand Islands Parkway. Use the Wolfe Island ferries Cape Vincent New York to Kingston Ontario as an alternative.

**Ivy Lea Campsite**
Thousand Islands Parkway at Road 3
www.stlawrenceparks.com
Tel: (613) 659 3057  (800) 437 2233

**Jasper** 49 X61 GPS 44.83273,-75.93421:  Village

**Johnstown** 50 Y64-65 GPS 44.74698,-75.46165: Village

Bicycles and pedestrians are prohibited on the Ogdensburg-Prescott International Bridge – Use Seaway International Bridge, Cornwall

**Grenville Provincial Park**
1 km east on St Lawrence
Tel: (613) 925 2000
Reservations- www.ontarioparks.com
Tel: (888) 668 7275

**Jones Falls** 37 A58 GPS 44.55244,-76.23928: Rideau Canal Locks 39-42 Scenic "Great Stone Arch Dam.", lockmaster's house and blacksmith shop group camping with prior approval
www.pc.gc.ca/lhn-nhs/on/rideau/index.aspx
Tel: (888) 773 8888  (613) 283 5170

**Jordan** 18 R32 GPS 43.14133,-79.37210: Village with attractive shops on Main Street

**Cave Spring Cellars winery**
836 Main Street
Jordon ON
www.cavespringcellars.com
Tel: (888) 806 9910 (905) 562 3581

**Creekside Estate Winery**
2170 Fourth Avenue  Jordon ON
www.creeksidewine.com
Tel: (905) 562 0035  (877) 262 9463

**Balls Falls Conservation Area**
waterfall, 1806 grist mill,
1846 Ball family home
uphill south on Glen Road
www.npca.ca  Tel: (905) 788 3135

**Inn On The Twenty**
On The Twenty Restaurant & Wine Bar
3836 Main Street  Jordan ON  L0R 1S0
www.innonthetwenty.com
Tel: (800) 701 8074  (905) 562 5336
restaurant - (905) 562 7313

**Martin House B&B**
2437 North Service Road
Jordan Station ON  L0R 1S0
www.bbcanada.com/themartinhouse
Tel: (905) 984 9972

**Best Western Beacon Harbourside**
2793 Beacon Boulevard (at North Service Road) P O Box 70 Jordan ON  L0R 1S0
www.bwbeacon.com
Tel: (888) 823 2266  (905) 562 4155

**Big Valley Campground**
2211 King Street  RR#1
St. Catharines ON  L2R 6P7
Tel: (905) 562 5616

**Kashabowie** 2 GPS 48.64918,-90.43403:  Village

**Keady** 39 A18,19 GPS 44.46491,-81.03996: Village, large regional farmers market Tuesdays

**Keady Farmers Market**
R.R. 4 Tara, Ontario
www.keadylivestock.com/farmers.html
Tel: (519) 934-2339

**Keene** 33 D42 GPS  44.24014,-78.16321:

**Elmhirst's Resort restaurant**
RR#1 Keene ON K0L 2G0
www.elmhirst.com
Tel: (800) 461 1940  (705) 295 4591

**Kemptville** 50 V63 GPS 45.01592,-75.64561: Town

**Howard Johnson Kemptville**
4022 County Road 43
Kemptville ON  K0G 1J0  www.hojo.com
Tel: (800) 446 4656  (613) 258 5939

**Clothier Inn Motel**
8 Clothier Street East Kemptville ON
Tel: (613) 258 0164

**Nestle Down**
4101 Highway 43  RR#3
Kemptville ON  K0G 1J0
www.bbcanada.com/6126.html
Tel: (613) 258 7778

**Rideau River Provincial Park**
RR#4 Kemptville ON  N0G 1J0
Tel: (613) 258 2740
Reservations- www.ontarioparks.com
Tel: (888) 668 7275

207 Prescott Street
Kemptville ON K0G 1G0
www.ngpl.ca        Tel: (613) 258 5577

**Kenora** 2 GPS 49.77066,-94.48930:  City on scenic Lake of the Woods,  tourist centre, pulp and paper mills

**Twenty murals depict Kenora's history**
**Ontario Travel Information Centre**
Ontario/Manitoba Border Highway 17
c/o General Delivery Keewatin P0X 1C0
www.ontariotravel.net
Tel: (807) 468 2495  (800) 668 2746

**Harbourfest celebration** on the harbour, first weekend in August  www.harbourfest.ca

**Northwoods Bed & Breakfast**
817 Highway 17 West  Box 1208
Keewatin ON  P0X 1C0

www.northwoodsbedandbreakfast.ca
Tel: (888) 303 4833  (807) 547 2992

**Kendall House Bed & Breakfast**
127 5th Avenue South
Kenora ON  P9N 2A3
www.bbcanada.com/3568.html
Tel: (807) 468 4645

**Super 8**
240 Lakeview Drive
Kenora ON  P9N 3W7
www.super8.com
Tel: (800) 889 9698 (807) 468 8016

**Southview Inn & Bistro restaurant**
Highway 17 West  Box 640
Keewatin ON  P0X 1C0
www.southviewinn.ca
Tel: (807) 547 2471

**The Plaza Restaurant**
125 Main Street South  Kenora
www.plazarestaurant.ca
Tel: (807) 468 8173

**Kent Bridge** 7 Y10 GPS 42.51506,-82.07304: Village

**Kettle Point First Nation** 13 R10
GPS 43.18040,-81.98959:
Native Canadian community

**Annual Pow Wow** held in early July at Kettle Point Ballpark

**Kettleby** 30 G31 GPS 44.01026,-79.55904: Village, picnic area

**Killaloe** 81 N49 GPS 45.56453,-77.41961:

**Killaloe Public Library**
1 John Street
Killaloe ON  K0J2A0
Tel: (613) 757 2211

**Kilmarnock** 49 W61 44.88677,-75.92686:
Rideau Canal Lock 24
group camping with prior approval
www.pc.gc.ca/lhn-nhs/on/rideau/index.aspx
Tel: (888) 773 8888  (613) 283 5170

**Kimberley** 40 B23 GPS 44.39136,-80.53672:
Village in the heart of the valley near ski resort

**Kincardine** 26 E14 GPS 44.18162,-81.63173:
Resort town on Lake Huron with Scottish heritage. Pipe band marches through town each Saturday at 8 PM - late June to Labour Day

**Scottish Festival** in July and Gathering of the Bands – massed pipes and drums in August
**Piper** at the lighthouse on sunny summer evenings and Marine Museum at the harbour

**Bluewater Summer Playhouse**
707A Queen Street
Kincardine Ontario, N2Z 1Z9
www.bluewatersp.on.ca
Tel: (877) 396 5722  (519) 396 5722

**Inverlyn Bed & Breakfast**
41 Inverlyn Crescent South
Kincardine ON  N2Z 1L1
www.bbcanada.com/inverlynbb
Tel: (519) 396 8754

**Best Western Governors Inn restaurant**
791 Durham Street
Kincardine ON  N2Z 1M4
www.bestwesternontario.com/kincardine-hotels Tel: (800) 780 7234  (519) 396 8242

Holiday Inn Express
2 Millenium Way Kincardine ON  M2Z 0B5
www.hiexpress.com  Tel: (519) 395 3545

**The Harbour Street Brasserie** -
patio overlooking the lake
217 Harbour Street  Kincardine ON
www.harbourstreetbrasserie.com
Tel: (519) 396 6000

**The Pelican's Roost**
851 Queen Street
Kincardine ON
Tel: (519) 396 3330

**Kincardine Home Hardware**
Highway 21 North
Kincardine ON

Tel: (519) 396 2032
727 Queen Street
Kincardine ON
library.brucecounty.on.ca/kilib
Tel: (519) 396 3289

## Kingston 36 D56 GPS 44.23154,-76.47933: City on Lake Ontario, visit Fort Henry, historic buildings and museums

**Kingston via Wolfe Island – Cape Vincent, New York USA Bicycle Crossing** - Kingston ferry terminal - Ontario Street and Barrack Street - to Marysville on Wolfe Island www.mto.gov.on.ca/english/traveller/ferry Tel: (613) 545 4664. Road 95 12 kilometers on Wolfe Island from Marysville to Port Alexandria. Port Alexandria, Wolfe Island ferry to Cape Vincent New York – dock at James Street www.hornesferry.com
Tel: (613) 385 2402  (315) 783 0638

**Rideau Canal Locks 46 to 49** - at Kingston Mills group camping with prior approval www.pc.gc.ca/lhn-nhs/on/rideau/index.aspx
Tel: (888) 773 8888  (613) 283 5170

**Tourist Information** –Kingston & Area tourism.kingstoncanada.com/en
Tel: (888) 855 4555  (613) 548 4415

**Rosemount Bed & Breakfast Inn**
46 Sydenham Street South
Kingston ON
www.rosemountinn.com
Tel: (888) 871 8844  (613) 531 8844

**Frontenac Club Inn**
225 King Street East
Kingston ON  K7L 3A7
www.frontenacclub.com
Tel: (613) 547 6167

**Four Points by Sheraton Kingston**
285 King Street East
Kingston ON
www.starwoodhotels.com/fourpoints
Tel: (800) 368 7764  (613) 544 4434

**St. Lawrence College – Residence Services**
23 Country Club Drive
Kingston ON K7M 9A4
www.slon.ca/residence/SummerAccomodations.htm
Tel: (613) 544 6600 ext. 4999

**Aquaterra**
1 Johnson Street Kingston ON  K7L 5H7
www.aquaterrabyclark.com
Tel: (613) 546 6243

**Chez Piggy**
68R Princess Street  Kingston ON  K7L 1A5
www.chezpiggy.com  Tel: (613) 549 7673

**Le Chien Noir** 69 Brock Street
Kingston ON  K7L 1R8
www.lechiennoir.com  Tel: (613) 549 5635

**The Cyclepath** bicycle rental
Kingston 471 Princess Street
Kingston ON  K7L 1C3
www.cyclepathkingston.com
Tel: (613) 542 3616

130 Johnson Street
Kingston ON  K7L 1X8
www.kfpl.ca  Tel: (613) 549 8888

## Kingsville 4 E4 GPS 42.03789,-82.74031: Town with attractive tree-lined streets

**Kingsville via Pelee Island – Sandusky, Ohio USA Bicycle Crossing.** Pelee Island Ferry service from Leamington and Kingsville to Pelee Island and Sandusky Ohio USA. March to December www.ontarioferries.com/jii/english/index.html
Tel: (800) 661 2220

**Jack Miner Bird Sanctuary**
Box 39  Road 3 West
over 5000 Canada geese and other birds that over winter here
www.jackminer.com  Tel: (519) 887 289 8328

**Colasanti's Tropical Gardens** restaurant, picnic area, tropical birds, zoo, greenhouses
1550 Road 3 East
Kingsville ON
www.colasanti.com  Tel: (519) 326 3287

**Mastronardi Wines**
1193 Concession 3
Kingsville ON
www.mastronardiwines.com
Tel: (800) 320 5040  (519) 733 9463

**Pelee Island Winery**
455 Seacliff Drive
Kingsville ON
www.peleeisland.com
Tel: (800) 597 3533  (519) 733 6551

**Bessie's Bed & Breakfast**
333 Millbrook Drive
Kingsville, ON N9Y 4A5
www.bbcanada.com/bessies
Tel: (519) 733 9403

**The Old Farmhouse B&B**
1389 Seacliff Drive
Kingsville ON N9Y2M4
www.oldfarmhouse.com  Tel: (519) 733 9660

**The Adams Golden Acres Mote**
GPS  42.0348267, -82.7578191
438 Main Street West County Rd 20
Kingsville ON  N9Y 2K2
www.adamsgoldenacres.com
Tel: (519) 733 6531 (888) 234 6018

**The Victorian Rose Tearoom & Restaurant**
64 Main Street East
www.victorianrosetearoom.ca
Tel: (519) 733 9035

**Mephisto's Grill Lounge**
15 Main Street West
www.mephistosgrill.com
Tel: (519) 733 0282

**Mettawas Station Restaurant**
169 Landsowne Avenue
Kingsville ON  N9Y1S4
www.mettawasstation.com  Tel: (519) 733 2459

28 Division Street South
Kingsville ON  N9Y 1P3
www.essexcountylibrary.ca  Tel: (519) 733 5620

## Komoka 8 T15 GPS 42.94566,-81.43055: Village

## Lake on the Mountain 35 F51
GPS 44.03726,-77.06291:  Restaurant, viewpoint and picnic area 200 feet above Glenora Ferry

## Lansdowne 37 B60 GPS 44.40574,-76.01893: Village

**Ontario Travel Information Centre**
20806 Road 2 & Highway 401 RR # 1
Lansdowne K0C 1N0
www.ontariotravel.net
Tel: (613) 347 3498  (800) 668 2746

**Charleston Lake Provincial Park**
RR 4 Lansdowne ON  K0E 1L0
Reservations- www.ontarioparks.com
Tel: (888) 668 7275

## Lakefield 44 B41 GPS 44.42251,-78.27278:

**Lock 26 on Trent Canal**
Group camping at most lock stations with prior approval
www.pc.gc.ca/eng/lhn-nhs/on/trentsevern/visit/visit6.aspx
Tel: (888) 773 8888 (705) 750 4900

**Harbour By The Lake B&B**
P.O.Box 1094, 4365 County Road 29
Lakefield ON  K0L 2H0
www.harbournebythelake.com
Tel: (888) 441 3686  (705) 652 0882

**The Village Inn**  restaurant
39 Queen Street
Lakefield ON  K0L 2H0
www.villageinn.ca
Tel: (800) 827 5678  (705) 652 1910

**Adventure Outfitters**
County Road  18 at Highway  507
Lakefield ON  K0L 2H0
www.adventureoutfitters.ca
Tel: (705) 652 7986

**Lakefield Public Library**
2 Queen Street  Lakefield ON
www.mypubliclibrary.ca  Tel: (705) 652 8623

## Latta 34 C49 GPS 44.29486,-77.34375: Village

## Leamington 5 E5 GPS 42.05416,-82.59971: Town with attractive waterfront

**Leamington via Pelee Island – Sandusky, Ohio USA Bicycle Crossing.** Pelee Island Ferry service from Leamington and Kingsville to Pelee Island and Sandusky Ohio USA. March to December www.ontarioferries.com/jii/english/index.html
Tel: (800) 661 2220

**Leamington Arts Centre**
72 Talbot Street West
Leaminton ON N8H 1M4
www.leamingtonartscentre.com
Tel: ( 519) 326 2711
ErieQuest, Heinz and Henry Collection of art, from jade to silver, sculpture and clothing, from India, China and southeast Asia.

**Annual Tomato Festival** – mid August
www.leamingtontomatofestival.com

**Point Pelee National Park**  paved road to the southernmost point in Canada; beaches, boardwalk trails, a bird watchers paradise.
www.pc.gc.ca/eng/pn-np/on/pelee/index.aspx
Tel: (519) 322 2365  (888) 773 8888

**Hillman March Conservation Area** canoeing, bird watching and beach - Road 37 at 2nd Concession Road - www.erca.org

**Comfort Inn**
GPS   42.0371646, -82.6008633
279 Erie Street South
Leamington ON  N8H 3C4
www.choicehotels.ca
Tel: (800) 424 6423  (519) 326 9071

**Marlborough House Bed & Breakfast**
GPS 42.05052,-82.60715
349 Marlborough Street West
Leamington ON
www.marlboroughhouse.ca
Tel: (866) 530 4389  (519) 322 3953

**Quersus Cottage**
168 Seacliffe Drive West
Leamington ON  N8H 3Y5
www.bbcanada.com/quercuscottage
Tel: (519) 324 0243

**Howard Johnson Inn Leamington**
201 Erie Street North
Leamington  N8H 3A5
www.howardjohnsonleamington.com
Tel: (800) 340 9841  (519) 325-0260

**Thirteen Russell Street**
13 Russell Street
Leamington ON N8H 1T7
Tel: (519) 326 8401

**Lakeside Bakery Cafe Deli**
286 Erie Street South
Leamington ON
www.lakesidebakery.com  Tel: (519) 326 2626

**Sturgeon Woods Campground Park**
Point Pelee Drive
www.sturgeonwoods.com/  Tel: (877) 521 4990

**The Bike Shop**
1111 Mersea Road 8, Leamington, ON
Tel: (519) 326-8385

1 John Street
Leamington ON N8H 1H1
www.essexcountylibrary.ca
Tel: (519) 326 3441

## Lighthouse Cove 5 B7 GPS 42.31388,-82.45239: Village at the mouth of the Thames River, 1818 Lighthouse

**Harbour Manor Bed & Breakfast**
21000 Harbour Drive
Lighthouse Cove ON
RR#5 Tilbury ON N0P 2L0
www.bbcanada.com/harbourmanorbb
Tel: (519) 682 0991

**Lighthouse Inn Restaurant**
Lighthouse Cove, ON, N0P 2L0
www.thelighthouseinn.ca
Tel: (519) 682 0600

## Lindsay 32 C37  GPS 44.35428,-78.74007: City in the Kawartha Lakes  convenience store, grocery store, restaurants, other stores

**Trent Severn Waterway  Lock 33**
Group camping at most lock stations with prior approval.    www.pc.gc.ca/eng/lhn-nhs/on/trentsevern/visit/visit6.aspx
Tel: (888) 773 8888  (705) 750 4900

**Academy Theatre**
2 Lindsay Street South
Lindsay ON K9V 2L6
www.academytheatre.ca
Tel: ( 877) 888 0038 (705) 324 9111

**Melton's Light House B&B**
17 Murdoch Court
Lindsay ON K9V 6L4
www.bbcanada.com/8664.html
Tel: (705) 878 3426

**Admiral Inn**
1754 Highway #7
R.R. #2 Lindsay ON K9V 4R2
www.admiralinn.ca
Tel: (866) 328 1743 (705) 328 1743

**Down To Earth Adventure Outfitters**
82 Kent Street West
Lindsay ON
Tel: (705) 328 0230

**Linwood** 22 L21 GPS 43.58146,-80.72828:
Town in Mennonite farming area

5279 Ament Line
Linwood ON N0B 2A0
www.rwl.library.on.ca Tel: (519) 698 2700

**Lions Head** 55 V17 GPS 44.98658,-81.25420: Village

**Cat's Pajamas Bed & Breakfast**
64 Main Street Box 321
Lion's Head ON N0H 1W0
www.bbcanada.com/8946.html
Tel: (519) 793 6700

**45th Parallel Bed & Breakfast**
21 Main Street
Lion's Head ON N0H 1W0
www.45thparallelbb.com
Tel: (519) 793 3529

90 Main Street
Lion's Head ON N0H 1W0
www.library.brucecounty.on.ca
Tel: (519) 793 3844

**Little Current** 84 J12 GPS 45.97939,-81.92538: Town

**Tourist Information** – Manitoulin Island
www.manitoulintourism.com
Tel: (705) 368 3021

**Gateway Information Centre**
Highway 6 north of Little Current

**Hawberry Motel**
36 Meredith Street Box 123
Little Current ON P0P 1K0
www.hawberrymotel.ca
Tel: (800) 769 7963 (705) 368 3388

**The Shaftesbury Inn restaurant**
historic 19 Robinson Street
Little Current ON P0P 1K0
www.rockgardenresort.on.ca
Tel: (705) 368 1945

50 Meredith Street West
Little Current ON Box 790 P0P 1K0
www.townofnemi.on.ca/library-0
Tel: (705) 368 2444

**Little Lake** 34 F45 GPS 45.97939,-81.92538:
Cottage area

**Little Lake Pavilion restaurant**
14226 Little Lake Road
RR#4 Brighton ON
Tel: (800) 263 6078 (613) 475 4053

**London** 8 T17 GPS 44.04047,-77.82303: The
Forest City, attractive tree lined streets,
museums and parks

**Tourist Information London**
www.londontourism.ca
Tel: (800) 265 2602 (519) 661 5000
Middlesex County -
www.middlesextourism.ca
Tel: (866) 205 1188 (519) 641 7190

**Online Cycling Map**
www.london.ca/d.aspx?s=/Transportation/
bikepage.htm

**Summer festivals** include the Festival at the
Forks July 1 weekend, SunFest World Music
Festival www.sunfest.on.ca and Home
Country Folk Festival www.homecounty.ca at
Victoria Park in July

**Best Western Stoneridge Inn restaurant**
6675 Burtwistle Lane
London ON N6L 1H5
www.stoneridgeinn.com
Tel: (888) 471 2378 (519) 652 6022

**Airport Inn**
2230 Dundas Street East at Airport Road
London ON N5V 1R5
www.airportinnandsuites.ca Tel: (519) 457
1200 (877) 464 1200

**Station Park Inn**
242 Pall Mall Street at Richmond
London ON
www.stationparkinn.ca
Tel: (800) 561 4574 (519) 642 4444

**Dufferin House Bed & Breakfast**
385 Dufferin Avenue London ON N6B 1Z5
www.bbcanada.com/dufferinhouse Tel, (519)
601-5511

**Fanshawe Conservation Area-**
recreation area, swimming, Fanshawe Lake,
Fanshawe Pioneer Village
1424 Clarke Road London ON
www.thamesriver.on.ca
Tel: (519) 451 2800
Reservations- Tel: (866) 668 2267

**Marienbad Restaurant**
122 Carling Street
London ON
www.marienbad.ca
Tel: (519) 679 9940

**Michaels on the Thames**
1 York Street London ON
www.michaelsonthethames.com
Tel: (519) 672 0111

**Mountain Equipment Coop**
1230 - 1300 Wellington Road
London ON N6E 1M3
www.mec.ca

**Reynold Cycle two locations**
688 Dundas Street
London ON N5W 2Z4
reynoldcycle.com Tel: (519) 645 1043
20 Meg Drive
London ON N6E 2X9 Tel: (519) 680 5100

251 Dundas Street
London ON N6A 6H9
www.londonpubliclibrary.ca
Tel: (519) 661 4600

**Long Sault** 52 U69 GPS 45.02998,-74.89832:
Village

**Long Sault Motel**
Box 700 Long Sault ON K0C 1P0
www.longsaultmotel.com
Tel: (613) 534 2546

**Long Sault Parkway - McLaren, Woodland &
Milles Roches**
www.stlawrenceparks.com
Tel: (800) 437 2233 (613) 543 4328

**L'Orignal** 68 N71 GPS 45.62028,-74.69604: Town

**Lowbanks** 18 U32 GPS 42.87495,-79.45297:
Hamlet

**Long Beach Conservation Area**
Erie Highway 3
Wainfleet ON
Reservations- (905) 899 3462
www.npca.ca

**Lucknow** 26 G15 GPS 43.96130,-81.51607:
Town

**Strawberry Summerfest** in early June
www.strawberrysummerfest.com

**Country "Music in the Fields"** in August
www.musicinthefields.ca

**Sommerville Court**
287 Ross Street (Huron Road 1)
Lucknow ON N0G 2H0
Tel: (866) 863 2557 (519) 357 7067

**Grey Ox Meadows**
875 Grey Ox Line RR#5
Lucknow ON
www.greyoxmeadows.com/bedbreakfast.html
Tel: (866) 433 0533 (519) 395 5007

526 Campbell Street

Lucknow ON
library.brucecounty.on.ca
Tel: (519) 528 3011

**Lyndhurst** 37 A59 GPS 44.55081,-76.12365:
Village

**Blair Cottage Bed & Breakfast Box**
39 169 Jonas Street
Lyndhurst ON K0E 1N0
www.bbonline.com/on/blaircottage/index.html
Tel: (613) 928 2622

**Mabee's Corners** 9, 10 V21 GPS 42.77882,
-80.680757: Village

**Maitland** 50 Z63 GPS 44.63637,-75.61140: Village

**Malden Centre** 4 E1 GPS 41.98527,-82.92686:
Village

**Colchester Ridge Estate Winery**
108 County Road 50 East
Harrow ON
www.colchesterridge.com
Tel: (519) 738 9800

**Erie Shore Vinyard**
1410 Road 50 West
Harrow, ON N0R 1G0
www.erieshore.ca
Tel: (519) 738 9858

**Sprucewood Shores Winery**
7258 Road 50 West
Harrow ON N0R 1G0
www.sprucewoodshores.com
Tel: (866) 938 9253 (519) 738 9253

**Viewpointe Estate Winery**
151 County Road 50 East
Harrow ON N0R 1G0
www.viewpointewinery.com
Tel: (866) 372 8439 (519) 738 0690

**Holiday Beach Conservation Area**
www.erca.org
6952 County Road 50
Camping reservations - essexcamping.ca/en
Tel: (866) 878 2470 (519) 736 3772

**Manotick** 66 E63 GPS 45.22739,-75.68430:
Historic operating Watson's Mill, village

**Chilver's Bed & Breakfast**
5220 McLean Crescent
Manotick ON K4M 1G2 Contact :
www.bbcanada.com/1059.html
Tel: (613) 692 3731

**Wright on the River Bed & Breakfast**
5224 McLean Crescent
Manotick ON K4M 1G2
www.bbcanada.com/11028.html
Tel: (613) 692 3781

**Marathon** 2 GPS 48.71993,-86.37570: Town

**Peninsula Inn**
Box 597 Highway 17
Marathon ON P0T 2E0
www.peninsulamotorinn.com
Tel: (807) 229 0651 (866) 866 8444

**Travelodge Marathon**
Box 700 Highway 17
Marathon ON P0T 2E0
www.travelodge.com
Tel: (888) 515 6375 (807) 229 1213

Box 400 22 Peninsula Road
Marathon ON P0T 2E0
www.marathon.ca/article/public-library-178.asp
Tel: (807) 229 0740

**Markdale** 28 C22 GPS 44.31913,-80.64889:
Town, craft shops and galleries

**Barrhead Pub & Grill**
735198 West Back Line RR# 6
Markdale ON N0C 1H0
Tel: (519) 986 3333

**Holly Hill Manor B&B**
66 Toronto St. South Markdale ON N0C 1H0
www.bbcanada.com/11178.htm
Tel: (519) 986 4777

75 Walker Street

**Markdale** ON  N0C 1H0
www.greyhighlandspubliclibrary.com
Tel: (519) 986 3436

**Marlbank**  47 B51 GPS 44.43494,-77.09292:

**Massey**  84 F10 GPS 46.21264,-82.07622: Village, museum

**Mohawk Motel**
Box 429
335 Sable Street
Massey ON  P0P 1P0
www.mohawkmotel.ca
Tel: (866) 865 2722  (705) 865 2722

**Massey Motel**
295 Sable Street West
Massey ON  P0P 1P0
www.masseymotel.com
Tel: (866) 590 2500  (705) 865 2500

185 Grove Street  Massey ON
www.masseylibrary.com
Tel: (705) 865 2641

**M'Chigeeng First Nation**  72 K10
GPS 45.82354,-82.16125: Village, native craft shops and galleries.  www.mchigeeng.ca

**Meaford**  40 Z22 GPS 44.60666,-80.59285: Attractive town with small boat harbour on Georgian Bay

**Meaford Motel  & Restaurant**
126 Sykes Street North
Meaford ON  N4L 1P3
www.meafordmotel.ca
Tel: (866) 970 5799  (519) 538 5799

**Millhollow Bed & Breakfast**
212 Miller Street
Meaford, Ontario N4L 1G9
www.millhollow.ca   Tel: (519) 538 0941

**Backstreet Cafe**
27 Nelson Street West
Meaford ON       Tel: (519) 538 4455

15 Trowbridge Street West
Meaford ON  N4L 1V4
www.meafordlibrary.on.ca
Tel: (519) 538 1060 x1123

**Meldrum Bay**  70  J2 GPS 45.92150,-83.11570:

**1873 Mississagi Lighthouse and Netshed Museum**

**Meldrum Bay Inn  restaurant**
25959 Hwy 540
Meldrum Bay ON  P0P 1R0
www.meldrumbayinn.com
Tel: (877) 557 1645  (705) 283 3190

**Merlin**  5 C8  6 C9 GPS 42.24221,-82.23281: Town

**Merrickville**  50 W61 GPS 44.91574,-75.83684: Historic and scenic lock town; stores, arts & crafts

**Rideau Canal Lock 21-23**
group camping with prior approval
www.pc.gc.ca/lhn-nhs/on/rideau/index.aspx
Tel: (888) 773 8888  (613) 283 5170

**Blockhouse Museum**
at town centre

**Baldachin Inn restaurant**
GPS 44.9124398, -75.8360327
111 St. Lawrence Street
Merrickville ON  www.baldachin.com
Tel: (877) 881 8874  (613) 269 4223

**Sam Jakes Inn**
118 Main Street East
Merrickville ON  K0G 1N0
www.samjakesinn.com
Tel: (800) 567 4667  (613) 269 3711

**Millisle Bed & Breakfast**
205 Mill Street  Box 341
Merrickville ON  K0G 1N0
www.bbcanada.com/millislebb
Tel: (613) 269 3627

111 Main Street East
Merrickville ON K0G 1N0
www.village.merrickville-wolford.on.ca/mpl/library.htm
Tel: (613) 269 3326

**Midland**  41 X28 GPS 44.74990,-79.88851:  Town

**Southern Georgian Bay Tourism**
208 King Street Midland ON  L4R 3L9
www.southerngeorgianbay.on.ca
Tel: (705) 526 7884

**Sainte-Marie Among the Hurons**
Highway 12 East
Midland ON  L4R 4K8
www.saintemarieamongthehurons.on.ca
Tel: (705) 526 7838

**The Martyrs' Shrine**
P.O. Box 7 Highway 12
Midland ON  L4R 4K6
www.martyrs-shrine.com
Tel: (705) 526 3788

**Little Lake Inn Bed & Breakfast**
669 Yonge Street
Midland ON  L4R 2E1
www.littlelakeinn.com
Tel: (888) 297-6130  (705) 526-2750

**The Cutters Rudder B&B**
78 Fifth Street
Midland ON  L4R 3V5
www.thecuttersrudder.com
Tel: (705) 527 7904

**Best Western Highland Inn & Conference Centre restaurant**
924 King Street, P.O. Box 515
Midland ON  L4R 4L3
www.bestwesternmidland.com
Tel: (800) 461 4265 (705) 526 9307

**The Riv Bistro**
249 King Street Midland ON
www.rivbistro.ca  Tel: (705) 526 9432

**Total Sports – The Bike Shop**
542 Bay Street
Midland ON  L4R 1L3
www.totalsportsmidland.com
Tel: (705) 528 0957

**Midland Public Library**
320 King Street
Midland ON  L4R 3M6
www.midlandlibrary.com
Tel: (705) 526 4216

**Mildmay**  27 F18 GPS 44.04200,-81.11934: Town

**Whispering Brook Bed & Breakfast**
7 Jane Street  Box 127  Mildmay ON  N0G 2J0
www.bbcanada.com/1049.html
Tel: (519) 367 2565

**Sandy's Family Restaurant**
96 Elora Street  Mildmay ON
Tel: (519) 367 5898

**Harley's Pub and Perk**
87 Elora Street  Mildmay ON
www.harleyspubandperk.com
Tel: (519) 367 2683

**Liesemer's Home Hardware Cycle & Sports**
98 Elora Street
Mildmay ON
Tel: (519) 367 5314

**Milford**  35 G51 GPS 43.93475,-77.09156: Village, restored Scott's Mill

**Milford Bistro**
3048 County Road 10
Milford ON       milfordbistro.com
Tel: (613) 476 0004

**Millbrook**  32 E40 GPS 44.15065,-78.44804: Historic mill town

**4TH Line Theatre**
1 Dufferin Street
Millbrook
www.4thlinetheatre.on.ca
Tel: (705) 932 4445  (800) 814 0055

**Miller Lake**  54 T15 GPS 45.10257,-81.44311:

**Mindemoya**  72 L10 GPS 45.74194,-82.14144: Village

**Farmers market** Saturday at arena, Pioneer Museum, Highway 551

**Manitoulin Inn**
Highway 551 Box 59

**Mindemoya** ON  P0P 1S0
www.manitoulininn.ca
Tel: (877) 270 0551  (705) 377 5500

**Mindemoya Motel**
Highway 542 RR#1
Mindemoya ON  P0P 1S0
Tel: (705) 377 4779

**Mine Centre**  2 GPS 48.76096,-92.64060:

**Mine Centre Resort**
Highway 11 Box 121  P0W 1H0
Tel: (807) 599 2826

**Mississauga**  24 L-M30 GPS 43.58828,-79.64372: City

**Monte Carlo Inn**
1886 Dundas Street East
Mississauga ON  L4X 1L9
www.montecarloinns.com/torontowest.html
Tel: (800) 363 6400  (905) 273 9500

**Carousels Bed & Breakfast**
2359 Bostock Crescent
Mississauga ON  L5J 3S8
www.bbcanada.com/carousels Tel: (905) 822 7654

**Gears Bike Shop**
176 Lakeshore Road West  Mississauga
ON  L5H 1G4  gearsbikeshop.com
Tel: (905) 271 2400

**Port Credit Branch Library**
20 Lakeshore Road East
www.mississauga.ca/portal/residents/branchlibraries
Tel: (905) 615 4835

**Mitchells Bay**  6 A7 GPS 42.47438,-82.40639: Village on Lake St. Clair

**Montreal River**  96 J13 GPS 47.24195,-84.64142: Village

**Mooretown**  12 U6 GPS 42.83985,-82.46576: Village

**Moore Museum** with 6 heritage buildings
94 Moore Line
www.twp.stclair.on.ca/mooretown_museum.htm
Tel: (519) 867 2020

**St. Clair Township Campground** - outdoor
pool  www.twp.stclair.on.ca/camping.htm
campground_2010.pdf
Tel: (866) 294 0938  Tel: (519) 867 2951

**Morpeth**  7 A12 GPS 42.39336,-81.84348: Village

**Greenview Aviaries & Zoo**
www.greenviewaviariesparkandzoo.com
Tel: (519) 674 3025

**Rondeau Provincial Park**
RR1 Morpeth ON  N0P 1X0
Tel: (519) 674 1770
Reservations- www.ontarioparks.com
Tel: (888) 668 7275

**Morrisburg**  51 W76 GPS 44.89983,-75.18717: Village

**McIntosh Country Inn**
PO Box 1140  County Road #2
Morrisburg ON  K0C 1XO
www.mcintoshcountryinn.com
Tel: (888) 229 2850  (613) 543 3788

**Russell Manor Bed & Breakfast restaurant**
36 First Street Box 219
Morrisburg ON  K0C 1X0
www.russellmanorbb.com
Tel: (866) 401 7472  (613) 543 3871

**Riverside-Cedar Park**
www.stlawrenceparks.com
Tel: (800) 437 2233  (613) 543 3287

28 Ottawa Street
Morrisburg ON
www.sdglibrary.ca  Tel: (613) 543 3384

**Moscow**  36 B53 GPS 44.42888,-76.80679:  Hamlet

**Mount Albert**  1 E33 GPS 44.13579,-79.30934: Town

**Mount Elgin** 9 T20-21 GPS 42.96019,-80.79071:

**Mount Pleasant** 16-17 S24
GPS 43.07792,-80.31349: Town

**Be My Guest Bed & Breakfast**
GPS 43.08215,-80.31092
538 Mt. Pleasant Road
RR#2 Brantford ON N3T 5L5
www.bbcanada.com/3933.html
Tel: (519) 753 6922

**Nanticoke** 11 V27 GPS 42.81074,-80.07198:
Hamlet, industrial area

**Selkirk Provincial Park**
RR1 Selkirk ON N0A 1P0
Tel: (905) 776 2600
Reservations- www.ontarioparks.com
Tel: (888) 668 7275

**Haldimand Conservation Area**
www.lprca.on.ca
Tel: (877) 990 9938 (905) 776 2700

**Napanee** 35 D52 GPS 44.24832,-76.95158:
Historic town

**Lennox and Addington Museum** in the old jail
on Thomas Street
www.lennox-addington.on.ca/must-see/l-a-
museum-archives.html

**c.1826 MacPherson House** on Elizabeth Street
macphersonhouse.ca

**Hampton Inn**
40 McPherson Drive
Napanee ON K7R 3L1
www.hamptoninnnapanee.com
Tel: (800) 560 7809 (613) 354 5554

**Twin Peaks Motel**
353 Dundas Street West
Napanee ON K7R 2B5
www.twinpeaksmotel.com
Tel: (613) 354 4066

25 River Road
Napanee ON K7R 3S6
www.lennox-addington.on.ca/library/location-
and-hours.html
Tel: (613) 354 2525

**Nestor Falls** 2 GPS 49.19676,-93.94612: Town

**Arrowhead Resort & Motel**
Box 66 L Nestor Falls ON P0X 1N0
www.arrowheadresortmotel.com
Tel: (807) 484 2132

**Caliper Lake Provincial Park**
Box 188 Nestor Falls ON P0X 1K0
Tel: (807) 484 2181
Reservations- www.ontarioparks.com
Tel: (888) 668 7275

**Neustadt** 27 F19 GPS 44.07730,-81.00298:
Village, Birthplace of John Diefenbaker,
Canada's seventeenth Prime Minister
www.crht.ca/CRH_Museum.html

**Neustadt Springs Brewery**
established in 1859
456 Jacob Street
www.neustadtsprings.com
Tel: (519) 799 5790

**Noah's Inn restaurant**
527 Mill Street Neustadt
www.noahsinn.ca Tel: (519) 799 5662

**The Monk and Nun Bistro**
5515 Mill Street Neustadt Tel: (519) 799 5217

**Newbury** 7 W12 GPS 42.68479,-81.80002: Town

**New Hamburg** 22 P21 GPS 43.37826,-80.71132: Town

**Oak Grove Cheese**
29 Bleams Road East
New Hamburg ON
www.oakgrovecheese.ca Tel: (519) 662 1212

**Ontario Mennonite Relief Sale** last weekend
in May
New Hamburg Arena 251 Jacob Street New
Hamburg ON N3A 1C6 www.nhmrs.com

**Puddicombe House B&B restaurant**
145 Peel Street
New Hamburg, ON N3A 1E7
www.puddicombehouse.com
Tel: (519) 662-2111

**The Waterlot Restaurant & Inn**
17 Huron Street New Hamburg ON
www.waterlot.com Tel: (519) 662 2020

145 Huron Street
New Hamburg ON N3A 1K1
www.rwl.library.on.ca Tel: (519) 662 1112

**Newboro** 48 Z57 GPS 44.65170,-76.31784:
Town Rideau Canal Lock 36
group camping with prior approval
www.pc.gc.ca/lhn-nhs/on/rideau/index.aspx
Tel: (888) 773 8888 (613) 283 5170
Stores, restaurant

**Rideau Lakes Union Library**
10 Brock Street
Newboro ON K0G 1P0
www.rideaulakeslibrary.ca
Tel: (613) 272-0241

**Newcastle** 32 G39 GPS 43.91822,-78.58920: Town

**Lilac Cottage Bed & Breakfast**
601 Mill Street South
Newcastle ON L1B 1C1
www.bbcanada.com/8602.html
Tel: (905) 987 1123

**Niagara Falls** 19 R34-35 GPS 43.10663,-79.06424:
City at the falls; falls illuminated nightly,
fireworks on Friday in summer

Casino Niagara and other tourist attractions
are located on Clifton Hill above the Niagara
Parkway

**Ontario Travel Information Centre**
Rainbow Bridge 5355
Stanley Avenue L2E 7C2
www.ontariotravel.net
Tel: (905) 358 3221 (800) 668 2746

**Tourist Information** – Niagara Region
www.tourismniagara.com
Tel: (800) 263 2988

**Niagara Region Bicycling Information**
www.rnbc.info

**GO Transit summer rail service Toronto to
Niagara Falls** permits bicycles www.gotransit.
com/public/en/travelling/seasonal.aspx,
4223 Bridge Street Niagara Falls, just west
of Niagara River at Whirlpool Bridge Union
Station 65 Front Street Toronto, just north of
Waterfront Trail at York Street

**Villa Gardenia Bed and Breakfast**
4741 Zimmerman
Niagara Falls ON L2E 3M8
www.VillaGardeniaBB.com
Tel: ( 905) 358 1723

**Danner House Bed & Breakfast**
12549 Niagara River Parkway
Niagara Falls ON L2E 6S6
www.dannerhouse.com
Tel: (866) 295 1805 (905) 295 1805

**Old Stone Inn**
5425 Robinson Street
Niagara Falls ON L2G 7L6
www.oldstoneinn.on.ca
Tel: (800) 263 6208 (905) 357 1234

**Country Inn & Suites**
5525 Victoria Avenue
Niagara Falls ON L2G 2L3
www.countryinns.com/niagara-falls-hotel-on-
l2g3l3/onniafal
Tel: (800) 596 2375 (905) 374-6040

**Secret Garden Restaurant**
5827 River Road
Niagara Falls ON L2G 3K9
www.secretgardenrestaurant.net
Tel: (905) 358 4588

**Elements on the Falls**
6650 Niagara River Parkway
Niagara Falls
www.niagaraparks.com/dining/elementsonthefalls.php
Tel: (905) 354 3631

**Pedlar Bicycle Shop**
4547 Queen Street
Niagara Falls ON

www.pedlarbicycle.com
Tel: (905) 357 1273

**Zoom Leisure bike rentals**
6289 Fallsview Boulevard
Niagara Falls ON L2G 3V7
www.zoomleisure.com
Tel: (866) 811 6993 (905) 468 2366

4848 Victoria Avenue
Niagara Falls ON L2E 4C5
www.nflibrary.ca Tel: (905) 356 8080

**Niagara on the Lake** 19 Q34-35
GPS 43.25540,-79.07212: 215 year old historic
town with unique shops

*Accommodation Rreservation Service -
accomm@niagaraonthelake.com
Tel: (905) 468 4263; reserve ahead accommodation
is booked heavily*

**Shaw Festival**
Box 774 10 Queen's Parade
Niagara-on-the-Lake ON L0S 1J0
www.shawfest.com
Tel: (800) 511 7429 (905) 468 2172

**Niagara on the Lake Chamber of Commerce**
26 Queen Street P.O. Box 1043
Niagara-on-the-Lake ON L0S 1J0
www.niagaraonthelake.com
Tel: (905) 468-1950

**Niagara Region Bicycling Information**
www.rnbc.info

**Fort George** on the Niagara Parkway south of
Niagara on the Lake restored to the War of
1812 www.friendsoffortgeorge.ca

**Niagara Apothecary** drug store museum
5 Queen Street www.niagaraapothecary.ca

**Chateau des Charmes Wines**
1025 York Road Niagara on the Lake ON
www.chateaudescharmes.com
Tel: (905) 262 4219

**Inniskillen Wines** started Ontario's quality wine
industry in 1975
1499 Line 3 Niagara Parkway
Niagara on the Lake ON L0S 1J0
www.inniskillin.com
Tel: (905) 468 2187 (888) 466 4754

**Konzelmann Estate Winery**
1096 Lakeshore Road RR#3
Niagara on the Lake ON L0S 1J0
www.konzelmannwines.com
Tel: (905) 935 2866

**Lailey Vinyard**
15940 Niagara Parkway
Niagara on the Lake ON
www.laileyvineyard.com
Tel: (905) 468 0503

**Palatine Hills Estate Winery**
911 Lakeshore Road
Niagara on the Lake ON
www.palatinehillsestatewinery.com
Tel:(905) 646 9617

**Reif Estate Winery**
Germanic style wine making
15608 Niagara Parkway
Niagara on the Lake ON L0S 1J0
www.reifwinery.com
Tel: (905) 468 7738

**Stonechurch Vineyards**
1270 Irvine Road at Lakeshore Road
RR#5 Niagara on the Lake
ON L0S 1J0
www.stonechurch.com
Tel: (866) 935 3500 (905) 935 3535

**Strewn Winery**
winery and cooking school
1339 Lakeshore Road
RR#3 Niagara on the Lake ON L0S 1J0
www.strewnwinery.com
Tel: (905) 468 1229

**Sunnybrook Farm Estate Winery**
specializing in fruit wines
1425 Lakeshore Road
RR#3 Niagara on the Lake ON L0S 1J0
www.sunnybrookfarmwinery.com
Tel: (905) 468 1122

**Williams Gate Bed & Breakfast**
GPS 43.25236,-79.07998
413 Gate Street Box 1885
Niagara on the Lake ON L0S 1J0
www.williamsgate.com
Tel: (888) 821 5261 (905) 468 3086

**The King's Way Bed & Breakfast**
308 Nassau Street
Niagara on the Lake ON
www.bbcanada.com/123.html
Tel: (905) 468 5478

**Best Western Colonel Butler Inn**
278 Mary Street  Box 642
Niagara on the Lake ON  L0S 1J0
www.bestwesternontario.com/niagara-on-the-lake-hotels Tel: (866) 556 8882  (905) 468 3251

**Moffat Inn & Restaurant**
60 Picton Street, PO Box 578
Niagara on the Lake ON  L0S 1J0
www.vintage-hotels.com/moffat/default.htm
Tel: (888) 669 5566  (905) 468 4116

**Oban Inn  restaurant**
160 Front Street PO Box 94
Niagara-on-the-Lake ON  L0S 1J0
www.obaninn.ca
Tel: (866) 359 6226  (905) 468 4116

**The Bike Shop**
996 Lakeshore Road
Niagara on the Lake ON
Tel: (905) 934 3815

**Zoom Leisure  bike rentals**
2017 Niagara Stone Road
Niagara-on-the-Lake ON  L0S 1J0
www.zoomleisure.com
Tel: (866) 811 6993  (905) 468 2366

**10 Anderson Lane**
Niagara on the Lake ON
www.notlpubliclibrary.org
Tel: (905) 468 2023

**Nipigon** 2 GPS 49.01375,-88.26249:  Town

**Scandia House Bed & Breakfast**
GPS 49.0114367, -88.2617595
17 Second Street
Nipigon ON  P0T 2J0
www.bbcanada.com/10834.html
Tel: (807) 887 3133

**Northland Motel**
Box 736  Highway 17  Nipigon ON  P0T 2J0
www.northland-motel.com
Tel: (866) 899 9902  (807) 887 2032

**Nipigon Public Library**
25 Third Street  Box 728
Nipigon ON  P0T 2J0
www.nipigon.net/content/Nipigon_Public_Library  Tel: (807) 887 3142

**Normandale** 10 W25 GPS 42.71076,-80.31143: Village

Local bog iron ore supplied an iron foundry
which operated from 1822 to 1853

**Normandale Century Inn B&B  restaurant**
2326 Front Road Normandale ON  N0E 1W0
www.bbcanada.com/normandaleinn
Tel: (519) 426 8345

**Union Hotel B&B**
Normandale ON
www.bbcanada.com/12352.html
Tel: (519) 426-5568

**North Buxton** 5 8B  6 8B
GPS 42.30868,-82.22418:  Hamlet

**Buxton National Historic Site and Museum**
21975 A. D. Shadd Road
www.buxtonmuseum.com
celebrating the underground railroad and
black settlements in Canada

**Norwich** 10 T22 GPS 42.98768,-80.59694: Town

**Carriage House Bed & Breakfast**
55 Stover Street North
Norwich ON
www.bbcanada.com/carriagehousebb
Tel: (877) 351 9831  (519) 863 5918

**10 Tidey Street  Highway 59**
Norwich ON  N0J 1P0
www.ocl.net/locations/Norwich
Tel: (519) 863 3307

**Norwood** 45 G61 GPS 44.3823-77.979913:  Town

**Asphodel Norwood Public Library**
2363 County Road 45 Norwood ON K0L 2V0
www.anpl.org  Tel: (705) 639 2228

**Oakland** 16 S24  17 S25 GPS 43.03171,-80.33153: Village

**Oakville** 24 N30 GPS 43.46617,-79.68958:  City

**The Oakville Inn**
162 Lakeshore Road East
Oakville ON  L6J 1H4
www.oakvilleinn.ca  Tel: (888) 625 4667

**Walnut House B&B**
134-136 Forsythe Street
Oakville ON  L6K 3K2
www.bbcanada.com/6842.html
Tel: (866) 925 6885  (905) 844 7687

**Beccofino**
263 Lakeshore Road East Oakville ON
www.beccofino.ca  Tel: (905) 842 2263

**Ristorante Julia**
312 Lakeshore Road East  Oakville ON
www.juliasristorante.com/main2.html
Tel: (905) 844 7401

**Racer Sportif**
151 Robinson Street Unit 1
Oakville ON  L6J 7N3
www.racersportif.com  Tel: (905) 815 2100

**120 Navy Street**
Oakville ON
www.opl.on.ca
Tel: (905) 815 2042

**Odessa** 36 D54 GPS 44.27697,-76.71892:  Town

**102 Main Street**
Odessa ON  K0H 2H0
www.lennox-addington.on.ca/library/
location-and-hours.html  Tel: (613) 386 3981

**Ohsweken** 17 S26 GPS 43.06914,-80.11797:
Central town for Six Nations Territory

**Six Nations Tourism**
www.sntourism.com
Tel: (866) 393 3001 (519)758 5444

**Grand River Champion of Champions Pow
Wow  late July**

**Six Nations Fall Fair weekend after Labour Day**

**The Bear's Inn**
1979 4th Line Road  PO Box 187
Ohsweken ON  N0A 1M0
www.thebearsinn.com  Tel: (519) 445 4133

**Chiefswood Tent and Trailer Park**
Ohsweken Road at Highway 54
www.sixnations.ca/prChiefswoodPark.htm
Tel: (519) 752 3969

**Pauline Johnson birthplace and home**
1037 Road 54  Box 640
Ohsweken ON  N0A 1M0
www.chiefswood.com  Tel: (519) 752 5005

**Omemee** 3245 C39  GPS 44.298884, -78.559769 Town

**Kawartha Lakes Public Library**
PO Box 520 1 Kings Street West
Omemee ON K0L 2W0
www.city.kawarthalakes.on.ca/residents/
library-services/hours-and-locations/omemee-library  Tel: (705) 799-5711

**Orangeville** 29 H26 GPS 43.92012,-80.09349:
Regional centre first settled in 1830

**Theatre Orangeville** in restored
1875 Town Hall Opera House
87 Broadway Avenue
Orangeville ON L9W 1K1
www.theatreorangeville.ca
Tel: (800) 424 1295  (519) 942 3423

**Farmers Market** - Saturday morning
www.thehillsofheadwaters.com/
orangevillefarmersmarket

**Best Western Orangeville Inn and Suites**
7 Buena Vista Drive
Orangeville ON  L9W 0A2
www.bestwesternorangeville.com
Tel: (800) 780 7234  (519) 941 3311

**McKitrick House Inn Bed & Breakfast**
255 Broadway Avenue
Orangeville ON
www.mckitrickhouseinn.com

Tel: (877) 625 4875  (519) 941 0620

**Irvine House Bed & Breakfast**
25 First Avenue
Orangeville ON L9W 1H9
www.irvinehousebb.ca        Tel: (519) 941 8833

**Hockley Valley Resort restaurant**
resort in Hockley Valley
RR1 Orangeville ON  L9W 2Y8
www.hockley.com
Tel: (866) 462 5539  (519) 942 0754

**Greystones Inn Restaurant**
63 Broadway
Orangeville ON
www.greystonesinn.ca
Tel: (519) 941 2235

**Bluebird Cafe**
102 Broadway  Orangeville ON
www.bluebirdcafeandgrill.com
Tel: (519) 941 3101

**John's Cycle Shop**
90 John Street
Orangeville ON  L9W 2P9
Tel: (519) 941 4417

**1 Mill Street**
Orangeville ON  L9W 2M2
www.orangeville.library.on.ca
Tel: (519) 941 0610

**Orillia** 42 Z32 GPS 44.60659,-79.41823:

**Anne's Cranberry House B&B**
25 Dalton Crescent South  Orillia ON  L3V 5J7
www.bbcanada.com/cranberryhousebb
Tel: (866) 876 5885 (705) 326 6871

**Casa Dizon B&B**
9 Tecunseh Street
Orillia ON  L3V 1X7
www.bbcanada.com/7918.html
Tel: (866) 833 2272  (705) 326 2841

**Best Western Couchiching Inn  restaurant**
440 Couchiching Point Road
Orillia ON L3V 6P8
www.bestwesternorillia.com
Tel: (888) 869 2306 (705) 325 6505

**Comfort Inn Orillia**
75 Progress Drive
Orillia ON  L3V 6H1
www.choicehotels.ca/hotels/
hotel?hotel=CN284
Tel: (800) 424 6423  (705) 327 7744

**Stone Gate Inn**
437 Laclie Street
Orillia ON  L3V 4P7
www.stonegateinn.com
Tel: (877) 674 5542  (705) 329 2535

**Sixteen Front Restaurant**
16 Front Street North Orillia ON  L3V 4R5
sixteenfront.com  Tel: (705) 326 3135

**Velocity Bike and Multisport**
161 Mississaga Street East
Orillia ON  L3V 1V8
www.velocitybicycle.com
Tel: (705) 329 0367

**Orton** 23 J25 GPS 43.78141,-80.22877:

**Oshawa** 32 H37 GPS 43.88868,-78.85950:  City

**Best Western Durham Hotel**
550 Bloor Steeet West
Oshawa ON L1J 5Y6
www.bestwesternontario.com/oshawa-hotels
Tel: (800) 780 7234  (905) 723 5271

**The White House Bed & Breakfast**
494 King Street East
Oshawa ON  L1H 1G1
www.bbcanada.com/10408.html
Tel: (905) 579 0062

**Bicycles Plus**
843 King Street West Unit 11
Oshawa ON  L1J 2L4
www.bicyclesplus.com Tel: (905) 436 6040

**Jess Hann Branch**
199 Wentworth StreetWest
Oshawa ON  L1J 6P4
www.oshawalibrary.on.ca
Tel: (905) 579 6111

**Ottawa** 66 Q62-63 GPS 45.42150,-75.69189:
City, Capital of Canada with many museums
and cultural attractions

🛈 🚲 🛡 ⭐ 🛏 🚴 📚

🛈 **Online Cycling Map-**
ottawa.ca/residents/onthemove/travelwise/
cycling/index_en.html

🛈 **The Capital Pathway**
National Capital Commission
Bike paths in the National Capital Region Region
www.canadascapital.gc.ca/bins/ncc_web_
content_page.asp?cid=16297-16299-9970-
9971-29551&lang=1

🛈 **Ottawa Tourism-**
Capital Information Kiosk
World Exchange Plaza 111 Albert Street
www.canadascapital.gc.ca
Tel: (800) 465 1867 (613) 239 5000

🛈 **Rideau Canal Locks 1-8**
www.pc.gc.ca/lhn-nhs/on/rideau/index.aspx
Tel: (888) 773 8888 (613) 283 5170

🛏 **Benner's Bed & Breakfast**
539/541 Besserer Street
Ottawa ON K1N 6C6
www.bennersbnb.com
Tel: (877) 891 5485 (613) 789 8320

🛏 **Auberge**
King Edward: Bed & Breakfast
525 King Edward Avenue
Ottawa ON K1N 7N3
www.kingedwardottawa.com
Tel: (800) 841 8786 (613) 565 6700

🛏 **Alexander House**
542 Besserer Street
Ottawa ON K1N 6C7
ottawabandb.com
Tel: (613) 797 5355

⭐ **Carleton University Tour & Conference Center**
1125 Colonel By Drive
261 Stormont Bldg.
Ottawa ON K1S 5B6
www2.carleton.ca/housing/conference-services
Tel: (866) 278 8687 (613) 520 5611

🚲 **Cycos**
5 Hawthorne Avenue
Ottawa ON K1S 0A9
www.cycosport.ca
Tel: (613) 567 8180

🚲 **Fosters Sport & Cycle**
305 Bank Street
Ottawa ON
www.fosterssports.ca Tel: (613) 236 9611

📚 120 Metcalfe
Ottawa ON K1P 5M2
www.biblioottawalibrary.ca
Tel: (613) 580 2945

**Owen Sound** 39 Z19 GPS 44.56488,-80.94260:
Scenic town located between two bluffs around
a beautiful natural harbour

🍽 🎭 🎪 🛈 📣 🛏 ⛺ 🚲 📚

🛈 **Tourist Information**
Owen Sound & Grey County
www.visitgrey.ca
Tel: (877) 733 4739 (519) 376 3265

🎭 **Tom Thomson Art Gallery**
www.tomthomson.org Tel: (519) 376 1932
Summerfolk Festival held in the middle of
August
840 First Avenue West Owen Sound
ON N4K 4K4 www.summerfolk.org

📣 **Kelso Beach Park**
18th Street West Owen Sound
Tel: (519) 376 1440

📣 **Inglis Falls Conservation Area**
spectacular 80 foot waterfall and hiking trails

🛏 **Brae-Briar Bed & Breakfast**
980 3rd Avenue West
Owen Sound ON N4K 4P6
www.bbcanada.com/622.html
Tel: (519) 371 0025

🛏 **The Highland Manor B&B**
867 4th Ave 'A' West
Owen Sound ON N4K 6L5
www.highlandmanor.ca
Tel: (877) 372 2699 (519) 372 2699

🛏 **Best Western Inn on the Bay**
1800 2nd Avenue East Box 516
Owen Sound ON N4K 5P1
www.bestwesternontario.com/hotels/best-
western-inn-on-the-bay
Tel: (800) 780 7234 (519) 371 9200

⛺ **Harrison Park**


2nd Avenue East
Tel: (519) 371 9734

🍽 **Nathaniel's Restaurant**
215 8th Street East
Owen Sound ON N4K 1L2
Tel: (519) 371 3440

🍽 **Rocky Racoon Café**
941 2nd Avenue East
Owen Sound ON N4K 2H5
www.rockyraccooncafe.com
Tel: (519) 374 0500

🚲 **Jolley's Alternative Wheels**
939 Second Avenue West
Owen Sound ON N4K 1S2
www.alternativewheels.com
Tel: (519) 371 1812

📚 824 First Avenue West
Owen Sound ON N4K 4K4
owensound.library.on.ca
Tel: (519) 376 6623

**Paincourt** 6 A8 GPS 42.39289,-82.29365:
French Canadian village

🛏

**Paisley** 27 C17 GPS 44.30653,-81.27205: Town
with old mills and attractive restored town hall

🍽 🛏 🛡 🛏

🛡 **Treasure Chest Museum**
407 Queen Street

🛏 **Gar-Ham Hall Bed & Breakfast**
GPS 44.31232,-81.27481
538 Queen Street North
Paisley ON N0G 2N0
www.bbcanada.com/2770.html
Tel: (519) 353 7243

⛺ **Paisley Rotary Campground**
Water Street
Paisley ON N0G 2N0
Tel: (519) 353 5575

🍽 **Marty's Bar & Grill**
526 Queen Street Paisley ON N0G 2N0
Tel: (519) 353 5012

🍽 **Back Eddie's**
660 Queen Street South Paisley ON N0G 2N0
www.backeddies.com Tel: (519) 353 4787

**Paris** 16 R24 GPS 43.19068,-80.38164: Town
in the valley of the Grand and Nith Rivers;
galleries

🛡 🍽 🛏 🎭 🛡 ⭐ 🚲 📚

🛡 **Historic cobblestone buildings** including the
1837 St. James Anglican Church, 5 Burwell
Street and 165 Grand River Street North

⭐ **Farmers market and Paris Fair** on Labour Day
weekend at fairgrounds, Grand River Street
North and Silver Street www.parisfair.com

🛏 **Asa Wolverton House**
52 Grand River Street South
Paris ON N3L 2B3
www.bbcanada.com/10616.html
Tel: (519) 442-1652 (519) 754-5773

🛏 **Behind The Pines Bed & Breakfast**
1 Homestead Road
Paris ON N3L 1P3
http://bbcanada.com/7539.html
Tel: (519) 442 1740

🚲 **Paris Sports Centre Inc.**
19 Broadway Street West Paris ON
Tel: (519) 442 0766

📚 12 William Street
Paris ON N3L 1K7
www.brant.library.on.ca Tel: (519) 442 2433

**Parry Sound** 57 R27 GPS 45.34364,-80.03576:

🛏 🛏 🛈 ⭐ 🚲 🍽 🛏 📚

🛈 **Tourist Information:**
Georgian Bay Country Tourism
1A Church Street
Parry Sound ON P2A 1Y2
www.gbcountry.com
Tel: (888) 746 4455 (705) 746 4455

⭐ **Festival of the Sound** music
festival in July and August
42 James Street
Parry Sound ON P2A 1T5
www.festivalofthesound.ca
Tel: (866) 364 0061 (705) 746 2410

🛏 **Drifters Bed & Breakfast**
37 Macklaim Drive
Parry Sound ON P2A 2Z7


www.bbcanada.com/drifters
Tel: (705) 746 4700

🛏 **40 Bay Street Bed & Breakfast**
40 Bay Street
Parry Sound ON P2A 1S5
www.40baystreet.com
Tel: (866) 371 2638 (705) 746 9247

🛏 **Comfort Inn**
120 Bowes Street Parry Sound ON
www.comfortinn.com/hotel-parry_sound-
canada-CN288?promo=gcicn288
Tel: (877) 424 6423 (705) 746 6221

🛏 **Microtel Inn And Suites**
292 Louisa Street
Parry Sound ON P2A 0A1
www.microtelinn.com
Tel: (800) 771 7171 (705) 746 2700

🚲 **Bialkowski Trysport**
77 Bowes Street
Parry Sound ON P2A 2L6
ontariotrysport.com
Tel: (877) 844 9887 (705) 746 8179

📚 **Parry Sound Public Library**
29 Mary Street
Parry Sound ON P2A 1E3
www.pspl.on.ca
Tel: (705) 746 9601

**Pelee Island** 5 H45 GPS 41.76848,-82.68887:
www.pelee.org The island is very flat and the
maximum distance around the outer ring of
roads is 30 kilometers (18 miles). The main
roads are paved or surface treated in the
summer. Roads are quiet, often tree lined
and along the shore. Suggested stops are the
Pelee Island Winery Pavilion just south of the
ferry dock, the Fish Point Nature Preserve
(unsafe for swimming), the public beach on
the East Shore Road, the museum and trading
post at the ferry dock and a hike to the ruins
at Lighthouse Point. There is no town on the
island and only a few stores and restaurants.

🛏 🍽 🛏 Ⓢ 🍷 ⭐ 🛡 ⛺

Ⓢ **Pelee Island – Sandusky, Ohio USA Bicycle
Crossing.** Pelee Island Ferry service from
Leamington and Kingsville to Pelee Island and
Sandusky Ohio USA April to December.
www.ontarioferries.com/jii/english/index.html
Tel: (800) 661 2220

🍷⭐ **Pelee Island Winery** - Pelee Island just south
of ferry dock, summer weekend events
www.peleeisland.com
Tel: (800) 597 3533 (519) 733 6551

🛏🍽 **Anchor & Wheel Inn**
The Island Restaurant
11 West Shore Road
www.anchorwheelinn.com
Tel: (519) 724 2195

🛏 **Stonehill Bed & Breakfast**
911 West Shore Road
½ kilometer north of the West Dock
www.stonehillpelee.bravehost.com
Tel: (519) 724 2193

🛏 **Island Memories Bed & Breakfast**
192 North Shore Road
www.island-memories.com
Tel: (519) 724 2667

⛺ **East Park Campground**
East Shore Road
primitive campground
Tel: (519) 724 2913

**Pembroke** 81 K51 GPS 45.82648,-77.11221:

🛏 🛏 🛈 🍽 📚

🛈 **Ottawa Valley Tourist Association**
9 International Drive
Pembroke ON K8A 6W5
www.ottawavalley.org
Tel: (800) 757 6580 (613) 732 4364

🛏 **Booth House Inn B&B**
272 Pembroke Street East
Pembroke ON K8A 3K1
www.bbcanada.com/boothhouseinn
Tel: (613) 735 1151

🛏 **Grey Gables Manor Inn B&B**
353 Mackay Street
Pembroke ON K8A 1C8
www.greygablesmanor.com
Tel: (613) 635 7011

🛏🍽 **Best Western Pembroke Inn** restaurant
RR#4 1 International Drive

Pembroke ON K8A 6W5
bestwesternontario.com/hotels/best-western-pembroke-inn-and-conference-centre
Tel: (800) 567 2378 (613) 735 0131

🛏 **Comfort Inn Pembroke**
959 Pembroke Street East
Pembroke ON
www.choicehotels.ca
Tel(800) 424 6423 (613) 735 1057

## Penetanguishene 41 X27
GPS 44.76812,-79.93536

🛏🍴🚲🏛🛶

🏛 **Discovery Harbour** 1828 British Naval Base
Homeport of magnificent replica ships H.M.S.
Bee and H.M.S. Tecumseth.
93 Jury Drive Penetanguishene ON L9M 1G1
www.discoveryharbour.on.ca
Tel: (705) 549-8064

🎭 **Kings Wharf Theatre**
97 Jury Drive, Penetanguishene ON L9M 1G7
www.draytonentertainment.com
Tel: (855) 372 9866 (705) 549 5555

🛏 **Georgian Terrace Guest House**
14 Water Street
Penetanguishene ON L9M 1V6
www.georgianterrace.ca
Tel: (888) 549 2440 (705) 549 2440

🚲 **Georgian Cycle**
21 Peel Street
Penetanguishene ON L9M 1A5
www.shopmidland.com/georgiancycle
Tel: (705) 549 7388

## Perth 49 W58 GPS 44.89894,-76.24833: Town
founded in 1816 on the Tay River

🏛🏛🛏🍴

🏛 **Perth Museum**
in 1840 Matheson House and shop at the
1880's Code Mill

ℹ **Tourist Information:** Rideau Heritage Route
www.beautifulperth.com

🛏 **Nevis Estate**
61 Drummond Street West
Perth ON K7H 2K5
www.nevisestate.com Tel: (613) 326 0017

🛏 **Perth Manor Boutique Hotel**
23 Drummond Street West
Perth ON K7H 2J6
www.perthmanor.com
Tel: (613) 264 0050

🍴 **Maximilian Dining Lounge**
99 Gore Street East
Perth ON K7H 1J1
Tel: (613) 267 2536

📚 30 Herriott Street
Perth ON
www.perthunionlibrary.ca Tel: (613) 267 1224

## Petawawa 81, 93 K50 GPS 45.894702,
-77.283249

🏛🍴🚲🛏

🛏 **Quality Inn & Suites**
3119B Petawawa Boulevard Petawawa, ON
www.petawawaqualityinnandsuites.com
Tel: (800) 424 6423 (613) 687 2855

🛏 **Petawawa River Inn & Suites**
3520 Petawawa Boulevard
Petawawa ON K8H 1W9
www.petawawariverinnandsuites.ca
Tel: (800) 573-9775 (613) 687-4686

🚲 **GearHeads**
3025 Petawawa Boulevard
Petawawa ON K8H 1X9
www.gearheads.ca

## Peterborough 33 C41 GPS 44.30073,-78.32131:
City

ℹ🏛🛏🍴🛏🚲📚

ℹ **Trent Canal Lock 19, 20, 21 and 22** - Lock 21 is
the highest hydraulic lift lock in the world
www.pc.gc.ca/eng/lhn-nhs/on/trentsevern/
visit/visit6/lock21.aspx
P.O. Box 567
Peterborough ON K9J 6Z6
camping permitted at most lock stations with
prior approval
Tel: (888) 773 8888 (705) 750 4900
Ont.Trentsevern@pc.gc.ca

ℹ **Tourist Information:**
Peterborough and The Kawarthas Tourism

1400 Crawford Drive
RR#5 Peterborough ON K9J 6X6
www.thekawarthas.net
Tel: (800) 461 6424 (705) 742 2201

🛏 **Beacon By The Bay B&B**
199 Crescent Street
Peterborough ON K9J 2G5
www.bbcanada.com/beaconbythebay
Tel: (866) 745 9165 (705) 745 9165

🛏 **King Bethune Guest House**
270 King Street West
Peterborough ON K9J 2S2
www.kingbethunehouse.com
Tel: (800) 574 3664 (705) 743 4101

🛏 **Moffat House Bed & Breakfast**
597 Weller Street
Peterborough ON K9H 2N9
www.moffathouse.ca
Tel: (705) 743 7228 (877) 415 1646

🛏🍴 **Best Western Otonabee Inn restaurant**
84 Lansdowne Street East
Peterborough ON
bestwesternontario.com/hotels/best-western-otonabee-inn
Tel: (800) 780 7234 (705) 742 3454

🚲 **Wild Rock Outfitters**
169 Charlotte Street
Peterborough ON K9J 2T7
www.wildrock.net
Tel: (888) 945 3762 (705) 745 9133

📚 **Peterborough Public Library**
345 Aylmer Street North
Peterborough ON
www.peterborough.library.on.ca
Tel: (705) 745 5560

## Philipsburg 22 N21 GPS 43.42126,-80.72067: Village
🏛

## Pickering 25 J34 GPS 43.83762,-79.08231: City
🛏🍴🚲📚

🍴 **Port Restaurant**
1289 Wharf Street
Pickering ON L1W 1A2
www.portrestaurant.ca Tel: (905) 839 7678

🚲 **Bay Cycle and Sports**
980 Brock Road South
Pickering ON L1W 2A3
www.baycyclesports.com Tel: (905) 837 1433

🚲 **Pedal Performance**
1050 Brock Road #1 Pickering ON L1W 3X4
www.pedalperformance.com
Tel: (905) 837 2906

## Picton 35 G51 GPS 44.00922,-77.13897:
Picturesque hub of Quinte's Isle on Picton Bay;
craft and antique shops

🛏🏛🍴🏛🏛🛏🛏🚲📚

ℹ **Tourist Information –**
Prince Edward County
116 Main Street Picton
www.pec.on.ca
Tel: (800) 640 4717 (613) 476 2421

🎭 **Prince Edward County Jazz Festival** late
August
Regent Theatre Picton and around Prince
Edward County
www.pecjazz.org

🏛 **Macaulay Heritage Park museum** in 1825
church, 1830 house
Church Street at Union Street
1823 Court House on Union Street
www.pecounty.on.ca/government/rec_parks_
culture/rec_culture/museums/macaulay.php

🍷 **Black Prince Winery**
13370 Loyalist Parkway RR#1
Picton ON K0K 2T0
www.blackprincewinery.com
Tel: (866) 470 9463 (613) 476 4888

🛏 **Pierce The Picton Harbour Inn**
33 Bridge Street Picton ON
www.pictonharbourinn.com
Tel: (800) 678 7906 (613) 476 2186

🛏 **Claramount Inn & Spa**
97 Bridge Street
Picton ON K0K 3V0
www.claramountinn.com
Tel: (800) 679 7556 (613) 476 2709

🛏 **Caruso's On King Bed & Breakfast and
Serenity Spa**

41 King Street
Picton ON K0K 2T0
www.bbcanada.com/carusos Tel: (613) 476 9986

🛏 **Eastlake House** 27 Centre Street
Picton ON K0K 2T0
www.eastlakehouse.com Tel: (613) 476 2004

🛏 **Brown's Manor Bed &Breakfast**
2 Johnson Street Picton ON K0K 2T0
www.brownsmanor.com Tel: (613) 476 0248

⛺ **Sandbanks Provincial Park**
RR1 Picton ON K0K 2T0
Tel: (613) 393 3319
Reservations- www.ontarioparks.com
Tel: (888) 668 7275

🍴 **Currah's Café & Restaurant**
252 Main Street West
Picton ON
www.currahs.ca Tel: (613) 476 6374

🍴 **Portabella Restaurant**
265 Main Street West
Picton ON
www.portabellaonmain.com
Tel: (613) 476 7057

🚲 **Ideal Bike** bicycle rental
172 Main Street
Picton ON
www.idealbike.com
Tel: (800) 301 3981 (613) 476 1913

📚 208 Main Street
Picton ON
www.peclibrary.org Tel: (613) 476 5962

## Point Clark 26 F13 GPS 44.06933,-81.75442:
Village, historic lighthouse

🏛🏛🛏

www.pc.gc.ca/eng/lhn-nhs/on/clark/natcul.aspx

## Pointe Fortune 69 P73
GPS 45.56503,-74.45229: Village

🏛🍴🛏⛺

🚢 **Ferry to Carillon, Quebec**
www.traversierlepasseur.com
Tel: (450) 537 3412

⛺ **Voyageur Provincial Park**
Box 130 Chute-a-Blondeau ON
K0B 1B0 Tel: (613) 674 2825
Reservations- www.ontarioparks.com
Tel: (888) 668 7275

## Poplar Hill 8 T14 GPS 43.00540,-81.51100: Village
🏛

## Port Bruce 9 X19 GPS 42.66098,-81.02280: Hamlet

📷 **Port Bruce Provincial Park**
sand beach on Lake Erie, no camping
P.O. Box 9 Port Burwell ON N0J 1T0
www.ontarioparks.com
Tel: (519) 874 4691

## Port Burwell 9 X20 GPS 42.64570,-80.80594:
Quaint village, 1852 lighthouse, museum,
fishing port, and beach

🛏🍴🏛🛏⛺📚

🛏 **Grey Gables Bed & Breakfast**
22 Erieus Street Box 297
Port Burwell ON
www.bbcanada.com/3912.html
Tel: (519) 874 4644

⛺ **Port Burwell Provincial Park**
PO Box 9 Port Burwell ON N0J 1T0
Tel: (519) 874 4691
Reservations- www.ontarioparks.com
Tel: (888) 668 7275

⛺ **Sand Hills Park**
unique 450 foot high sand dunes, family
camping, swimming (lake)
RR#2
Port Burwell ON N0J 1T0
www.sandhillpark.com
Tel: (519) 586 3891

🍴 **Lighthouse Restaurant Pub**
36 Robinson Street Port Burwell ON
Tel: (519) 874 4348

📚 21 Pitt Street
Port Burwell ON N0J 1T0
www.library.elgin-county.on.ca
Tel: (519) 874 4754

## Port Colborne 19 U33-34 GPS 42.88509,-79.25198:
City on Lake Erie at entrance to Welland Canal

🛏🍴🏛🚢🏛🛏ℹ🚲🛶⛺🚲⭐

**Welland Canal Lock 8 and information centre**
in Fountain View Park at Main Street
**Historical and Marine Museum**
280 King Street Port Colborne ON L3K 3J9
www.portcolborne.com/page/museum
Tel: (905) 834-7604
**Farmers Market** Friday Morning Downtown in
front of City Hall. 66 Charlotte Street
www.portcolborne.com/page/farmers_market
**Nickel Beach on Lake Erie** at the south end of
Welland Street
**Canal Days Festival** on the August holiday
weekend
www.portcolborne.com/page/canal_days
**Showboat Festival Theatre**
Roselawn Centre
296 Fielden Avenue
Port Colborne ON L3K5X7
www.roselawncentre.com
Tel: (888) 870 8181 (905) 834 0833
**Talwood Manor Bed & Breakfast**
GPS 42.88862,-79.25708
303 Fielden Avenue
Port Colborne ON L3K 4T5
www.talwoodmanor.com
Tel: (905) 834 6049
**Lakebreeze Bed & Breakfast**
GPS 42.88571,-79.26012
234 Steele Street
Port Colborne ON L3K 4X7
www.lakebreezeniagara.com
Tel: (877) 834 1233 (905) 834 1233
**At Twenty-Seven**
27 Main Street West
Port Colborne ON L3K 3T8
www.attwentyseven.com
Tel: (905) 835 2700
**West Harbour Restaurant**
3 Marina Road
Port Colborne ON L3K 6C6
Tel: (905) 835 1895
**Sherkston Shores**
490 Empire Road
Sherkston ON L0S 1R0
www.sherkston.com
Tel: (877) 482 3224 (905) 894 0972
310 King Street
Port Colborne ON L3K 4H1
www.portcolbornelibrary.org
Tel: (905) 834 6512

**Port Credit** 24 M30 GPS 43.55143,-79.58593:

**Monte Carlo Inn**
1886 Dundas Street East
Mississauga ON L4X 1L9
www.montecarloinns.com/torontowest.html
Tel: (800) 363 6400 (905) 273 9500
**Carousels Bed & Breakfast**
2359 Bostock Crescent
Mississauga ON L5J 3S8
www.bbcanada.com/carousels
Tel: (905) 822 7654
**Waterside Inn**
15 Stavebank Road South Mississauga ON
www.watersideinn.ca/breakwater/index.shtml
Tel: (905) 891 7770
**Ten Restaurant and Wine Bar**
139 Lakeshore Road East
www.tenrestaurantandwinebar.com
Tel: (905) 271 0016
**Port Credit Branch Library**
20 Lakeshore Road East
www.mississauga.ca/portal/residents/
branchlibraries
Tel: (905) 615 4835

**Port Dalhousie** 19 Q33
GPS 43.20190,-79.26810: Early port settlement
on Lake Ontario

**Antique carousel;**
park with public beach
www.stcatharines.ca/en/experiencein/
LakesideParkCarousel.asp
**Old Port B&B**
73 Main Street
St. Catharines ON L2N 4V1
www.bbcanada.com/oldprtbb
Tel: (905) 934 5761
**Wooton House Bed & Breakfast**

2 Elgin Street
St.Catharines, ON L2N 5G3
www.wootonhouse.com
Tel: (905) 937-4696
23 Brock Street
Port Dalhousie ON
www.stcatharines.library.on.ca
Tel: (905) 646 0220

**Port Darlington** 32 H38
GPS 43.88991,-78.66365: Harbour

**Port Dover** 11 V26 GPS 42.78498,-80.20116:
Popular tourist resort and fishing port, sand beach

**Tourist Information**
Port Dover and Norfolk County
www.norfolktourism.ca
Tel: (800) 699 9038
**Lighthouse Festival Theatre**
247 Main Street Port Dover
www.lighthousetheatre.com
Tel: (888) 779 7703 ext 226 (519) 583 2221
**Goldora Place B&B**
57 Prospect Street Port Dover ON N0A 1N6
www.bbcanada.com/8906.html
Tel: (519) 583 3415
**Angels Nest Rooms by the Beach**
316 St. George Street PO Box 1313
Port Dover ON N0A 1N0
www.bbcanada.com/9954.html
Tel: (519) 583 2640
**Erie Beach Hotel, restaurant**
19 Walker Street
Port Dover ON N0A 1N0
www.eriebeachhotel.com
Tel: (519) 583 1391
**Beach House Restaurant**
2 Walker Street
Port Dover ON
Tel: (519) 583 0880
413 Main Street
Port Dover ON N0A 1N0
www.norfolk.library.on.ca
Tel: (519) 583 0622

**Port Elgin** 38 B16 GPS 44.43710,-81.38816:
Popular resort town with beach on Lake Huron

**Spruce Hall Bed & Breakfast**
824 Goderich Street
Port Elgin ON N0H 2C0
www.bbcanada.com/2643.html/
Tel: (866) 389 4250 (519) 832 9835
**The George House**
657 Mill Street Box 511
Port Elgin ON N0H 2C0
www.bbcanada.com/3317.html
Tel: (877) 884 2913 (519) 389 4896
**Windspire Inn**
276 Mill Street Box 2366
Port Elgin ON N0H 2C0
www.windspireinn.com
Tel: (888) 389 7111 (519) 389 3898
**Port Elgin Super 8**
5129 Highway 21 Port Elgin ON N0H 2C0
www.portelginsuper8.com Tel: (888) 388 3608
**Port Elgin Municipal Tourist Camp**
584 Bruce Street
Tel: (519) 832 2512
**Macgregor Point Provincial Park**
1593 Bruce Road 33
RR#1 Port Elgin ON N0H 2C5
Tel: (519) 389 9056
Reservations- www.ontarioparks.com
Tel: (888) 668 7275
**Brucedale Conservation Area**
south on Lake Huron, sand beach
www.svca.on.ca Tel: (888) 364 2155
**Andre's Swiss Country Dining**
442 Goderich Street
Port Elgin ON N0H 2C4
www.andresswissdining.com
Tel: (519) 832 2461
**Rick's Bikes** (Richard Diotte)
761 Goderich Street
Port Elgin ON Tel: (519) 832 2744
708 Goderich Avenue
Port Elgin ON N0H 2C0
library.brucecounty.on.ca Tel: (519) 832 2201

**Port Hope** 33 G41 GPS 43.95012,-78.29161:
Historic town, antique shops

**All Canadian Jazz Festival** Downtown Port
Hope late Septemberv www.allcanadianjazz.ca
**Canadian Firefighters Museum** - 95 Mill Street
www.firemuseumcanada.com
Tel: (905) 885 8985
**Restored 1930's atmospheric Capitol Theater**
20 Queen Street
www.capitoltheatre.com
Tel: (800) 434 5092 (905) 885 1071
**The Hill and Dale Manor Bed & Breakfast**
GPS 43.95220,-78.29781
47 Pine Street
Port Hope ON L1A 2E6
www.hillanddalemanor.com
Tel: (877) 238 9132 (905) 885 5992
**The Waddell restaurant**
1 Walden Street Port Hope ON
thewaddell.ca
Tel: (800) 361 1957 (905) 885 2449
**Dr. Penstowe Bed & Breakfast**
98 Ontario Street Port Hope ON L1A 2V2
www.penstowe.com Tel: (905) 885 4317
31 Queen Street Port Hope ON
www.phpl.ca Tel: (905) 885 4712

**Port Lambton** 6 W6 GPS 42.65674,-82.50571:
Village

**Port Perry** 31 E36 GPS 44.10682,-78.94273:
Charming town on Lake Scugog

**Tourist Information:**
www.discoverportperry.ca Tel: (905) 985 4971
**A Country Place Bed & Breakfast**
291 Mary Street
Port Perry ON L9L 1B7
www.bbcanada.com/1035.html/
Tel: (905) 448 3114
**Lakeshore Bed & Breakfast**
435 Lakeshore Drive
Port Perry ON L9L 1N7
www.bbcanada.com/lakeshorebb/
Tel: (905) 985 7684
231 Water Street
Port Perry ON L9L 1A8
www.scugoglibrary.ca Tel: (905) 985 7686

**Port Robinson** 19 S34 GPS 43.03839,-
79.21010: Village on Welland Canal

**Pedestrian and bicycle ferry crossing Welland
Canal**, April to December on demand, no charge
Confirm schedule in advance if you need to cross
on this ferry.
www.thorold.com - Tel: (905) 384 2929 [dock]

**Port Rowan** 10 X23 GPS 42.62402,-80.45047:
Village which dates from 1819, fishing port

**Backus Conservation Area**
park featuring a museum and restored 1798
water powered grist mill
www.lprca.on.ca/backus.htm
Tel: (519) 586 2201
**Abigails Bed & Breakfast**
GPS 42.62402,-80.45047
1056 Main Street
Port Rowan ON N0E 1M0
www.abigailsbandb.ca Tel: (519) 586 8777
**The Bay House Bed & Breakfast**
PO Box 375 14 Archibald Drive
Port Rowan ON N0E 1M0
www.bbcanada.com/thebayhouse
Tel: (519) 586 3337
**Long Point Provincial Park**
on 40 kilometer peninsula, a UN biosphere reserve.
PO Box 99 Port Rowan ON N0E 1M0
Tel: (519) 586 2133
Reservations- www.ontarioparks.com
Tel: (888) 668 7275
1034 Bay Street
Port Rowan ON N0E 1M0
www.norfolk.library.on.ca
Tel: (519) 586 3201

**Port Severn** 41 X29 GPS 44.80303,-79.71502:
Lock 45 on Trent Canal

Group camping at most lock stations with prior approval
www.pc.gc.ca/eng/lhn-nhs/on/trentsevern/visit/visit6.aspx
Tel: (888) 773 8888 (705) 750 4900

**Port Stanley** 8 X18 GPS 42.66575,-81.21258: Village

⭐ CALIPSO Days Festival - first weekend in August

⭐ Port Stanley Festival Theatre
6-302 Bridge Street  Port Stanley ON
www.portstanleytheatre.ca
Tel: (519) 782 4353

⭐ Port Stanley Terminal Rail
309 Bridge Street
Port Stanley ON  N5L 1C5
www.pstr.on.ca
Tel: (877) 244 4478 (519) 782 3730

Kettle Creek Inn restaurant
216 Joseph Street
Port Stanley ON  N5L 1C4
www.kettlecreekinn.com
Tel: (866) 414 0417 (519) 782 3388

Windjammer B&B restaurant
324 Smith Street
Port Stanley ON
www.thewindjammerinn.com
Tel: (519) 782 4173

302 Bridge Street
Port Stanley ON  N5L 1C3
www.library.elgin-county.on.ca
Tel: (519) 782 4241

**Pottageville** 30 G30
GPS 43.99192,-79.62307: Hamlet

**Prescott** 50 Y64 GPS 44.70942,-75.51842:
Historic town dating from 1784. Bicycles and pedestrians are prohibited on the Ogdensburg-Prescott International Bridge – Use Seaway International Bridge, Cornwall

Ontario Travel Information Centre
1033 Highway 16  Box 1600 K0E 1T0
www.ontariotravel.net
Tel: (613) 925 3346  (800) 668 2746

⭐ St. Lawrence Shakespeare Festival
riverfront amphitheatre
www.stlawrenceshakespeare.ca
Tel: (613) 925 5788

Forwarders Museum & Tourist Information Centre
201 Water Street  Tel: (613) 925 1861

Fort Wellington
King Street at VanKoughnet Street
www.pc.gc.ca/lhn-nhs/on/wellington/index_E.asp

Ashbury Inn on the River B&B
GPS 44.69197,-75.54628
R.R. 1 G5 1665 County Road 2
Prescott ON  K0E 1T0
www.ashburyinnbb.com
Tel: (866) 731 7410  (613) 925 2566

The Colonel's Inn Bed & Breakfast
408 East Street
Prescott ON  K0E 1T0
www.bbcanada.com/thecolonelsinn
Tel: (613) 482 9539

Dewar's Inn on the River
1649 Road 2
Prescott ON  K0E 1T0
www.dewarsinn.com
Tel: (877) 433 9277  (613) 925 3228

The Red George Pub
197 Water Street West Suite 102
Prescott ON  K0E 1T0   Tel:  (613) 925 8800

The Wok House
238 King Street West Prescott ON
Tel: (613) 925 2532

300 Dibble Street West  Prescott ON
www.prescott.ca/residential/library.aspx
Tel: (613) 925 4340

**Prince Albert** 31 F36 GPS 44.08389,-78.95416:

**Providence Bay** 72 M9

Auberge Inn
71 McNevin Street
Providence Bay ON  P0P 1T0
www.aubergeinn.ca

---

Tel: (705) 377 4392 (877) 977 4392

**Queenston** 19 R35 GPS 43.16362,-79.05350:
Quaint historic village

Brock's Monument, in Queenston Heights Park

Laura Secord Homestead 29 Queenston Street
www.niagaraparks.com/heritage-trail/laura-secord-homestead.html

Riverbrink - Samuel E. Weir Museum and Art Gallery
116 Queenston Street
Queenston ON
www.riverbrink.org
Tel: (905) 262 4510

MacKenzie Printery & Newspaper Museum
1 Queenston Street
www.mackenzieprintery.org
Tel: (905) 262 5676

South Landing Inn
21 Front Street  Box 269
Queenston ON  L0S 1L0
www.southlandinginn.com
Tel: (905) 262 4634

Queenston Heights Restaurant
14184 Niagara Parkway  Queenston ON
www.niagaraparks.com/dining/queenstonres.php
Tel: (905) 262 4374

**Reeces Corners** 12 T9 GPS 42.97953,-82.11765:

Country View Motel Resort camping
RR 1 Wyoming
Reeces Corners ON  N0N 1T0
www.countryviewmotelandrvresort.com
Tel: (519) 845 3394

**Renfrew** 82 P55 GPS 45.47418,-76.68695:

Lochiel Street Bed and Breakfast
270 Lochiel Street South.
Renfrew ON  K7V 1W8
www.bbcanada.com/8563.html
Tel: (866) 433 3752  (613) 433 3752

Best Western Renfrew Inn  restaurant
760 Gibbons Road
Renfrew ON  K7V 4A2
www.bestwesternontario.com/renfrew-hotels
Tel: (800) 780-7234 (613) 432 8109

Martin Cycle and Small Engine
31 Patrick Avenue
Renfrew ON  K7V 3G6
Tel: (613) 432 4855

Renfrew Public Library
3 Railway Ave
Renfrew ON  K7V 3A9
www.town.renfrew.on.ca/library
Tel: (613) 432 8151

**Renton** 10 U25 GPS 42.85948,-80.22011:  Village

**Rideau Ferry** 49 W59 GPS 44.84980,-76.14207:

**Ridgetown** 7 A11 GPS 42.43957,-81.88657:  Town

Ridge House Museum  1875 Victorian House
53 Erie Street South
www.chatham-kent.ca/ridgehouse
Tel: (519) 674 2223

Dempster House
66 Main Street East
Box 358 Ridgetown ON  N0P 2C0
www.dempsterhouse.on.ca
Tel: (519) 674 5196

54 Main Street
Ridgetown ON  N0P 2C0
www.chatham-kent.ca/community+services/library/Library.htm
Tel: (519) 674 3121

**Ridgeway** 19 U35 GPS 42.87810,-79.05181:  Town

Fort Erie Historical Museum
402 Ridge Road  Ridgeway ON
www.museum.forterie.ca/historical.html

89 Ridge Road South
Ridgeway ON  L0S 1N0
www.forterie.library.on.ca
Tel: (905) 894 1281

---

**Rockford** 39  A19-20 GPS 44.52385,-80.91774:

**Rockland** 67 P66 GPS 45.54603,-75.29304:
Bilingual town on Ottawa River

Clarence Rockland Public Library
1525 Avenue du Parc
Rockland ON  K4K 1C3
Tel: (613) 446 5680

**Rockport** 37 C61 GPS 44.38037,-75.93590: Village

⭐ Rockport Boat Line  1000 Island boat cruises
23 Front Street  www.rockportcruises.com
Tel: (613) 659 3402  (800) 563 8687

Boathouse Country Inn & Tavern  restaurant
19 Front Street
Rockport ON  K0E 1V0
www.boathousecountryinn.com
Tel: (613) 659 2348

**Rodney** 7 Y13 GPS 42.56803,-81.68309:  Village

A Touch of Home Bed & Breakfast
184 Furnival Road
Box 310 Rodney ON  N0L 2C0
www.bbcanada.com/3301.html
Tel: (519) 785 0823

Lions Gate Estate B&B
12663 Furnival Road
RR#1 Rodney ON  N0L 2C0
www.bbcanada.com/5657.html
Tel: (519) 785 0531

207 Furnival Road
Rodney ON  N0L 2C0
www.library.elgin-county.on.ca
Tel: (519) 785 2100

**Rossmore** 34 E49 GPS 44.13935,-77.38770:
Village

**Rossport** 99 H-10 GPS 48.83491,-87.51991:
Village

**St. Catharines** 19 Q33 GPS 43.15633,-79.24867
Attractive city with full range of services

Ontario Travel Information Centre
Westbound QEW at end of Garden City Skyway RR # 4
Niagara-on-the-Lake L0S 1J0
www.ontariotravel.net
Tel: (905) 684 6354  (800) 668 2746

Welland Canals Centre - canal view, tourist information, picnic area, snack bar, St. Catharines Museum
932 Welland Canals Parkway
St. Catharines ON  L2R 7K6
www.stcatharineslock3museum.ca
Tel: (905) 984 8880  (800) 305 5134

Brock University Conference & Event Services
50 Glenridge Avenue
St. Catharines ON  L2S 3A1
www.brocku.ca/conference-services/individual
Tel: (905) 688 5550 x3369

Ski Pro Shop
278 Geneva Street
St. Catharines ON
www.skiproshop.com
Tel: (905) 934 2682

**St. Clair Beach** 4 B3 GPS 42.31528,-82.86126:
Hamlet

**St. Clements** 22 M22 GPS 43.52378,-80.65191:
Village in Mennonite farming area

3605 Lobsinger Line
St. Clements ON  N0B 2M0
www.rwl.library.on.ca
Tel: (519) 699 4341

**St. Davids** 19 R35 GPS 43.16062,-79.10156:
Village

Old Firehall Restaurant
268 Creek Road at York Road
St. Davids ON

www.oldfirehall.com Tel: (905) 262 5443

**St. Jacobs** 22 M22 GPS 43.53920,-80.55360: Tourist town which serves the Mennonite farming area

⭐🍴🚴🛏🍴🚶

⭐ **The Meeting Place** on King Street for presentation on Mennonite history

🏛 **Old Factory** on Spring Street for the Maple Syrup Museum and antique showcase

🛏🍴 **St Jacobs Restaurants**
**Benjamins Restaurant and Inn**
1430 King Street Tel: (519) 664 3731
**Stone Crock**
1396 King Street
Tel: (519) 664 2286 (866) 664 2286
**Jacob's Grill**
1398 King Street Tel: (519) 6644 2575
www.stjacobs.com/restaurants

🛏 **Evenholme Esatate & Spa**
16 Isabella Street St. Jacobs ON
www.evenholmeestate.com
Tel: (519) 664 2208

🛏 **Queensway Landing Bed & Breakfast**
46 Queensway Drive
St. Jacobs ON N0B 2N0
www.bbcanada.com/9444.html
Tel: (519) 664 2824

🍴 **Harvest Moon Restaurant**
5 Parkside Drive St Jacobs ON N0B 2N0
www.harvestmoonrestaurant.ca
Tel: (519) 664 2373

🚶 29 Queensway Drive St. Jacobs ON N0B 2N0
www.rwl.library.on.ca Tel: (519) 664 3443

**St. Marys** 15 Q18 GPS 43.25950,-81.14142: Town with Victorian stone architecture

🛏🍴🚴⭐🚴🛏🚶

⭐ **Park with swimming pool** in an abandoned quarry at the edge of town; riverside promenade

⭐ **Heritage Festival**
in early July

🏛 **Canadian Baseball Hall of Fame and Museum**
386 Church Street South
St. Marys ON N4X 1C2
www.baseballhalloffame.ca
Tel: (877) 250 2255 (519) 284 1838

🛏🍴 **The Westover Inn restaurant**
300 Thomas Street
St. Marys N4X 1B1
www.westoverinn.com
Tel: (800) 268 8243 (519) 284 2977

🛏 **Hathaway House Bed & Breakfast**
44 St. Andrew Street South, P.O. Box 2616
St. Marys ON N4X 1A4
www.hathawaybedandbreakfast.com
Tel: (519) 284 1137

🛏🍴 **Stone Willow Inn & Wild Stone Bar & Grill**
940 Queen Street East
St. Marys ON N4X 1B3
www.stonewillow.com
Tel: (800) 409 3366 (519) 284 4140

🍴 **Woolfy's At Wildwood**
Highway 7 at Road 118/119
RR2 St. Marys ON N4X 1C5
www.woolfys.com
Tel: (519) 349 2467

🚶 15 Church Street
Box 700 St. Marys ON N4X 1B4
www.stmarys.library.on.ca
Tel: (519) 284 3346

**St. Thomas** 8 V17 GPS 42.77894,-81.19315: City

🛏🍴🛈🚴⭐🛏🚴🚶

🛈 **Tourist Information –**
St. Thomas and Elgin County
www.elgintourist.com
Tel: (877) 463 5446 x 168
(519) 631 1460 x 168

🏛 **Elgin County Railway Museum**
225 Wellington Street
www.ecrm5700.org
Tel: (519) 637-6284

⭐ **Iron Horse Festival** late August
www.ironhorsefestival.com

🛏 **Cardinal Court Motel**
10401 Sunset Road
RR # 7 St. Thomas ON N5P 3T2
www.cardinalcourt.ca
Tel: (877) 774 8380 (519) 633 0740

🚴 **Paul's Bicycle Repair & Sports Exchange -**

115 Ross Street
St Thomas ON N5R 3X8
Tel: (519) 631 3307

🚶 **St. Thomas Public Library**
153 Curtis Street St. Thomas ON
www.st-thomas.library.on.ca
Tel: (519) 631 6050

**St. Williams** 10 W24 GPS 42.66786,-80.41552: Village

🏛

**Salem** 22 K23 GPS 43.69196,-80.44189: Hamlet

🍴

**Saltford** 20 J13 GPS 43.74444,-81.69279: Village

🍴

**Sandfield** 73 M11 GPS 45.70471,-81.99865: Hamlet, store

🛏

**Sandford** 31 E33 GPS 44.13506,-79.20110:

🏛

**Sarnia** 12 T7 GPS 42.97877,-82.40336: Port city on St. Clair River

🛏🍴🛏🚴🛈🚴🛈🚴🚴🚶

🚴 **Sarnia – Port Huron, Michigan USA Bicycle Crossing**
Riders and bicycles will be transported at the convenience of the Blue Water Bridge Authority - (810) 984 3131.
For alternatives see Sombra for the Marine City Ferry and Walpole Island for the Algonac Ferry.

🛈 **Ontario Travel Information Centre**
Blue Water Bridge
1455 Venetian Boulevard N7T 7W7
www.ontariotravel.net
Tel: (519) 344 7403 (800) 668 2746

🛈 **Tourist Information –**
Sarnia and Lambton County
www.tourism-sarnia-lambton.com
Tel: (800) 265 0316 (519) 336 3232

🎭 **Imperial Theatre**
168 North Christina Street
Box 43 Sarnia ON N7T 7H8
www.imperialtheatre.net
Tel: (519) 344 7469

🎰 **Point Edward Casino**
2000 Venetian Boulevard
Tel: (888) 394 6244

🛏 **Best Western Guildwood Inn restaurant**
1400 Venetian Boulevard
Sarnia ON N7T 7W6
www.bestwesternontario.com/hotels/best-western-guildwood-inn
Tel: (800) 780 7234 (519) 337 7577

🛏 **Super 8 Motel**
420 North Christina Street
Sarnia ON N7T 5W1
www.super8.com Tel: (800) 889 9698

🛏 **Twin Lakes Retreat Bed & Breakfast**
1404 Errol Road East
Sarnia ON N7S 5T2
www.bbcanada.com/11084.html
Tel: (519) 542 8014

🍴 **Mama Rosa's**
499 Front Street North
Sarnia ON Tel: (519) 337 7166

🚴 **The Bicycle Shop**
410 Front Street
Sarnia ON www.thebicycleshopsarnia.ca
Tel: (519) 344 0515

🚶 124 Christina Street South
Sarnia ON N7T 8E1
www.lclmg.org Tel: (519) 337 3291

**Sauble Beach** 38 Z17 GPS 44.62966,-81.26325: Long sand beach

🛏🍴🛏🚶

🛏 **Knights Inn**
11 Sauble Falls Parkway Box 9
RR#1 Sauble Beach ON N0H 2G0
www.bmts.com/~knightsinn
Tel: (877) 239 9921 (519) 422 2311

🍴 **Sauble Dunes Restaurant**
11 Southampton Parkway
Sauble Beach ON N0H 2N0
www.saubledunes.ca Tel: (519) 422 2745

🚶 27 Community Center Drive Sauble Beach ON

Tel: (519) 422 1283

**Sauble Falls** 38 Y17 GPS 44.68428,-81.25557: Cascading waterfall

🏛⛺

⛺ **Sauble Falls Provincial Park**
RR#3 Wiarton ON N0H 2T0
Tel: (519) 422 1952
Reservations- www.ontarioparks.com
Tel: (888) 668 7275

**Sault Ste Marie** 2 GPS 46.51797,-84.34797: Centre of Algoma region and services

🛏🚴⭐🛏🚴🚴🚴⛺

🚴 **Sault Ste. Marie – Sault Ste. Marie, Michigan USA Bicycle Crossing.**
Bicycles are permitted on the International Bridge.
Tel: (906) 635 5255

🛈 **Ontario Travel Information Centre**
Sault Ste. Marie International Bridge
261 Queen Street West P6A 1A3
www.ontariotravel.net
Tel: (705) 945 6941 (800) 668 2746

⭐ **Roberta Bondar Tent Pavilion**, tickets for Lock Tours and a Farmers Market Saturday and Wednesday mornings. Casino and Museum Ship Norgoma nearby.

🏛 **Canadian Bushplane Heritage Centre**
50 Pim Street
www.bushplane.com Tel: (705) 945 6242

⭐ **Agawa Canyon Train Tour**
P.O. Box 130 129 Bay Street
Sault Ste. Marie ON P6A 6Y2
www.algomacentralrailway.com
Tel: (705) 946 7300 (800) 242 9287

🛏 **Little Brown Dog Bed and Breakfast**
742 Wellington Street West
Sault Ste. Marie ON P6C 3V4
www.bbcanada.com/littlebrowndog
Tel: (705) 949-9591

🛏 **Quality Inn Bay Front**
180 Bay St. Sault Ste. Marie ON
www.qualityinnssm.com
Tel: (800) 228 5151 (705) 945 9264

🛏 **Sleep Inn**
727 Bay Street Sault
Ste. Marie ON P6A 6Y3
www.sleepinnssmarie.ca
Tel: (800) 753 3746 (705) 253 7533

🚴 **Duke of Windsor Sports Shop**
655 Queen Street East
Sault Ste. Marie ON P6A 2A6
Tel: (705) 942 1610

🚶 50 East Street
Sault Ste. Marie ON P6A 3C3
www.ssmpl.ca Tel: (705) 759 5230

**Schomberg** 30 G30 GPS 44.00281,-79.68410: Town

🛏🍴

**Schreiber** 2 GPS 48.81386,-87.26647: Town

🛏🍴🛏

**Scone** 27 C18 GPS 44.30527,-81.07301: Village with scenic waterfall and mill ruins

🛏🚴

🛏 **Sconeview Bed & Breakfast**
RR#3 Chesley ON N0G 1L0
www.bbcanada.com/sconeviewbb
Tel: (519) 363 6992

**Seaforth** 20 M15 GPS 43.55304,-81.39370:

🏛🛏🍴🛏🚶

🛏 **Peggoty's Bed And Breakfast**
145 Main Street North
Seaforth ON N0K 1W0
www.bbcanada.com/7751.html
Tel: (519) 527 1072

🚶 **Seaforth Public Library**
108 Main Street South
Box 490 Seaforth ON N0K 1W0
www.huroncounty.ca/library
Tel: (519) 527 1430

**Scotland** 16 S24 GPS 43.02577,-80.37540: Village

🏛🍴

**Shabaqua Corner** 2 GPS 48.60147,-89.89700: Village

🍴

**Sharon** 30 E-F32 GPS 44.09960,-79.44052: Town

⬛🍴♿🚲

🏛 **Historic Sharon Temple**
18974 Leslie Street  Sharon ON  L0G 1V0
www.sharontemple.ca    Tel: (905) 478 2389

🚲 **Spoke O Motion**
17915 Leslie Street Newmarket ON  N3Y 3E3
www.spokeomotion.com Tel: (905) 853 9545

## Shebandowan  2 GPS 48.62463,-90.07244: Village
🍴

## Simcoe  17 U25  GPS N42° 50.146', W080° 18.4108'
⬛🍴🚍🏛♿🅂

🍴 **The Blue Elephant Restaurant**
6 Norfolk Street South Simcoe ON N3Y 2W2
www.blueelephant.ca Tel: (519) 428 2886

🛏🍴 **Best Western Little River Inn**
203 Queensway West Simcoe ON N3Y2M9
bestwesternontario.com/hotels/best-western-
little-river-inn  Tel: (519) 426-2125

📚 **Norfolk County Public Library**
49 Colborne Street
South Simcoe ON  N3Y 4H3
www.ncpl.ca  Tel: (519) 426 5206

## Sioux Narrows  2 GPS 49.41902,-94.09607:
🏛🅰

🅰 **Sioux Narrows Provincial Park**
Box 5160 Kenora ON  P9N 3X9
Tel: (807) 226 5223
Reservations- www.ontarioparks.com
Tel: (888) 668 7275

## Smiths Falls  49 W60: Town
⬛🛈🍴🚍📚

🛈 **Rideau Canal Museum, Locks 26, 27, 29 and**
31 group camping with prior approval
www.pc.gc.ca/lhn-nhs/on/rideau/index.aspx
Tel: (888) 773 8888  (613) 283 5170

🛈 **Tourist Information:**
www.smithsfalls.ca/visiting-here.cfm

🛏 **Best Western Colonel By Inn**
88 Lombard Street
Smith Falls ON  K7A 4G5
www.bestwesternontario.com/hotels/best-
western-colonel-by-inn/
Tel: (800) 780 7234  (613) 284 0001

🛏 **Comfort Inn**
33 Centre Street Smiths Falls ON K7A 3B8
comfortinn.com  Tel: (613) 283-5150

🚲 **Sport X**
11 Chambers Street Smiths Falls ON  K7A2Y2
www.sportx.ca  Tel: (613) 284 1632

📚 **Smiths Falls Public Library**
81 Beckwith Street North
Smiths Falls ON  K7A2B9
www.smithsfallslibrary.ca Tel: (613) 283 2911

## Smithville  18 S31  GPS 43.09392,-79.54890:
Grocery store, other stores, restaurant
⬛🛏🍴

🛏 **Niagara's Nest B&B**
103 Wade Road  Smithville ON  L0R 2A0
www.bbcanada.com/niagarasnest
Tel: (905) 957 7130

## Sombra  6 W6 GPS 42.71401,-82.47841: Village
⬛🍴🅂🚍🌟♿🚍🅰📚

🅂 **Sombra – Marine City, Michigan USA**
**Bicycle Crossing**
www.bluewaterferry.com
Tel: (877) 892 3879  (519) 892 3879

🌟 **Bridge to Bay Trail**
Marine City to Algonac Michigan USA
www.stclaircounty.org/Offices/parks/btob.aspx

🏛 **Sombra Museum**
www.twp.stclair.on.ca/sombra_museum.htm
Tel: (519) 892 3982

🛏 **Sheboane Bed & Breakfast**
2955 St. Clair Gardens Sombra ON  N0P 2H0
www.sheboane.ca  Tel: (519) 892 3389

🅰 **Branton Cundick Park**
54 West Wilkesport Line Sombra ON
www.twp.stclair.on.ca/camping.htm
Tel: (519) 892 3968

🅰 **Cathcart Park**  955 St. Clair Parkway
Sombra ON  N0P 2H0
www.twp.stclair.on.ca/camping.htm
Tel: (519) 892 3342

📚 **Lambton County Library**
3536 St. Clair Parkway  Sombra ON  N0P 2H0

---

www.lclmg.org  Tel: (519) 892 3711

## South Baymouth  73 N11
GPS 45.57011,-82.01320: Ferry terminal and village
⬛🍴♿🅂🛏🅰

🏛 **Little Schoolhouse and Museum**
www.manitoulin-island.com/museums/little_
schoolhouse.htm  Tel: (705) 859 2344

🅂 **Tobermorey-South Baymouth Ferry:**
Ferry service between South Baymouth
on Manitoulin Island and Tobermorey.
Departures early May to mid October, 1.75
hour crossing. Reservations and information
www.ontarioferries.com/chi/english/index.html
Tel: (800) 265 3163

🛏 **Huron Motor Lodge**
South Baymouth ON P0P 1Z0
www.manitoulin.com/hml
Tel: (800) 387 2756  (705) 859 3131

🛏 **Buckhorn Motel**
Box 40  South Baymouth ON  P0P 1Z0
www.buckhornmotel.com  Tel: (705) 859 3635

🛏 **South Bay Guest House**
15 Given Road
South Baymouth ON  P0P 1Z0
www.southbayguesthouse.com
Tel: (877) 656 8324  (705) 859 2363

🅰 **John Budd Memorial Park**
First Street, 1 km north of ferry dock

## South Lancaster  52 T72 GPS 45.13026,-74.49153:
🏛🍴🅰

🅰 **Glengarry Park Campsite**
South Service Road
www.stlawrenceparks.com Tel: (519) 347 2595

## Southampton  38 A16 GPS 44.49774,-81.36985:
Attractive lakeshore town with sand beach
⬛🌟🚍🍴🅰♿🚲

🌟 **Saugeen First Nations Pow Wow** in August
and Saugeen Amphitheatre gardens east on
Highway 21
www.saugeenfirstnation.ca

🛏 **Chantry Breezes Bed & Breakfast**
107 High Street Box 1576
Southampton ON  N0H 2L0
www.chantrybreezes.com
Tel: (866) 242-6879  (519) 797 1818

🛏 **Southampton Inn**
118 High Street  Southampton ON  N0H 2L0
www.thesouthamptoninn.com
Tel: (888) 214 3816

🛏 **Huron Haven Motel**
21 Huron Street South
Box 479 Southampton ON  N0H 2G0
www.bmts.com/~huronhaven
Tel: (888) 815 3717  (519) 797 2248

🍴 **Walker House**
146 High Street  Southampton ON  N0H 2L0
Tel: (519) 797 2772

🍴 **Armen's Café**
224 High Street Southampton ON N0H 2L0
Tel. (519) 797 3864

🅰 **Southampton Municipal Campground**
227 Lake Street  Southampton ON  N0H 2L0
Tel: (866) 832 2008  (519) 797 3648

🚲 **Martin's Bicycle Shop**
23 High Street  Southampton ON  N0H 2L0
www.martins.ca  Tel: (519) 797 3200

📚 **215 High Street**
Southampton ON  N0H 2L0
www.library.brucecounty.on.ca
Tel: (519) 797 3586

## Southwold  8 V16 GPS 42.81031,-81.35703: Village
🏛

## Spanish  2 GPS 46.19310,-82.33808: Village
⬛🛏📚

🛏 **Le Bel Abri Bed & Breakfast**
3 Garnier Street  Spanish  P0P 2A0
www.bbcanada.com/1482.html
Tel: (705) 844 2545

📚 **8 Trunk Road**
Spanish ON  P0P 2A0
www.town.spanish.on.ca
Tel: (705) 844 2555

## Sparta  9 W18 GPS 42.70244,-81.07954: Historic
Quaker village, blacksmith shop museum, arts
and crafts shops
⬛🛏♿

---

## Spencerville  50 X64 GPS 44.84306,-75.54668:
Village with mill and historic stone buildings
⬛♿

## Springbrook  46 B47 GPS 44.40001,-77.61396:
Village
🏛🍴

## Stirling  34 C47 GPS 44.29630,-77.54678:  Town
⬛🍴♿🎭🚍

🏛 **Hastings County Museum of Agricultural Heritage**
Stirling Fairgrounds 435 West Front
Stirling ON K0K 3E0
www.agmuseum.ca Tel: (613) 395 0015

🎭 **The Stirling Festival Theatre**
Box 95  41 West Front Street
Stirling ON  K0K 3E0
www.stirlingfestivaltheatre.com
Tel: (877) 312 1162  (613) 395 2100

🛏 **La Dolce Vita Bed & Breakfast**
54 Wellington Street
Stirling ON  K0K 3E0
www.ldvbb.com
Tel: (613) 395-2138

## Stockdale  34 D47 GPS 44.20017,-77.62922:  Hamlet
🏛

## Stoney Point  5 B6 GPS 42.31428,-82.55171:
🏛

## Stratford  21 P19 GPS 43.37013,-80.98193:  The
Festival City, internationally famous theatre
attracting 500 000 people each season
🎭🛈🌟🚍🍴🚲♿

🛈 **Tourist Information – Stratford and Area**
www.welcometostratford.com
Tel: (800) 561 7926

🌟🎭 **Stratford Shakespeare Festival**
55 Queen Street  Stratford ON  N5A 6V2
www.stratfordfestival.ca
Tel: (800) 567 1600

🛈 **Stratford Festival Accommodation Bureau**
www. stratfordaccommodations.com
Tel: (800) 567 1600

🌟 **Farmers Market** Saturday mornings at
Fairgrounds - 20 Glastonbury Drive

🛏 **Avon And John Bed & Breakfast**
72 Avon Street  Stratford ON  N5A 5N4
www.avonjohn.com
Tel: (877) 275 2954  (519) 275 2954

🛏 **Dufton House B&B**
12 Elizabeth Street  Stratford ON  N5A 4Z2
www.duftonhouse.com
Tel: (519) 271-7413

🛏🍴 **Adren Park Inn restaurant**
552 Ontario Street Stratford ON  N5A 6W4
www.ardenpark.on.ca
Tel: (877) 788 8818  (519) 275 2936

🍴 **The Church Restaurant and Belfry**
Box 724 Stratford ON  N5A 6V6
www.churchrestaurant.com
Tel: (519) 273 3424

🍴 **The Prune**
151 Albert Street  Stratford ON  N5A 3K5
www.oldprune.on.ca
Tel: (519) 271 5052

🚲 **Totally Spoke'D**
29 Ontario Street  Stratford ON
www.totallyspoked.ca  Tel: (519) 273 2001

📚 **19 St. Andrew Street**
Stratford ON  N5A 1A2
www.stratford.library.on.ca  Tel: (519) 271 0220

## Strathroy  8 T14 GPS 42.95577,-81.62230: Town
⬛🍴🚍🅰♿

🛏🍴 **ClockTower Inn -**
**Strathroy Ale House & Pub**
71 Frank Street  Strathroy ON  N7G 2R5
www.clocktower-inn.com
Tel: (888) 776 8515 (519) 245 5656

🛏 **Strathroy Motor Inn**
28540 Centre Road Strathroy ON N7G 3H6
www.strathroymotorinn.com
Tel: (519) 245 4480

🅰 **Trout Haven Park**
24749 Park Street  RR#3
Strathroy ON N7G 3H5
www.trouthaven.ca  Tel: (519) 245 4070

📚 **34 Frank Street**
Strathroy ON  N7G 2R4

www.middlesex.library.on.ca
Tel: (519) 245 1290

### Summerstown 52 U72 GPS 45.05772,-74.56559:
Mountainveiw B&B
19263 County Road 2 Summerstown ON K0C 2E0 www.mountainviewbb.ca
Tel: (613) 931 9686

### Sweaburg 15, 16 S21 GPS 43.067233, -80.759614

### Sydenham 36 B55 GPS 44.31816,-76.54086:
Town, Convenience store, grocery store, restaurant, other stores

### Tamworth 47 A52 GPS 44.48738,-76.99482: Town
At Home Bed & Breakfast
12 Ottawa Street Tamworth ON K0K 3G0
www.athomebedandbreakfast.ca
Tel: (613) 379 2035
1 Ottawa Street
Tamworth ON K0K 3G0
www.lennox-addington.on.ca/library/about-the-library.html

### Tara 39 A18 GPS 44.47652,-81.14525: Village
Bruce County Public Library –
Tara Branch
69 Yonge Street Tara ON
www.library.brucecounty.on.ca/telib
Tel: (519) 934 2626

### Teeswater 26 G16 GPS 43.99034,-81.30226:
Teeswater Creamery/Gay Lea Retail Store.
21 Clinton Street North
Teeswater ON N0G 2S0 www.gaylea.com
Tel: (519) 392 6864
Bruce County Public Library –
Teeswater Branch
2 Clinton Street South Teeswater ON
www.library.brucecounty.on.ca/telib
Tel: (519) 392 6801

### Tehkummah 73 M11 45.64955,-82.00350: Village
Gordons Park Bed & Breakfast –
Campground 18777 Highway 6
Tehkumah ON P0P 2C0
www.gordonspark.com Tel: (705) 859 2470

### Terra Cotta 23 K28 GPS 43.71651,-79.93595: Village

### Terrace Bay 2 GPS 48.78335,-87.09792: Town
Imperial Motel restaurant
Highway 17 Terrace Bay ON
Tel: (877) 825 1625 (807) 825 3226
Rainbow Falls Provincial Park
west on Highway 17 Box 280
Terrace Bay ON P0T 2W0
Tel: (807) 824 2298
Reservations- www.ontarioparks.com
Tel: (888) 668 7275
Neys Provincial Park
east on Highway 17 Box 280
Terrace Bay ON P0T 2W0
Tel: (807) 229 1624
Reservations- www.ontarioparks.com
Tel: (888) 668 7275
1010B Highway 17
Box 369 Terrace Bay ON
www.terracebay.ca/?pgid=78
Tel: (807) 825 3315, Ext. 222

### Thamesville 7 Y11 GPS 42.55182,-81.97105:
Thamesville Public Library
3 London Road
Thamesville ON N0P 2K0
www.chatham-kent.ca/community+services/library/hours+and+locations/Thamesville+Library.htm
Tel: (519) 692 4251

### Thedford 13 R12 GPS 43.16396,-81.85515: Town

### Thessalon 2 GPS 46.26541,-83.54646: Village
North Shore Bed & Breakfast
299 River Street P.O. Box 24
Thessalon ON P0R 1L0
www.bbcanada.com/10782.html
Tel: (705) 842 3173
Carolyn Beach Motel restaurant
1 Lakeside Drive, Box 10
Thessalon ON P0R 1L0
www.carolynbeach.ca
Tel: (800) 461 2217 (705) 842 3330
Lakeside Park
Highway 17B at Stanley Street
Tel: (705) 842 2523
187 Main Street Thessalon ON P0R 1L0
www.thesslibcap.com Tel: (705) 842 2306

### Thorndale 15 S18 GPS 43.10513,-81.14118: Village
Silver Rock Bed & Breakfast
21814 Fairview Road
Thorndale ON N0M 2P0
www.angelfire.com/on/hamilton
Tel: (519) 461 0331
21790 Fairview Road
Thorndale ON N0M 2P0
www.middlesex.library.on.ca
Tel: (519) 461 1150

### Thorold 19 R34 GPS 43.12429,-79.19772:
The canal city
Tourist Information: Lock 7 Tourist Center
50 Chapel Street South Thorold ON L2V 2C6
www.thoroldtourism.ca Tel: (888) 680 9477
The Inn At Lock 7
24 Chapel Street South Thorold ON L2V 2C6
overlooking Welland Canal Lock 7
www.innatlock7.com
Tel: (877) 465 6257 (905) 227 6177
Robinsong Bed & Breakfast
41 Welland Street South Thorold ON L2V 2B6
www.bbcanada.com/robinsong
Tel: (905) 680 2427
Clarkson Cycle
103A Pine Street South Thorold ON
clarksoncycle.com Tel: (905) 227 0810
14 Ormond Street North Thorold ON L2V 1Y8
www.thoroldpubliclibrary.ca
Tel: (905) 227 2581

### Thunder Bay 2 GPS 48.38170,-89.24548:
Port city on Lake Superior
Ontario Travel Information Centre
7671 Highway 61 RR # 7 Pigeon River
Thunder Bay "F" P7C 5V5
www.ontariotravel.net
Tel: (807) 964 2094 (800) 668 2746
Fort William Historical Park
recreated fur trading post
Broadway Avenue off Hwy. 61 South
www.fwhp.ca Tel: (807) 473 2344
McVicar Manor Bed & Breakfast
146 Court Street North
Thunder Bay ON P7A 4V2
www.bbcanada.com/3918.html
Tel: (807) 344 9300
The Little Pearl Bed & Breakfast
268 Pearl Street Thunder Bay ON P7B 1E6
www.thelittlepearl.ca
Tel: (807) 346 8700
Best Western Crossroads Motor Inn
655 West Arthur Street
Thunder Bay ON P7E 5R6
www.bestwesternontario.com/hotels/best-western-crossroads-motor-inn
Tel: (800) 780 7234 (807) 577 4241
Super 8 Motel
439 Memorial Avenue
Thunder Bay ON P7B 3Y6
www.super8.com
Tel: (800) 889 9698 (807) 344 2612
Thunder Bay KOA
162 Spruce River Road
Thunder Bay ON P7B 5E4
www.koa.com/where/on/55120/reserve
Reservations-
Tel: (800) 562 4162 (807) 683 6221

Kakabeka Falls Provincial Park
32 kilometers west on Highway 11/17
Tel: (807) 473 9231
Reservations- www.ontarioparks.com
Tel: (888) 668 7275
Bistro One
555 Dunlop Street Thunder Bay ON
www.bistroone.ca Tel: (807) 622 2478
Armando Fine Italian Cuisine
28 Cumberland Street North Thunder Bay ON
Tel: (807) 344 5833
Fresh Air Experience
311 Victoria Avenue East
Thunder Bay ON P7C 1A4
www.freshairexp.com
Tel: (877) 311 9393 (807) 623 9393
Waverley Resource Library
285 Red River Road
Thunder Bay ON P7B 1A9
www.tbpl.ca Tel: (807) 344 3585

### Tilbury 5-6 C7 GPS 42.26166,-82.43200: Town,
convenience store, grocery store, other stores
175 year old clock in the shopping district and murals depicting the local history

antique mall south of Highway 401 at exit 56
4625 Richardson Sideroad
l-kantiques.tripod.com (519) 682 1827

Katharine's Bed & Breakfast
8 Carlyle Street Tilbury ON
www.bbcanada.com/3088.html
Tel: (519) 682 3706 (519) 401 3061
Ossobuco Italian Reataurant
58 Queen Street North
Tilbury ON
Tel: (519) 682 4433

### Tillsonburg 9, 10, 15, 16 U21 GPS 42.861942, -80.727507: Town
Tourist Information – Annandale National Historic Site
30 Tillson Avenue Tilsonburg ON N4G 2Z8
www.tillsonburg.ca/site/1251/default.aspx
Tel: (519) 842 2294
Howard Johnson Tillsonburg
92 Simcoe Street Tillsonburg ON N4G 2J1
www.hojotillsonburg.ca
Tel: (866) 942 7366 (519) 842 7366
The Mill Tales Inn restaurant
20 John Pound Road Tillsonburg ON
www.milltalesinn.webs.com
Tel: (519) 842 1782
Niko's Eatery and Bar
102 Broadway Street Tillsonburg ON
www.nikoseatery.com Tel: (519) 688 9393
The Manse
38 Ridout Street West
Tillsonburg ON N4G 2E1
Tel. (519) 842-2900

### Tobermory 54 S14 GPS 45.25382,-81.66509:
Charming port
Fathom Five National Marine Park
www.pc.gc.ca/amnc-nmca/on/fathomfive/index.aspx
diving centre to explore shipwrecks. Flowerpot Island and glass bottom boat tours
Tobermory-South Baymouth Ferry:
Ferry service between South Baymouth on Manitoulin Island and Tobermory. Departures early May to mid October, 1.75 hour crossing.
Reservations and information
www.ontarioferries.com/chi/english/index.html
Tel: (800) 265 3163
Harbourside Motel
24 Carlton Street Tobermory ON N0H 2R0
www.blueherronco.com/motel.htm
Tel: (519) 596 2422
Blue Bay Motel
32 Bay Street Box 58
Tobermory ON N0H 2R0
www.bluebay-motel.com Tel: (519) 596 2392
Tobermory Lodge restaurant
65 Elgin St. Box 190 Tobermory ON N0H 2R0
www.tobermorylodge.com
Tel: (800) 572 2166 (519) 596 2224

**Innisfree Bed & Breakfast**
46 Bay Street  Tobermory ON  N0H 2R0
www.tobermoryaccommodations.com
Tel: (519) 596 8190

**Tobermory Village Campground**
7159 Highway 6 - 3 km south
www.tobermoryvillagecamp.com
Tel: (519) 596 2689

**Bruce Peninsula National Park**
407 Cyprus Lake Road at Highway 6
Tobermory ON  N0H 2R0
www.pc.gc.ca/pn-np/on/bruce/index_E.asp
Tel: (877) 737 3783  (519) 596 2233

**Tobermory Public Library**
Bay Street  Tobermory ON
library.brucecounty.on.ca/tolib
Tel: (519) 596 2446

**Toledo** 49 Y60 GPS 44.74629,-76.00128:

**Toronto** 24 K32 GPS 43.64899,-79.35356:
Capital and largest city in Ontario with a great
variety of things to see and do

**Online Cycling Map**
www.toronto.ca/cycling/map/index.htm

**Ontario Travel Information Centre**
Atrium On Bay
20 Dundas Street West M5G 2C2
www.ontariotravel.net
Tel: (416) 314 5899  (800) 668 2746

**Toronto Tourism**
www.seetorontonow.com
Tel: (800) 363 1990  (416) 203 2500

**GO Transit** regional train and bus service
Union Station
Summer train service to Niagara: Bicycles
permitted on trains off peak and in off peak
direction during peak hours
www.gotransit.com
Tel: (888) 438 6646  (416) 869 3200

**TTC** subway, streetcar & bus transit
www3.ttc.ca Tel: (416) 393 4636
Toronto Island Ferry south end of Bay Street
www.toronto.ca/parks/island
Tel: (416) 392 8193

**Novotel Toronto Centre**
45 The Esplanade  Toronto ON  M5E 1W2
www.novotel.com/gb/hotel-0931-novotel-
toronto-centre/index.shtml
Tel  (416) 367 8900

**Radisson Hotel Admiral**
249 Queens Quay West  Toronto M5J 2N5
www.radisson.com/torontoca_admiral
Tel: (888) 201 1718  (416) 203 3333

**Toronto Bed & Breakfast**
Box 269  253 College Street
Toronto ON  M5T 1R5
www.torontobandb.com
Tel: (877) 922 6522  (705) 738 9449
economical student residence May to August

**Neill-Wycik College**
96 Gerrard Street East  Toronto ON  M5B 1G7
www.neill-wycik.com
Tel: (800) 268 4358  (416) 977 2320

**Cycle Solutions**
444 Parliament Street  Toronto ON  M5A 3A2
www.cycle-solutions.ca
Tel: (416) 972 6948

**Cycle Solutions**
615 Kingston Road  Toronto ON  M4E 1R3
www.cycle-solutions.ca    Tel: (416) 691 0019

**Wheel Excitement** bicycle rentals
249 Queen's Quay West
Unit 110 Toronto ON  M5J 2N5
www.wheelexcitement.ca
Tel: (416) 260 9000

**Mountain Equipment Co-Op**
400 King Street West  Toronto ON  M5V 1K2
www.mec.ca
Tel: (888) 847 0770 (416) 340-2667

www.torontopubliclibrary.ca
171 Front Street East  Tel: (416) 393 7655
2161 Queen Street East  Tel: (416) 393 7703

**Tottenham** 30 F29 GPS 44.02287,-79.80578:
Town

18 Queen Street North
Tottenham ON  L0G 1W0

---

www.ntpl.ca
Tel: (905) 936 2291

**Turkey Point** 10 W24 GPS 42.68459,-80.33105:
Convenience store, restaurant

**Turkey Point Provincial Park**
Tel: (519) 426 3239
PO Box 5 Turkey Point ON N0E 1T0
Reservations- www.ontarioparks.com
Tel: (888) 668 7275

**Tweed** 46 A49 GPS 44.47550,-77.31102:
Resort town on Stoco Lake

**Newton House Bed & Breakfast**
246 Colborne Street Box 429
Tweed ON  K0K 3J0
www.newtonhouse.ca Tel: (613) 478 1691

**Holiday House Bed & Breakfast**
42 St. Edmunds Road RR#4
Tweed ON  K0K 3J0
www3.sympatico.ca/edward.zak/
Tel: (866) 272 7613  (613) 478 5025

255 Metcalf Street  Tweed ON  K0K 3J0
www.tweedlibrary.ca  Tel: (613) 478 1066

**Upper Canada Village** 51 V68
GPS 44.94864,-75.06949:  Museum village,
many buildings from the St. Lawrence Seaway

www.uppercanadavillage.com
13740 County Road 2
Morrisburg ON  K0C 1X0
Tel: (800) 437 2233  (613) 543 4328

**Willard's Hotel** full service restaurant
in 1860's historic tavern  Tel: (613) 543 0660

**Village Café**
Tel: (613) 543 0660

**Uxbridge** 31 E34 GPS 44.10616,-79.12386:
Historic town

**Foster Memorial**, inspired by the Taj Mahal
north on Road 1
www.uxbridge.com/people/tfoster.html

**Leaskdale Manse Museum**
north on Road 1 - home of LM Montgomery,
author of the Anne of Green Gables books
www.uxbridge.com/people/maud.html

**Just Mary Bed & Breakfast**
49 Main Street North  Uxbridge ON  L9P 1J7
www.bbcanada.com/justmary
Tel: (905) 852 5349

9 Toronto Street
Uxbridge ON  L9P 1P7
www.uxlib.com  Tel: (905) 852 9747

**Vankleek Hill** 68 P71 GPS 45.52099,-74.65144:
Town

**Varna** 20 M14 GPS 43.53387,-81.59593: Village

**Vernonville** 33 F44 GPS 44.04707,-77.98319:
Hamlet

**Verona** 36 A 54 GPS 44.48005,-76.69421:  Town

**Victoria Harbour** 41 X29 GPS 44.75070,-79.77444:

**Tay Township Public Library** - Victoria Harbour
145 Albert Street
Victoria Harbour ON  L0K2A0
Tel: (705) 534 3581

**Vienna** 9 W20 W20 GPS 42.67992,-80.78888:
Village

**Edison Museum of Vienna**
Where Thomas Edison visited his grandfather,
Captain Samuel Edison
14 Snow Street  Vienna ON  N0J 1Z0
www.edisonmuseum.ca Tel: (519) 866-5521

**Villa Nova** 10 T25 GPS 42.94285,-80.16037:
Village

**Vineland Station** 18 R32

---

GPS 43.15995,-79.39440:  Shopping and
antiques north of QEW at Prudhommes
Landing

**Virgil** 19 Q34 GPS 43.22119,-79.12422:  Town,
convenience store, restaurant, other stores

**Vittoria** 10 V24 GPS 42.76215,-80.32357:
Historic village, capital of London District
1815 to 1825

**Wallaceburg** 6 X7 GPS 42.59297,-82.39503:
Town

**WAMBO** antique motor and boat outing
in early August   www.kent.net/wambo/

**Wallaceburg District Museum**
505 King Street  Wallaceburg
www.kent.net/wallaceburg-museum
Tel: (519) 672 8962

**Oaks Inn restaurant**
80 McNaughton Avenue
Wallaceburg ON  N8A 1R9
www.oaksinnhotel.com
Tel: (888) 627 1433  (519) 627 1433

**Days Inn**
76 McNaughton Avenue
Wallaceburg ON  N8A 1R9
www.daysinnwallaceburg.com
Tel: (866) 627 0781  (519) 627 0781

209 James Street
Wallaceburg ON  N8A 2N4
www.chatham-kent.ca/community+services/library/
hours+and+locations/Wallaceburg+Library.htm
Tel: (519) 627 5292

**Wallacetown** 8 X15 GPS 42.63405,-81.46614:
Vllage

**Walpole Island First Nation** 6 X6
GPS 42.59442,-82.49857

www.bkejwanong.com

Walpole Island – Algonac, Michigan USA
Bicycle Crossing - www.walpolealgonacferry.com
Tel: (519) 677 5781

**Bay to Bridge Trail**  Marine City to Algonac
Michigan USA - www.stclaircountyparks.org
Three Fires Confederacy of Potawatami, Ottawa
and Ojibwa people Pow Wow in late July

**Walters Falls** 39 A21 GPS 44.48807,-80.70750:
Village

**Rainbow's End Cabin**
RR#8 Owen Sound ON
www.rainbowsendcabin.com
Tel: (519) 538 3523

**Warkworth** 33 D44 GPS 44.20073,-77.88984: Village
**Warkworth Long Lunch** late August
www.warkworth.ca/annual-events/longlunch

**Oak Heights Estate Winery**
West on County Road 29
337 Covert Hill Road  RR #1
Warkworth ON  K0K 3K0
www.oakheights.ca
Tel: (866) 625 6051 (705) 924 9625

**Thornton Inn**
44 Main Street Box 420
Warkworth ON  K0K 3K0
www.thorntoninn.com Tel: (705) 924 3980

**Jeannine's Backtalk Cafe**
9 Main Street Warkworth ON
Tel: (705) 924 2166

**Town Hall Centre for the Arts** -Library
40 Main Street  Warkworth ON  K0K 3K0
www.trenthillslibrary.ca Tel: (705) 924 3116

**Warsaw** 45 G42 GPS 44.430061, -78.1373
Village

**Warsaw Caves Conservation Area**
289 Caves Road Warsaw ON
www.warsawcaves.com
Tel: (705) 652 3161 (877) 816 7604

**Sunflower Bay B&B**

967 Water Street  P.O. Box 36
Warsaw ON  K0L 3A0
www.sunflowerbay.ca  Tel: (705) 652 1022

**Warwick** 13 T11 GPS 43.00288,-81.94458:

**Wasaga Beach** 41 A27 GPS 44.52080,-80.01579:

**Mallards Nest Guest House**
23 31st Street South
Wasaga Beach ON  L9Z 2C6
www.mallardsnest.ca
Tel: (416) 529 8926

**Serenity in the Beach B&B**
536 Oxbow Park Drive
Wasaga Beach ON  L9Z 2T8
www.serenityinthebeach.com
Tel: (705) 429 0017

**Donato House**
1080 Mosley Street
Wasaga Beach ON
www.donatohouse.com
Tel: (877) 372 4411 (705) 429 4411

**Wasaga Beach Public Library**
120 Glenwood Drive
Wasaga Beach ON  L9Z 2K5
www.wasagabeach.library.on.ca
Tel: (705) 429 5481

**Washago** 42 X32 GPS 44.74965,-79.33452:

**Waterdown** 23 P27 GPS 43.33523,-79.89295:

**Waterdown Motel**
219 Dundas Street East  Waterdown ON
Tel: (905) 689 5278

**Bicycle Works**
316 Dundas Street East  Waterdown ON
www.thebicycleworks.ca   Tel: (905) 689 1991

**Hamilton Public Library –**
Waterdown Branch  25 Mill Street North
Waterdown ON  L0R 2H0
www.inform.hamilton.ca/record/HAM0563
Tel: (905) 689 6269

**Waterford** 17 T25 GPS N42° 55.8982', W080°
17.3736'

**Norfolk County Public Library**
15 Main Street South Waterford ON N0E 1Y0
www.ncpl.ca  Tel: (519) 426 3506

**Waterloo** 22 N23 GPS 43.46339,-80.52076:
Waterloo and adjacent Kitchener are both
cities with a variety of stores and services

**Tourist Information -**
Waterloo, Kitchener and  Area
www.kwtourism.ca   Tel: (800) 265 6959

**Uptown Waterloo Jazz Festival**  mid July
www.uptownwaterloojazz.ca

**Hillcrest House Bed & Breakfast**
73 George Street  Waterloo ON  N2J 1K8
www.hillcresthouse.ca
Tel: (866) 624 3534   (519) 744 3534

**Best Western St. Jacobs Country Inn**
50 Benjamin Road  Waterloo ON  N2V 2J9
www.stjacobscountryinn.com
Tel: (800) 972 5371   (519) 884 9295

**Wilfred Laurier University Conference Services**
75 University Avenue West
Waterloo ON  N2L 3C5
www.wlu.ca/conferences
Tel: (519) 884 1970 x 3958

**Laurel Creek Conservation Area**
625 Westmount Road  Waterloo ON
www.grandriver.ca
Tel: (866) 668 2267   (519) 884 6620

**Sole Restaurant & Wine Bar**
83 Erb Street West  Waterloo ON
www.sole.ca   Tel: (519) 747 5622

**Hannah's Bella Bistro**
4 King Street North  Waterloo ON
Tel: (519) 746 3504

**McPhail's Cycle & Sports**
98 King Street North  Waterloo ON  N2J 2X4
www.mcphailscycle.com
Tel: (519) 886 4340

**Waterloo Public Library**
35 Albert Street  Waterloo ON  N2L 5E2

www.wpl.ca  Tel: (519) 886 1310

**Waupoos** 35 G52 GPS 44.00130,-77.00103:
Hamlet

**Waupoos Winery restaurant**
3016 Road 8  RR#4  Picton ON  K0K 2T0
www.waupooswinery.com  Tel: (613) 478 8338

**County Cider Company  lunch**
657 Bongards X Road at Road 8  RR 4
Picton ON K0K 2T0
www.countycider.com  Tel: (613) 476 1022

**Fifth Town Artisan Cheese**
4309 Road 8  RR #4  Picton  ON  K0K 2T0
www.fifthtown.ca
Tel: (800) 584 8696  (613) 476 5755

**The Duke of Marysburgh Pub & Bistro**
2470 Road 8
www.dukeofmarysburgh.com
Te: (613) 476 8991

**Wawa** 2 GPS 47.99098,-84.77267: Town

**Northern Lights Motel & Chalets**
1014 Highway 17 North
Wawa ON  P0S 1K0 CA
www.nlmotel.com
Tel: (800) 937 2414  (705) 856 1900

**Best Northern Motel**
Highway 17 South  Wawa ON  P0S 1K0 CA
www.bestnorthern.ca
Tel: (800) 434 8240  (705) 856 7302

**Lake Superior Provincial Park**
Box 267 Wawa ON  P0S 1K0
Tel: (705) 856 2284
Reservations- www.ontarioparks.com
Tel: (888) 668 7275

**Wawa Public Library**
40 Broadway Avenue Wawa ON  P0S 1K0
www.mtpl.on.ca  Tel: (705) 856 2062
Internet access at Visitor Information Centre
Highway 17 at Highway 101

**Webbwood** 84 E12 GPS 46.26913,-81.89021:
Village

**Welland** 19 T33-34 GPS 42.99348,-79.23924:
City with, parks, picnic areas and bike paths

**Welland Rose Festival** is held in June
www.wellandrosefestival.on.ca
Tel: (905) 732 7673

**Anderson's Bed & Breakfast**
GPS  42.93295,-79.24424
324 Kingsway Road  Welland ON  L3B 3N9
www.bbcanada.com/3336.html
Tel: (905) 732 3730

**Best Western Rose City Suites**
GPS  42.97547,-79.25756
300 Prince Charles Drive
Welland ON  L3C 7B3
www.bestwesternniagara.com
Tel: (800) 780 7234  (905) 732 0922

**Days Inn Welland**
1030 Niagara Street  Welland ON L3C 1M6
www.daysinnwelland.ca
Tel: (800) 329 7466  (905) 735 6666

50 The Boardwalk
Welland ON  L3B 6J1
www.welland.library.on.ca  Tel: (905) 734 6210

**Wellesley** 22 M21 GPS 43.47665,-80.76454:
Village

**Apple Butter and Cheese Festival**
in September.
www.wellesleyabcfestival.ca

**Wellesley Apple Products**
apple butter and cider
3800 Nafziger Road North
www.wellappleproducts.com

**The Nith River Chop House Wellesley**
1193 Queen's Bush Road
Wellesley ON  N0B 2T0
www.nithchophouse.com  Tel: (519) 656 9057

1137 Henry Street
Wellesley ON N0B 2T0
www.rwl.library.on.ca  Tel: (519) 656 2001

**Wellington** 34 G49 GPS 43.95130,-77.35130:
Village

**Breeze Off The Lake Bed & Breakfast**
449 Main Street
Wellington ON  K0K 3L0
www.breezeoffthelake.ca
Tel: (613) 399 2960

**Devonshire on the Lake  restaurant**
24 Wharf  Street
Wellington ON  K0K 3L0
www.devonshire-inn.com
Tel: (800) 544 9937 (613) 399 1851

**Karlo Estates Winery**
561 Danforth Road  Wellington ON
www.karloestates.com
Tel: (613) 399 3000
west on Road 33 (Loyalist Parkway)

**By Chadsey's Cairns Winery**
17432 Loyalist Parkway RR#1
Wellington ON  K0K 3L0
www.bychadseyscairns.com
Tel: (613) 399 2992

**Sandbanks Estate Winery**
17598 Loyalist Parkway RR#1
Wellington ON  K0K 3L0
www.sandbankswinery.com
Tel: (613) 399 1839

261 Main Street
Wellington ON
www.peclibrary.org   Tel: (613) 399 2023

**Wendover** 67 N67  GPS 45.57034,-75.14541:
French Canadian village

**West Lake** 34 G49  35 G50
GPS 43.94216,-77.24350:  Resort area

**Isaiah Tubbs Resort restaurant**
642 County Road 12  Picton ON  K0K 2T0
www.isaiahtubbs.com
Tel: (800) 724 2393  (613) 393 2090

**West Lorne** 8 X14 GPS 42.60471,-81.60800:
Village

160 Main Street
West Lorne ON  N0L 2P0
www.library.elgin-county.on.ca
Tel: (519) 768 1150

**West Montrose** 22 M22 GPS 43.58756,-80.48192:
Village with Ontario's last remaining covered
bridge

**Westport** 48 Y57  GPS 44.67968,-76.39745:
Scenic resort town on Rideau Lake

**Rideau District Museum**
29 Bedford Street
www.village.westport.on.ca/about-westport/
rideau-district-museum

**The Rothwell's Stone Cottage B&B**
15 Main Street, Box 368
Westport ON  K0G 1X0
www.rothwellstonecottagebb.ca
Tel: (613) 273 3081

**A Victorian Reflection Bed & Breakfast**
16 Church Street  Westport ON K0G 1X0
www.avictorianreflection.com
Tel: (613) 273 8383

**The Cove Country Inn restaurant**
2 Bedford Street  Westport ON K0G 1X0
www.coveinn.com
Tel: (888) 298 3466  (613) 273 3636

**Tangled Garden Café**
7 Church Street  Westport ON
www.tangledgardencafe.com
Tel: (613) 273 7733

3 Spring Street
Westport ON  village.westport.on.ca/about-
westport/westport-public-library
Tel: (613) 273 3223

**Wheatley** 5 E7  GPS 42.09454,-82.46295:
Town

**By The Bay B&B**
493 Gregory Line RR1
Wheatley ON  N0P 2P0
www.dentsbythebay.com
Tel: (866) 298 4322   (519) 825 7729

**Wheatley Provincial Park**
PO Box 640 Wheatley ON N0P 2P0
Reservations- www.ontarioparks.com
Tel: (888) 668 7275 (519) 825 4659

**Car Barn Restaurant and Tavern**
23 Talbot Street East Wheatley ON
Tel: (519) 825 4946

35 Talbot Street West
Wheatley ON N0P 2P0
www.chatham-kent.ca/community+services/
library/Library.htm
Tel: (519) 825 7131

**Whitby** 25 H36 GPS 43.89926,-78.94255: City

**Ezra Anne's House Bed & Breakfast**
239 Wellington Street Whitby ON L1N 5L7
www.ezraannes.com
Tel: (800) 213 1257 (905) 430 1653

**Impala Bicycles**
1818 Dundas Street East Whitby ON K7G 2G2
www.impalabicycles.com
Tel: (866) 652 2453 (905) 434 4530

405 Dundas Street West
Whitby ON L1N 6A1
www.whitbylibrary.on.ca Tel: (905) 430 7913

**White River** 2 GPS 48.59312,-85.27481:
Village

**White River Motel**
Box 608 White River ON P0M 3G0
www.whiterivermotel.com
Tel: (800) 822 5887 (807) 822 2333

**White Lake Provincial Park**
west on Highway 17 Box 340
White River ON P0M 3G0
Tel: (807) 822 2447
Reservations- www.ontarioparks.com
Tel: (888) 668 7275

**Obatanga Provincial Park**
east on Highway 17
Box 340
White River ON P0M 3G0
Tel: (807) 822 2592
Reservations- www.ontarioparks.com
Tel: (888) 668 7275

**Whitefish Falls** 84 G13 GPS 46.11509,-81.72925:
Village

**Whitney** 79 P41 GPS 45.49919,-78.24499

**Algonquin East Gate Motel**
P.O. Box 193 Whitney ON K0J 2M0
www.algonquineastgatemotel.com
Tel: (613) 637 2652

**South Algonquin Public Library**
Whitney ON K0J 2M0
www.olsn.ca/southalgonquin
Tel: (613) 637 5471

**Wiarton** 39 X18 GPS 44.74013,-81.13978:
Attractive town on Colpoy's Bay

**Tourist Information –**
Wiarton and Bruce County
www.explorethebruce.com
Tel: (800) 268 3838 (519) 534 5344

**Wiarton Willy**
world famous albino groundhog weather
forecaster
www.wiarton-willie.org

**Wiarton Willy Inn**
Highway 6 south Wiarton ON
www.wiartonwillys.com
Tel: (888) 534 3907 (519) 534 3907

**Bruce Gables Bed & Breakfast**
410 Berford Street Box 448
Wiarton ON N0H 2T0
www.bbcanada.com/948.html
Tel: (519) 534 0429

**Maplehurst B&B**
277 Frank Street PO Box 803
Wiarton ON N0H 2T0
www.bbcanada.com/1898.html
Tel: (519) 534 1210

**Green Door Café**
563 Berford Street Wiarton ON N0H 2T0
www.thegreendoorcafe.com Tel: 519 534 3278

**Pacific Inn & Lucille's Dining**
624 Berford Street Wiarton ON N0H 2T0
www.pacificinnwiarton.com
Tel: (519) 534 9050

578 Brown Street
Wiarton ON
www.library.brucecounty.on.ca
Tel: (519) 534 2602

**Wilton** 36 C54 GPS 44.31709,-76.73006:
Village,

**Wilton cheese factory** - www.wiltoncheese.com

**Windsor** 4 B1-2 GPS 42.31782,-83.03391:
City

**Windsor – Detroit, Michigan USA Bicycle
Crossing.** Bicycles disassembled are permitted
on the Tunnel Bus at the driver's discretion
[avoid busy times].
Information at (519) 944 4111
tw@city.windsor.on.ca.
Bicycles and pedestrians are prohibited on the
Ambassador Bridge. For an alternative see
Pelee Island for the Pelee Island Ferry from
Leamington and Kingsville to Sandusky, Ohio.

**Ontario Travel Information Centre**
www.ontariotravel.net Tel: (800) 668 2746

**Detroit-Windsor Tunnel**
110 Park Street East N9A 3A9
Tel: (519) 973 1338

**Tourist Information –**
Windsor and Essex County
www.visitwindsor.com
Tel: (800) 265 3633 (519) 225 6530

**Riverside Drive bikeway and parks** with a
spectacular view of the Detroit skyline. Take
your chances at nearby Casino Windsor

**Ojibway Park and Nature Preserve** picnic area,
Carolinian forest and large tallgrass prairie park.

**Branteaney's Bed & Breakfast**
1649 Chappus Street Windsor ON N9C 3T1
Tel: (519) 966 2334

**Inn on the River Bed & Breakfast**
3857 Riverside Drive East
Windsor ON N8Y 1B1
www.windsorinnontheriver.com
Tel: (866) 635 0055 (519) 945 2110

**Travelodge Ambassador Bridge**
2330 Huron Church Road Windsor ON
www.travelodge.ca
Tel: (800) 578 7878 (519) 972 1100

**Il Gabbiano Restorante**
875 Erie Street East Windsor ON
www.ilgabbiano.com Tel: (519) 256 9757

**Mick's Irish Pub**
28 Chatham Street East Windsor ON
www.micksirishpubwindsor.com
Tel: (519) 534 3278

**Pasticcio Ristorante**
854 Erie Street East Windsor ON
Tel: (519) 253 3329

**Courtesy Bicycles**
3154 Sandwich Street Windsor ON
Tel: (519) 254 8056

3312 Sandwich Street
Windsor ON N9C 1B1
www.windsorpubliclibrary.com
Tel: (519) 255 6770

**Wolfe Island** 36 E56-57
GPS 44.17999,-76.43677:

www.wolfeisland.com

**Kingston via Wolfe Island – Cape Vincent,
New York USA Bicycle Crossing.**
Kingston ferry terminal - Ontario Street and
Barrack Street - to Marysville on Wolfe Island
www.mto.gov.on.ca/english/traveller/ferry
Tel: (613) 545 4664.
Road 95 12 kilometers on Wolfe Island from
Marysville to Port Alexandria.
Port Alexandria, Wolfe Island ferry to Cape
Vincent New York – dock at James Street
www.hornesferry.com
Tel: (613) 385 2402 (315) 783 0638

**Woodstock** 16 R21 GPS 43.13011,-80.75656:
City

**Tourist Information -**
Woodstock Oxford County Area
www.tourismoxford.ca
Tel: (519) 539 9800 x3355

**Microtel Inn & Suites**
GPS 43.1126835, -80.7438781
811 Athlone Avenue Woodstock ON N4V 0B6
www.microtelwoodstock.ca
Tel: (519) 537 2320

**Chateau Carbide Willson Bed & Breakfast**
210 Vansittart Avenue
Woodstock ON N4S 6E
www.bbcanada.com/8118.html
Tel: (519) 533 0800

**Holiday Inn Express Hotel & Suites**
510 Norwich Avenue
Woodstock ON N4S 3W5
www.hiexpress.com Tel: (800) 345 8082

**Pittock Conservation Area**
725138 Pittock Park Road
Woodstock ON www.thamesriver.on.ca
Tel: (519) 539 5088

**Pedal Power Bikes & Boards**
590 Dundas Street Woodstock ON N4S 1C8
www.pedalpower.ca Tel: (519) 539 3681

**Woodstock Public Library**
445 Hunter Street Woodstock ON
www.woodstock.library.on.ca
Tel: (519) 539 4801

**Wooler** 34 E46 GPS 44.15687,-77.70042:
Village

**Yarker** 36 C54 GPS 44.37174,-76.77110:
Village

2824 County Road # 6
Yarker ON K0K 3N0
www.lennox-addington.on.ca
Tel: (613) 377 6698

**York** 17 S28 GPS 43.02674,-79.89189:
Village

**Zurich** 20 N14 GPS 43.42113,-81.62515:
Town

**Brokenshire House Bed & Breakfast**
19 Rosalie Street Zurich ON N0M 2T0
www.bbcanada.com/3901.html
Tel: (519) 236 4734

CPSIA information can be obtained
at www.ICGtesting.com
Printed in the USA
264922LV00007B